Business Models for Strategic Innovation

This book extends our understanding of how different cross-functional business and management disciplines, such as innovation and entrepreneurship, strategic management, marketing and HRM, individually and collectively underpin innovation in business management.

Business Models for Strategic Innovation develops insights from cross-disciplinary business knowledge streams and their cutting edge discipline-specific practical implications to create a cross-functional business innovation management model. Novel cross-disciplinary knowledge plays an imperative role in business innovation and we know that innovative management processes have significant implications for effective cross-functional management. In this context, each chapter of the book presents fresh insights on diverse business knowledge-streams as well as their applied implications on cross-functional business innovation management. Finally, centred on these cross-disciplinary business theories and their cutting edge implications, the last chapter of this book proposes a model of strategic cross-functional business innovation management process.

This academically rigorous work uses innovative theoretical propositions and state-of-the-art empirical analysis in order to enable cross-functional management teams to support organisation-wide business innovation processes.

S. M. Riad Shams is a Senior Research Fellow at the Ural Federal University, Russia. He is the lead-editor of the Annals of Business Research and has been serving as the track-chair in the leading international academic conferences.

Demetris Vrontis is a Professor and an Executive Dean at the University of Nicosia in Cyprus. He is the President of the EuroMed Research Business Institute and the Editor-in-Chief of the EuroMed Journal of Business.

Yaakov Weber is Professor at the School of Business Administration, College of Management, Israel. He has also served in various Editorial positions in leading journals such as CMR, JWB, HRM, BJM.

Evangelos Tsoukatos is an Associate Professor at the University of Applied Sciences, Crete, Greece where he teaches Management and adjunct faculty at the University of Nicosia, Cyprus and the Hellenic Open University.

The Annals of Business Research
Series Editors:
S. M. Riad Shams, *Ural Federal University, Yekaterinburg, Russian Federation*
Demetris Vrontis, *University of Nicosia*
Yaakov Weber, *the College of Management, Academic Studies, Israel*
Evangelos Tsoukatos, *the Technical Educational Institute of Crete, School of Management and Economics*

Business Models for Strategic Innovation
Cross-Functional Perspectives
Edited by S. M. Riad Shams, Demetris Vrontis, Yaakov Weber and Evangelos Tsoukatos

For more information about this series, please visit www.routledge.com/The-Annals-of-Business-Research/book-series/BUSRES

Business Models for Strategic Innovation

Cross-Functional Perspectives

Edited by S. M. Riad Shams,
Demetris Vrontis, Yaakov Weber
and Evangelos Tsoukatos

LONDON AND NEW YORK

First published 2018
by Routledge
2 Park Square, Milton Park, Abingdon, Oxon OX14 4RN

and by Routledge
711 Third Avenue, New York, NY 10017

Routledge is an imprint of the Taylor & Francis Group, an informa business

© 2018 selection and editorial matter, S. M. Riad Shams, Demetris Vrontis, Yaakov Weber and Evangelos Tsoukatos; individual chapters, the contributors

The right of S. M. Riad Shams, Demetris Vrontis, Yaakov Weber and Evangelos Tsoukatos to be identified as the authors of the editorial material, and of the authors for their individual chapters, has been asserted in accordance with sections 77 and 78 of the Copyright, Designs and Patents Act 1988.

All rights reserved. No part of this book may be reprinted or reproduced or utilised in any form or by any electronic, mechanical, or other means, now known or hereafter invented, including photocopying and recording, or in any information storage or retrieval system, without permission in writing from the publishers.

Trademark notice: Product or corporate names may be trademarks or registered trademarks, and are used only for identification and explanation without intent to infringe.

British Library Cataloguing-in-Publication Data
A catalogue record for this book is available from the British Library

Library of Congress Cataloging-in-Publication Data
Names: Shams, S. M. Riad, 1979– editor.
Title: Business models for strategic innovation: cross-functional perspectives / edited by S. M. Riad Shams [and three others].
Description: Abingdon, Oxon ; New York, NY : Routledge, 2018. |
Series: The annals of business research | Includes bibliographical references and index.
Identifiers: LCCN 2017059729 (print) | LCCN 2018000379 (ebook) |
ISBN 9781351257923 (Ebook) | ISBN 9780815367215 (hardback : alk. paper)
Subjects: LCSH: Strategic planning. | Diffusion of innovations–Management. |
Technological innovations–Management. | Organizational change.
Classification: LCC HD30.28 (ebook) | LCC HD30.28 .B84387 2018 (print) |
DDC 658.4/063–dc23
LC record available at https://lccn.loc.gov/2017059729

ISBN: 978-0-815-36721-5 (hbk)
ISBN: 978-1-351-25792-3 (ebk)

Typeset in Times New Roman
by Out of House Publishing

Contents

List of figures	ix
List of tables	x
Notes on contributors	xii
Foreword	xviii
Acknowledgement	xx
Editorial note	xxi

1 Strategic innovation management: a cross-functional vision to be materialised   1

S. M. RIAD SHAMS, DEMETRIS VRONTIS, YAAKOV WEBER AND EVANGELOS TSOUKATOS

Introduction 1
The definition of innovation and innovation management in business 2
The significance of cross-functional teams in business innovation 4
The need for further research on cross-functional business management 5
Conclusion 7
References 8

2 Neuromarketing applications of neuroprosthetic devices: an assessment of neural implants' capacities for gathering data and influencing behavior   11

MATTHEW E. GLADDEN

Introduction 11
An overview of neuromarketing 12
An overview of neuroprosthetic devices 13
A framework for analyzing neuroprostheses' neuromarketing applications 15

vi *Contents*

An assessment of neuromarketing applications by neural implant type 18
Conclusion 21
References 22

**3 The role of information sharing and communication strategies for
improving stakeholder engagement** 25

FRANCESCO CAPUTO, FEDERICA EVANGELISTA AND
GIUSEPPE RUSSO

Introduction 25
Conceptual and theoretical framework 27
Methodology 30
Findings 31
Discussion 32
Final remarks and future lines of research 34
References 36

**4 Assessing the dynamic of agri-food export trends before and after
the EU Eastern Enlargement** 44

ANTONINO GALATI, MARCELLA GIACOMARRA AND
MARIA CRESCIMANNO

Introduction 44
Literature review 45
Data and methods 46
Results and discussion 50
Conclusion 53
References 54

**5 How does entrepreneurial orientation influence knowledge
exploitation?** 58

ORLANDO LIMA RUA AND ALEXANDRA FRANÇA

Introduction 58
Theoretical framework 59
Methodology 62
Results 63
Discussion and conclusion 65
References 67

6 Profitability of the Italian credit cooperative banks 71

GIOVANNI OSSOLA, GUIDO GIOVANDO AND CHIARA CROVINI

Introduction 71
Literature review and theoretical background 72

Contents vii

Methodology 74
Findings 77
Discussion 80
Conclusions 81
References 81

7 Applying persuasion science in marketing communications: a comparison of marketing communications professionals in Armenia and Greece   85

ARMINE PETROSYAN AND NIKOLAOS DIMITRIADIS

The modern challenge of persuasion 85
Persuasion theories and marketing communications 87
Cialdini's principles 87
Neuromarketing: Persuasion in the human brain 88
Measurement of persuasion methods 90
Methodology 92
Research results and discussion 93
Practical implications 98
Conclusions 99
References 100

8 Innovative tertiary strategies on improving satisfaction level of students   106

DEMETRIS VRONTIS, SAM EL NEMAR AND AMANI MALLAT

Introduction 106
Literature review 107
Research methodology 112
Analysis and results 113
Conclusion 118
Limitations 121
References 121

9 Relationship marketing and entrepreneurial innovation: a B2B context of stakeholder relationship management   125

HASINA IDRIS AND S. M. RIAD SHAMS

Introduction 125
Evaluative viewpoint 125
The case of the England and Wales Cricket Board (ECB) 132
Findings 139
Discussion and conclusion 144
References 146

viii   *Contents*

10 Disclosure of electric mobility in annual reports of automotive companies: risks, strategies, and environment   152

GIUSEPPE IANNIELLO, MICHELA PICCAROZZI AND FABRIZIO ROSSI

Introduction 152
Literature review 153
Electric mobility: Risks, strategies, and environment 154
Research method and sample selection 156
Empirical results 158
Conclusion 163
References 165

11 Human and task integration during post-merger integration   168

YAAKOV WEBER

Introduction 168
Contextual ambidexterity 169
Discussion and conclusion 174
References 175

12 An integrated cross-functional model of strategic innovation management in business: the implications of ten cross-functional business areas   176

S. M. RIAD SHAMS, DEMETRIS VRONTIS, YAAKOV WEBER AND EVANGELOS TSOUKATOS

Introduction 176
The ten cross-functional perspectives in business 177
An integrated cross-functional model of strategic innovation management in business 178
Conclusions, limitations and future research 183
References 185

Index   187

Figures

1.1	The constructs, process and outcome of strategic innovation management in business	3
2.1	Examples of potential neuromarketing applications for neuroprostheses	17
3.1	The conceptual model	31
4.1	Bulgaria. Agri-food export dynamic towards NMS (2000–2011 period)	52
4.2	Bulgaria. Agri-food export dynamic towards OMS (2000–2011 period)	52
4.3	Latvia. Agri-food export dynamic towards NMS (2000–2011 period)	53
4.4	Latvia. Agri-food export dynamic towards OMS (2000–2011 period)	53
6.1	The trend of net banking income and profit/loss of BCCs in the period between 2009 and 2014	79
6.2	The trend of ROE and the profit margin ratio of BCCs in the period between 2009 and 2014	79
8.1	Student satisfaction conceptual framework	112
8.2	Student satisfaction model – factors of satisfaction from weakest to strongest	118
9.1	Growth in annual reserves of the England and Wales Cricket Board	140
9.2	Mutually beneficial relationship value-centred B2B innovation process	145
11.1	Corporate cultural differences, national cultural distance and optional integration approaches	171
12.1	Cross-functional driving and mediating factors of strategic innovation management in business	181

Tables

3.1	Relationships among study constructs	32
3.2	Results of SEM	32
3.3	Fitness indexes	33
4.1	Indicators used in the analysis	47
4.2	DEA Window results (%)	50
4.3	Groups of countries according to their average efficiency scores	51
5.1	Data summary	63
5.2	Internal consistency test by construct (Cronbach's alpha)	64
5.3	Summary and ANOVA of multiple regression analysis	65
5.4	Standardized beta coefficient	65
6.1	Main items considered in the financial statement analysis	78
6.2	The Pearson correlation ratio between profit/loss and net banking income	80
8.1	Reliability of institutional factors, out of school activities and expectations	113
8.2	Correlation of variables with student satisfaction	114
8.3	Correlation of student satisfaction and students' recommendations	115
8.4	Chi-square tests: student satisfaction and institutional factors	115
8.5	Chi-square tests: student satisfaction and school activities	116
8.6	Chi-square tests: student satisfaction and expectations	117
8.7	Chi-square tests: student satisfaction and demographics	117
9.1	Multifarious goals of ECB and their stakeholders	144
10.1	Registration of electric vehicles (electrically charged vehicles*) in Europe	153
10.2	Description of annual report 2013 and frequency of key words	160
10.3	Sentences for each key word	161
10.4	Information features	162
10.5	Panel A Economic performance and indicators of the content analysis of annual reports	164

Tables xi

10.5 Panel B Correlation (Spearman's rank) between economic
performance and indicators of the content analysis of annual
reports   164
12.1 Cross-functional business perspectives for strategic
cross-functional innovation management in business   179

Contributors

Francesco Caputo (PhD) is a Research Fellow at the Department of Pharmacy, University of Salerno, Italy. His main research interests include but are not limited to complexity, knowledge management, healthcare management, network theory, corporate communication, strategy, and systems thinking. He is member of the Editorial Boards of several international journals and he serves as reviewer for several journals. He is Secretary of the ASVSA, Association for research on Viable Systems (www.asvsa.org). He was also a finalist at the 2012/2013 Emerald/EMRBI Business Research Awards and he won the best presentation award at the 2016 B.S. Lab. Symposium "Governing Business Systems. Theories and Challenges for Systems Thinking in Practice", the best paper award at the 19th Toulon-Verona (ICQSS) Conference "Excellence in Services", and the best commended paper at the 2017 WOSC Congress "Science with and for Society: Contributions of Cybernetics and Systems".

Maria Crescimanno is a Full Professor at the Department of Agricultural, Food and Forest Sciences, University of Palermo (Italy). She is Coordinator of the graduate programs in agro-engineering and Forestry and environmental sciences. She was the delegate of the Chancellor of the University of Palermo for the planning and organization of the University's Masters and a Fellow of the EuroMed Academy of Business (EMRBI). Her research interests include international and European agricultural policy, foreign agri-food trade, agribusiness, market competitiveness, logistic, and fishery policy and market analysis. Her research has been published in many international peer-reviewed journals.

Chiara Crovini is a PhD candidate in Business and Management at the Department of Management, University of Turin, Italy. Her research area covers all the topics related to corporate governance, internal control systems, risk management, internal auditing, statutory audit of SMEs, banks and credit institutions. She is a Chartered Accountant and Statutory Auditor. She is a member of the European Risk Research Network (ERRN), of Business System Laboratory (B.S. Lab.), of the International Academy of Business and Economics (IABE), of Accademia Italiana di Economia Aziendale Giovani (AIDEA Giovani), and of SIDREA (Società Italiana dei Docenti di Ragioneria e di Economia Aziendale).

Nikolaos Dimitriadis is an award-winning communications professional, educator and consultant. He is the author of the book "Neuroscience for Leaders: A Brain Adaptive Leadership Approach" (Kogan Page, London) together with Prof. Alexandros Psychogios, and spoke at TEDx University of Strathclyde for the urgent need for Brain-Based Communication. He is a certified NeuroMarketer and a contributor to the NeuroMarketing Manager Program at Hamburg Media School. He has worked with international brands such as IKEA, IBM, JTI, Nestlé, Johnson & Johnson, Pierre Fabre, Coca-Cola, Banca Intesa Sanpaolo, Raiffeisen Bank, Rauch, Teekanne, USAID and others. He is a mentor of startups at the ICT HUB, Belgrade, Serbia. He is the CEO of Trizma Neuro, a cutting-edge Neuromarketing company, and the Regional Director at The University of Sheffield International Faculty City College for the Western Balkans. Dr. Dimitriadis is a strong advocate of brain-based solutions to business challenges.

Federica Evangelista has a PhD in Business Administration in the Department of Economics and Law at the University of Cassino and Southern Lazio in Italy. Her research interests cover the following topics: business administration, business management, corporate governance, corporate social responsibility, intellectual capital and intellectual property rights, intellectual asset management and knowledge management, international accounting, and leadership. She is the author of articles regarding corporate governance, intellectual capital and management of intangible assets.

Alexandra França obtained a Master's degree in Management from Porto Accounting and Business School and she is a PhD student of Marketing and Strategy at University of Minho. She has a solid background in industry and services leveraged by working as a consultant for multinational companies. Her research interests are international marketing, business strategy and entrepreneurship. Her research has been published in national and international scientific conferences and journals.

Antonino Galati is an Associate Professor of Agricultural economics and valuation at the Department of Agricultural, Food and Forest Sciences, University of Palermo (Italy). He holds a PhD in Agricultural Economic and Policy (2007) from the University of Palermo and is also Co-Chair of the Research Interest Committee in Agribusiness of the EuroMed Academy of Business. At the University of Palermo he is Professor in the Fundamentals of Economics, Environmental voluntary certifications, and Strategic Management of the Agro-forestry companies. His research interests include market competitiveness, agribusiness, marketing strategies, management, logistics and market analysis. His research has been

xiv *Contributors*

published in a wide range of international peer-reviewed journals and conference proceedings.

Marcella Giacomarra is Teaching Assistant at the Department of Agricultural and Forest Sciences (University of Palermo). In 2006, she acquired a degree in International and Diplomatic Sciences (University of Bologna, Italy), with a specialization in European Economic Studies. In 2017 she started relevant scientific collaborations with European bodies specialized in international studies. In 2015, she successfully completed her PhD studies in Statistics for Experimental and Technological Research (University of Palermo, Department of Economic, Business and Statistics science). During the PhD course, she started relevant collaborations with the Department of Agricultural and Forest Sciences (Palermo). Her main research interests are: innovative business models applied in the food sector; international relations; European Union economic policies comparison in both the food sector and the renewable energy one; and impact of both voluntary and regulated certifications/labels in the food sector. She is the author of numerous scientific papers and a reviewer for internationally recognized scientific journals.

Guido Giovando is an Associate Professor in Business Administration at the Department of Management, University of Turin, Italy. Currently, he is teaching Business Administration and Cost Accounting in the Bachelor degree courses and Accounting and Financial Statements of Banks and Credit Institutions in the Master degree courses. He is a Chartered Accountant and Statutory Auditor in many companies. He is the author of many national and international publications in the banking and assurance field, financial accounting and airport infrastructure. He is an Associate EuroMed Academy of Business (EMAB) Fellow of the EuroMed Academy of Business (EMAB).

Matthew E. Gladden studies the structure, dynamics, and implications of emerging technologically posthumanized digital-physical ecosystems in which human beings' experience of their environment is mediated by technologies for ubiquitous computing, virtual reality, and neurocybernetic enhancement and in which human beings co-inhabit such ecosystems with social robots, artificial intelligences, and other synthetic social agents. He is an award-winning author whose books include *Posthuman Management* and *From Strategic Analysis to Organizational Foresight*. His research has been published by Ashgate, IOS, and The MIT Press. He lectures in organizational robotics and has taught philosophical ethics. He serves as CEO of management consulting firm NeuraXenetica LLC and has filled senior executive and administrative roles at research institutions including Georgetown University and the Woodstock Theological Center. He studied at Wabash College (BA, Philosophy), the Polish Academy of Sciences (MBA, Innovation and Data Analysis), and Georgetown

University (certificates in Nonprofit Management and Advanced Business Management).

Giuseppe Ianniello (PhD) is a full professor of Economia Aziendale (Accounting and Business Administration) at the Department of Economics, Engineering, Society and Business, University of Tuscia, Viterbo, Italy, where he teaches undergraduate and graduate level courses in financial accounting and financial statement analysis. He received a Laurea Degree from the University of Siena, School of Banking and Finance (Italy) in 1991 and a PhD in Accounting and Business Administration from the University of Pisa (Italy) in 1995. His research deals with international accounting, financial reporting, accounting communication and principles of external auditing.

Hasina Idris holds MBA and BBA (honours in marketing). She is a Senior Lecturer at the European University of Bangladesh. Her key research areas are principles of marketing, service marketing, entrepreneurship, retail marketing, advertising and human resource management. Alongside her academic experience, she has worked extensively in the industry.

Amani Mallat holds a Master's degree in Business Administration and a Master's Degree in Biology (Molecular Biology). Research interests include, pricing, distribution and factors that impact the satisfaction level of university students. Other research interests include Pricing Strategies in the Pharmaceutical Industry.

Sam El Nemar is an Assistant Professor of Marketing. His prime research interests are in the Marketing of higher education, student university choices and satisfaction.

Giovanni Ossola is a Full Professor in Business Administration at the Department of Management, University of Turin, Italy. At present, he is teaching Business Administration in the Bachelor degree courses and Financial Accounting and Financial Statements of Banks and Credit Institutions in the Master degree courses. He is a Chartered Accountant and Statutory Auditor in many companies. He is a member of Accademia Italiana di Economia Aziendale (AIDEA). He is the author of many national and international publications in the banking and assurance field, financial accounting and airport infrastructure.

Armine Petrosyan is a Communications and SM Strategist with a strong academic and practical experience. She recently graduated from the University of Sheffield, Business Administration and Economics Department, with an MA in Marketing, PR and Advertising (Awarded MA Degree with Distinction). Her main research interests are Neuromarketing and Persuasion Methods. One of her latest achievements is getting certified by Microsoft as a Digital Marketing Specialist. Armine was a speaker during the 9th annual conference of the EuroMed Academy of Business (EMAB),

xvi *Contributors*

track: *Innovative Communications*: Innovation, Entrepreneurship and Digital Ecosystems. Armine was published in the book proceedings of the 10th Annual Conference of the EuroMed Academy of Business.

Michela Piccarozzi (PhD) is Assistant Professor of Management at the Department of Economics, Engineering, Society and Business, University of Tuscia, Viterbo, where she teaches courses in management and merger and acquisition. She received a Laurea Degree from the University of Tuscia, Economy and Management (Italy) in 2006 and a PhD in Planning and Control from the University of Florence (Italy) in 2010. Her research has developed along three lines: first, University Spin-offs (USOs); second, strategic planning, business plan and firms creation process; and third, innovative start-up.

Fabrizio Rossi (PhD) is Assistant Professor of Economia Aziendale (Accounting and Business Administration) at the Department of Economics, Engineering, Society and Business, University of Tuscia, Viterbo, where he teaches courses in Internal Auditing and Accounting. He received a Laurea Degree from the University of Florence, in 1999 and a PhD in Planning and Control from the University of Florence (Italy) in 2002. His research deals with continuous auditing and reporting and Corporate governance aspects.

Orlando Lima Rua is a Professor of Management at the Porto Accounting and Business School (ISCAP), Porto, Portugal. He holds a PhD in Economics and Management. His research interests are entrepreneurship, innovation and strategy. His research has been published in national and international scientific conferences and journals.

Giuseppe Russo is Associate Professor of Business Management in the Department of Economics and Law at the University of Cassino and Southern Lazio (Italy). He is Master coordinator of I Level both in Social Enterprise Management and in Innovation and in Public Administration Management. He is author of books and articles regarding business management, knowledge economy, intellectual capital planning and control. He is responsible for and member of several research projects.

S. M. Riad Shams (DProf) is a senior research fellow at the Ural Federal University, Russia. He completed his doctoral research from the Central Queensland University, Australia in 2011. His MBA and BBA (honours in marketing) have been awarded by the University of Dhaka, Bangladesh in 2004 and 2003, respectively. He is an Associate Research Fellow at the EuroMed Academy of Business, Cyprus. The key research areas of Dr Shams are stakeholder relationship management, business sustainability, strategic management, corporate reputation, image and brand positioning. He has published in and guest edited for various leading journals, namely, the Journal of Business Research, the International Marketing Review and so forth. He is the lead-editor of the Annals of Business Research and has been serving as the track-chair in the leading international academic conferences.

Evangelos Tsoukatos (PhD) teaches Management at the University of Applied Sciences Crete, Greece and is adjunct faculty at the University of Nicosia, Cyprus and the Hellenic Open University. He earned a BSc in Mathematics from the Aristotle University of Thessaloniki, Greece, a Postgraduate Diploma and MSc in Operational Research from Lancaster University Management School, UK, where from he also earned his PhD in Management Science. Prior to joining academia Dr Tsoukatos had extensive experience as consultant and in senior management positions. His research interests are in Services Management, Quality Management, Cross-Cultural Management and Entrepreneurship. He holds the position of Vice President – Operations and Development at the EuroMed Research Business Institute. He is Associate Editor of the EuroMed Journal of Business (EMJB) and editorial board member in a number of international scholarly journals. More information at http://teicrete.academia.edu/EvangelosTsoukatos.

Demetris Vrontis is a Professor and an Executive Dean at the University of Nicosia in Cyprus, where he has also served as Head of the Marketing Department and as Dean of the School of Business. He is the President of the EuroMed Research Business Institute and the Editor-in-Chief of the EuroMed Journal of Business. Prof. Vrontis is also a Visiting Professor, Visiting Research Fellow and collaborates with various universities and organisations around the globe. He is a certified Chartered Marketer and Business Consultant and has widely published in over 180 refereed journals and 25 books and gave numerous presentations in international conferences.

Yaakov Weber serves in various Editorial positions in leading journals such as California Management Review, Journal of World Business, Human Resource Management, British Journal of Management, and more. He published in top journals such as Strategic Management Journal, Management Science, Journal of Management, Human Relations, Journal of Business Research. His research received about 4500 citations. Other papers achieved "2nd most cited in last 5 years (2010–2015) and "most read" (2011–2015), or "most download", in leading journals. Prof. Weber is the winner of an "Outstanding Author Contribution Award" in his area of expertise. Prof. Weber is Co-Founder and Co-President of the EuroMed Business Research Institute (www.emrbi.org), the EuroMed Academy of Business and the EuroMed Research Centre. Prof. Weber has been senior consultant to CEOs, top executives and directors in leading companies such as Motorola, Coca-Cola, Society of Israel Plastics & Rubber Manufacturers, the largest international engineering company in Israel, and the USA-Israel Chamber of Commerce.

Foreword

It is a pleasure to write this introductory comment for the new book by my colleague Demetris Vrontis and his co-authors/editors. Professor Vrontis has developed a consistently high quality track record in his research, writing and teaching of business management issues. Through his work he has positioned himself as one of the important and innovative contributors to the literature.

So it comes as no surprise to have him address the field of business innovation in his latest work, where he and his co-authors explore innovation in business for products and services, technological process and operational process innovation and how they help to attain and sustain the competitive advantage of firms. This book explains how innovation management in business is an ongoing creative process of capacity building in all business functional areas. Thus, cross-functional research and practice in business innovation are imperative to proactively and effectively contribute to the overall operation of a business firm. From this perspective, this book discusses the issues and challenges in strategic business innovation management. It also offers insights on the diverse factors which motivate, drive and mediate innovation across the diverse functional areas of business. The book then offers contemporary insights on how strategic innovation management can be enhanced through innovation incubators. Recommendations are made on how to design, develop, commercialize, manage and evaluate innovation for it to be accepted by the target markets.

This book systematically explores current innovations in the field of innovation. To paraphrase former Secretary of Defense Donald Rumsfeld:

> There are known knowns which are things we know that we know. Then there are known unknowns, that is to say there are things that we now know that we don't know. But there are also unknown unknowns. These are things of which we do not know that we don't know them.

Professor Vrontis very elegantly and in a determined fashion, addresses all three of these categories, culminating in a strategic cross-functional business innovation model that is presented in the final chapter of this book. With a call for a new entrepreneurial mindset in innovation management that incorporates a cross-functional perspective of strategic initiatives, this book broadens and innovates our understanding of the core issues forming and surrounding innovation. This book encourages and allows the development of a cross-functional entrepreneurial mindset to cope with the innovation management challenges of the 21st century. This book will be a key information source for the new directions of cross-functional innovation. Congratulations to the authors!

Professor Michael R. Czinkota
Washington, D.C.
January 4, 2018

Michael R. Czinkota is a distinguished professor at the faculty of marketing and international business at Georgetown University in the USA, and at the University of Kent in the UK. He served in the U.S. Government as Deputy Assistant Secretary of Commerce, as head of the U.S. Delegation to the OECD Industry Committee in Paris and as senior advisor for Export Controls.

Professor Czinkota has testified twelve times before the U.S. Congress, and has been listed as one of the three most published contributors to international business research in the world by the *Journal of International Business Studies.*

Professor Czinkota was born and raised in Germany and educated in Austria, Scotland, Spain, and the United States. His Ph.D. is from the Ohio State University. His key book, with Ilkka Ronkainen, is International Marketing, 10th edition, CENGAGE.

Acknowledgement

We gratefully acknowledge the generous support of colleagues, who extended their hands to help us to make this book successful. We sincerely thank the contributors for their invaluable contributions. Without their disciplined effort, this book project would not have been accomplished. We would like to express our gratitude to all subject experts for volunteering in the double-blind review process. We also would like to acknowledge the friendly and supportive role of editorial staff of Routledge. Last, but not least, we appreciate all our family members for their encouragement to make this project a success.

Editorial note

Cross-disciplinary research for cross-functional innovation management

This book develops insights from cross-disciplinary business knowledge streams to originate a cross-functional business innovation management model, in order to underpin research and practice in business innovation. In general, novel cross-disciplinary business and management knowledge plays an imperative role in business and management innovation. Also, we know that innovative management processes have significant implications for effective cross-functional management, and overall business and management success. Following this context, each chapter of this book presents different novel theoretical insights on diverse business knowledge streams and their innovative applied implications on cross-functional business innovation management practices. Following these cross-disciplinary business theories and their cutting-edge, discipline-specific practical implications, this book proposes a cross-functional business innovation management model (Figure 12.1).

In terms of academic research, these cross-disciplinary contexts of theoretical developments offer a number of innovative theoretical propositions, which are comprehensively supported by rigorous conceptual developments and state-of-the-art empirical analyses, focusing on the diverse management functional areas. Alongside presenting the new research, this book also offers generous scope for further research in innovative business models and cross-functional management. In terms of practical implications, first, the different chapters offer the varied business discipline-specific fresh insights and their relevant management functional area-specific implications. For example, the new insights from neuroscience as an academic discipline and the implications of those new insights for marketing management as a business functional area. Second, the cross-functional business innovation management model (Figure 12.1) of this book appears as instrumental to enable the cross-functional management teams to proactively underpin the organization-wide business innovation process.

In order to develop insights focusing on the discussion thus far, this book pursues the aim to extend our understandings on how different xxii *Editorial note*

cross-functional business and management areas, such as strategic management, marketing, HRM, entrepreneurship and innovation and so forth individually and collectively can underpin innovation in business management, in order to proactively explore/exploit business opportunities and/or offset business risks. To pursue this aim, except the introductory first and the concluding last chapters, the rest of the cross-disciplinary middle chapters of this book are carefully commissioned, focusing on the cutting-edge research on innovative business management issues from the perspectives of the diverse business management functional areas. The first chapter of the book overviews the significance of research in innovative cross-functional management, based on cross-disciplinary theoretical gaps, and relevant issues. The last chapter summarises the overall findings of the rest of the cross-disciplinary middle chapters of the book to propose an innovative business model (Figure 12.1) that will have implications for cross-functional management practice.

From this context, Chapter 1 discusses that, on one hand, innovation in business is a crucial factor for successful implementation of business policies and strategies. On the other hand, cross-functional business innovation has received much interest among researchers and practitioners, because of its effective and innovative contribution, based on diverse business functional areas, to the overall innovation management process of a business firm. A concise literature review on the relevant topics illustrates the significance of cross-functional innovation in the contemporary business innovation management process; however, the review simultaneously accentuates the lack of current research on cross-functional business innovation, in order to fully exploit the diverse cross-functional innovation perspectives for proactively planning, implementing and managing the strategic innovation management process in business. Following this background, this chapter also proposes a cross-functional strategic innovation management vision, and provides an overview on the rest of the chapters of this book, in order to portray how the different chapters develop strategic innovation management insights, based on diverse business function-specific issues and arguments, with an aim to propose and justify an integrated cross-functional model of strategic innovation management in business.

Chapter 2 argues that neuromarketing utilizes innovative technologies to accomplish two tasks: 1) gathering data about how particular stimuli affect human beings' cognition; and 2) creating and delivering stimuli to influence the behavior of potential consumers. We argue that it will increasingly be possible to perform both tasks by accessing and exploiting neuroprosthetic devices already possessed by members of society. A conceptual framework is developed for identifying neuroprostheses' capacities for performing neuromarketing-related functions: one axis delineates functional types of neural implants; the other describes the two key neuromarketing activities. The framework is then utilized to identify neuromarketing applications for existing and anticipated neuroprosthetic technologies.

Editorial note xxiii

Chapter 3 of this book focuses on the increasing competitiveness in market configuration that impels companies to explore new ways to improve their competitive advantage and their chances of survival. According to managerial studies and empirical evidence offered by managerial literature, a possible strategy to improve companies' performances requires the involvement of stakeholders as complex actors endowed with relevant resources and knowledge. Starting from this key point, the chapter proposes a study on a sample of Italian companies with the aim to investigate the role of information sharing and communication strategies in supporting the emergence of the preconditions for stakeholder engagement.

Chapter 4 examines the evolution in development of intra-European Union agri-food export during the period 2000–2011. By using Data Envelopment Window Analysis, this chapter at first provides a more comprehensive picture on agri-food trade performance of sampled New Member States, focusing the attention on the pre and post phase of the enlargement process. Two specific country case studies will be released, revealing different patterns of performance among New EU Member States. The majority of New EU Member States differed in their approach in benefiting from the opportunity to enter into the EU enlarged market, not only according to their initial agricultural structural conditions, but also as a consequence of pre-and post-accession political and economic trade agreements. Many countries preferred to strengthen established trade relations with a past group of partner countries, as defined by agreements that are already in force. In the future, the increase in the export flows of quality products together with the ability to enter new end-markets within the EU will largely depend on the agri-food sector units' abilities to efficiently compete and sustain competitiveness in the European and global markets. In the years coming, the overall performance could be improved by strengthening the quality side of exported goods, to better comply with EU quality standards and to acquire a more competitive advantage in the single market. A challenge that New Member States are able to deal with also thanks to the recent increase in employment and education levels.

In Chapter 5, it is argued that, in a modern and turbulent business environment, knowledge has been designated as a dominant source of competitive advantage. The exploitation of knowledge must be carried out by proactive, innovative and risk-taking firms. Building on well-established theories, our research explores the influence of entrepreneurial orientation in the exploitation of knowledge of Portuguese small and medium enterprises (SMEs). Based on survey data, our empirical results indicate that entrepreneurial orientation has a positive and significant influence on exploitation of knowledge, specifically innovation and risk-taking.

Chapter 6 represents a theoretical contribution and considers the Italian banking sector, with a focus on the credit cooperative banks (BCCs). There were 364 credit cooperative banks in Italy in 2015 with a total of over 4,400 branches throughout the Italian territory and over 37,000 employees. This study helps understand the context and the main business in which these

xxiv *Editorial note*

banks operate. The sample analysed includes 264 Italian BCCs and data were extracted from Bankscope, which is a database containing comprehensive information on financial companies in Italy. The aim is to show that the BCCs are relevant in the Italian banking sector and enhance growth and value-creation for the local community in which they operate thanks to their activities. To do that, two indicators (the profit margin and return on equity [ROE]) were compared to see how they have changed over the years. Furthermore, by calculating the Pearson correlation ratio between profit/loss and net banking income of each year, this research analyzes the possible correlation of net banking income on the profitability of the banks, in order to assess the effects of a policy that is carried out by the corporate governance to face the difficulties that the banking system has been going through.

Chapter 7 of this book explores the adoption of both contemporary and traditional persuasion methods by marketing communication professionals in Armenia and Greece. The study used semi-structured, in-depth personal interviews with a sample of 20 participants in four marketing communication areas: public relations, advertising, digital media, and marketing/consulting. Results indicate that approaches of marketing communications professionals in both countries coincide to some extent and that there is a need for more education related to action-based persuasion techniques among those professionals. The study extends the body of knowledge of adoption of persuasion methods by marketing communication professionals, offering empirical findings from both Armenia and Greece.

The purpose of Chapter 8 is to identify the factors that positively impact student satisfaction in higher education and to measure the level of satisfaction by determining students' attitudes towards certain factors. With the rise in the number of students enrolling in educational institutions, strategic innovative quality considerations in the delivery of teaching, research programs and services are becoming an important aspect of higher educational institutions nowadays. Customer satisfaction is becoming a major interest for most colleges and higher education institutions so that they can understand how satisfied customers react to offered services or products. The purpose of this study is to identify the factors that positively impact student satisfaction in Lebanese higher education institutions and to measure satisfaction levels and opinions concerning certain factors. For this reason, a conceptual model was built and a quantitative study was adopted to explore the factors and how they are correlated. It was found that among institutional factors, out of school activities, demographic factors, and expectations, high satisfaction is positively associated with the services offered by institutions. This study contributes to a model of satisfaction on Lebanese students that can be added later on as a reference for further research related to the same topic.

Chapter 9 develops insights on the stakeholder focused entrepreneurial initiatives of the England and Wales Cricket Board (ECB) in a business-to-business (B2B) setting that engage their stakeholders/partners in a way where relationship marketing (RM) extends their mutually beneficial stakeholder relationship value, with the purpose of jointly innovating further product/ service value for their target markets. This case study aims to recognize the implications of RM against the ECB's entrepreneurial initiatives, stakeholder relationships, interactions and subsequent mutually beneficial relationship value to nurture their B2B product/service innovation. Eleven RM perspectives are recognized that impact on their relationship value, while the stakeholders work interdependently in the innovation process. The identified RM perspectives are recognized as value-innovating constructs in a B2B setting to reinforce the stakeholder relationship value, and collectively to uphold entrepreneurial initiatives, in order to innovate value through product/ service innovation. Such a relational approach of entrepreneurial innovation in the B2B context appears as feasible across industries and markets.

Chapter 10 intends to use the narrative section of annual reports to capture the role of electric mobility from the perspective of automobile companies. In particular, the explorative analysis focuses on the following aspects of electric vehicles (EV): risks, strategies, and environmental impact. From the analysis of the relation between the disclosure of electric mobility and economic performance, it appears that there is no significant link between company performance and an emphasis on electric mobility. The research method is based on thematic content analysis applied to the narrative section of annual reports. For the empirical analysis, we used a sample of major companies active in the European automobile market. Content analysis shows that automobile companies emphasize the strategic role and the environmental impact of electric mobility, whereas the risks involved are discussed less. The information disclosed is mainly qualitative and non-financial and has a historical time orientation.

Chapter 11 of this book deals with the complexity and contradictions of the post-merger integration (PMI) process faced by leaders and HR managers. Different streams of management research, in isolation from each other, failed to explain the high failure rate of mergers and acquisitions (M&A). This chapter combines knowledge from different streams and builds on the concept of contextual ambidexterity to deal with the complexity of PMI. It offers more sophisticated conceptualization of the effects of human integration and task integration on M&A performance in the context of various integration approaches.

Finally, the last chapter of this book, Chapter 12, provides an overview of the entire book. Based on the cross-functional research significance and research gap in business innovation management that is discussed in Chapter 1, and the contemporary cross-functional research insights on business innovation management that is derived from the arguments of Chapter 2 to Chapter 11, this chapter offers and justifies an integrated cross-functional model (Figure 12.1) of strategic innovation management in business. Centred on ten cross-functional perspectives, twelve cross-functional driving factors and ten cross-functional mediating factors of strategic innovation management, which are learnt from the insights of Chapter 2 to Chapter 11, Table 12.1 and xxvi *Editorial note*

Figure 12.1 of this chapter summarize the overall arguments of the book, in relation to the core theme of this book: "strategic cross-functional innovation management in business". This chapter discusses the research limitations and future research areas as well.

S. M. Riad Shams
Ural Federal University, Russia

Demetris Vrontis
University of Nicosia, Cyprus

Yaakov Weber
The College of Management Academic Studies, Israel

Evangelos Tsoukatos
University of Applied Sciences Crete, Greece

1 Strategic innovation management

A cross-functional vision to be materialised

S. M. Riad Shams, Demetris Vrontis,
Yaakov Weber and Evangelos Tsoukatos

Introduction

"Parallel to an expanding volume of research on innovation, the academic debate on the subject is becoming everlasting" (Conta et al., 2015, p. 107); however, in general, "innovation can be a critical driver in the successful handling of the constantly appearing new (business) challenges" (Conta et al., 2015, p. 107). As a result, ongoing research on business innovation management is imperative to focus on the relevant issues of this research-stream and the related topic-specific debates, in order to deliver the value to the associated stakeholders that is expected and accepted by them. Continuous innovation in business management is crucial for any business firm, not only for their survival, but also to ensure their ongoing progress.

For long-term success, "(strategic) innovation has become systemic and drives capitalist economic advantage" (Romer, 1990; Burton-Jones, 2001, as cited in Shams, 2015, p. 161). In general, strategic innovation in business needs a proper understanding of the needs, wants and expectations of the target market (Bresciani et al., 2012), in order to satisfy those needs through the commercialisation of the outcome of a business innovation process. In addition to the business innovation management centred on the issues related to a single business functional area, the cross-functional input from different functional areas of a business firm is, in general, instrumental to proactively plan, implement and monitor the strategic innovation management process in business, in order to enhance and sustain the impact of a newly innovated product/service, idea, technology or management process on long-term business success. However, a concise review of the extant literature in this chapter suggests that the cross-functional business innovation teams play an imperative role in the organisation-wide strategic innovation management process; the review also reveals that the current research in this field is not adequate to proactively explore the diverse issues in business, related to the overall implications of cross-functional business teams for strategic innovation management, focusing on diverse socio-economic environments and business settings.

2 S. M. Riad Shams et al.

From this context, the remainder of this chapter

- firstly, defines innovation in business and extends the discussion to the relevant areas of business management;
- secondly, accentuates significance of cross-functional teams for business innovation;
- thirdly, discusses the lack of current research on cross-functional business management for strategic innovation management, in order to set a cross-functional vision for strategic innovation in business;
- and finally, presents the conclusion of the overall discussions of the chapter.

Furthermore, this introductory chapter provides an overview of the contexts that are embraced in the rest of the chapters of this book, in order to develop insights on diverse business-function-specific innovation processes, with an aim to integrate the core issues of those processes into an inclusive cross-functional model of strategic innovation management in business.

The definition of innovation and innovation management in business

In general, strategic innovation management in business is defined as:

> [...] a firm's tendency to engage in and support new ideas, novelty, experimentation and creative processes that may result in new products, services or technological processes. Innovativeness represents a basic willingness to depart from existing practices and venture beyond the current state of the art (in order to sustain the competitive advantage underlying the innovation).
>
> (Lumpkin and Dess, 1996, p. 142, as cited in Vrontis et al., 2012, pp. 422–423; Shams and Kaufmann, 2016, p. 1257)

Business models innovation has emerged as an important means for firms to commercialise new ideas and technologies (Chesbrough, 2010, p. 354) in order to use the innovation outcome and the underlying innovation value internally and externally at a profit, in a way that would be expected and accepted by all associated stakeholders, including the customers (Kaufmann and Shams, 2015). From this context, the business model innovation management "represents the logic of the firm to propose customer value and to set up a viable revenue and cost structure for value capture (Teece, 2010), into the focus of attention of management practitioners and scholars alike" (Spietch et al., 2014, p. 237). Value is defined as

> an anticipated outcome of any sort of planned and organized activity. The activity could be derived from monetary, psychic, or physical resources. The more the outcome meets initial anticipation, the more the possibility of win-win outcomes or value optimization for all involved stakeholders.
>
> (Shams, 2013a, p. 244; 2013b, p. 263)

As a result, the innovation management process in business predominantly focuses on planning and implementing a unique course of action that could optimize value for all associated stakeholders. In order to ensure that a firm could optimize value for their key stakeholders through business innovation, the firms in the contemporary business environment administer an innovation management process, which is a "continuous process to develop innovative capacities in socio-economic settings through on-going development and adaptation of strategies and processes that enable higher advantage in collective and individual levels, compared to the prior strategies and processes to enhance socio-economic development" (Shams, 2016a, p. 671). Furthermore, it is important to ensure that "the innovation of unique strategic (business) models, which do not simply fit new competitive conditions, but perpetually and automatically predict and adapt… according to the pace and nature of change" (Thrassou et al., 2014, p. 352, as cited in Shams and Lombardi, 2016, p. 221).

Following the discussion thus far, it can be argued that the key issues that are depicted in Figure 1.1 play a central role in the process of strategic innovation management in contemporary business practices.

The arguments presented in this section from the extant literature suggest that innovative idea generation, screening and selection of the appropriate idea for developing novel product/service or relevant technology is an integral part of successful innovation management in business. In terms of selecting the appropriate idea, considering the needs, wants and expectations of the associated stakeholders (Sanchez et al., 2012; Christofi et al., 2015; Santoro et al., 2017) is crucial, in order to experiment and commercialise the innovative idea and the resulting product, service or technology, so that the outcome of the innovation management process would be expected and accepted by the key stakeholders (Shams and Belyaeva, 2017, Shams, 2017; 2016b; 2011). Figure 1.1 (the constructs, process and outcome of strategic innovation

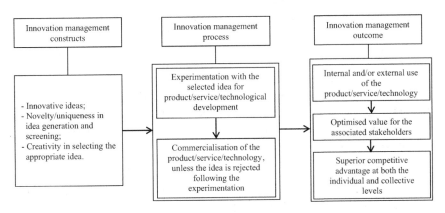

Figure 1.1 The constructs, process and outcome of strategic innovation management in business

4 *S. M. Riad Shams et al.*

management in business) portrays this procedure of strategic innovation management.

The significance of cross-functional teams in business innovation

The innovation management process and its subsequent "rewarding value-delivery process does not rely solely on an organization's or its entrepreneur's inspired efforts. Stakeholders, the most important associates of a value-delivery network and their significant contributions, are certainly required for a win–win outcome" (Kaufmann and Shams, 2015, p. 10, as cited in Shams et al., 2017, np). As a consequence, the internal and external stakeholders of a firm have significant implications for planning, implementing and monitoring the strategic innovation management process. For example, "increased use of cross-functional teams (within and across a firm) in new product development is related to higher project success" (McDonough, 2000, p. 221). In relation to this view, researchers further argue that

> on the basis of a study of 141 cross-functional product development teams, the authors find that innovativeness is positively related to the strength of superordinate identity in the team, encouragement to take risk, customers' influence, and active monitoring of the project by senior management.
>
> (Sethi et al., 2001, p. 73)

In fact, cross-functional teaming or "cross-boundary teaming, within and across organizations, is an increasingly popular strategy for innovation" (Edmondson and Harvey, 2017, p. 1), since, "the relationship between cross-functional collaboration and…innovativeness is stronger" (Clercq et al., 2011, p. 680). In terms of change management in business operation, cross-functional teams play a positive role to implement proactive and effective change management strategies (Piercy et al., 2013). In terms of technology innovation and operational effectiveness, "cross functional teams have an indirect influence on continuous improvement of operational performance through the alignment between technology innovation effectiveness and operational effectiveness" (Santa et al., 2011, p. 122). In terms of purchasing management, "a positive impact was found of cross-functional integration and functional coordination on purchasing performance, and of purchasing performance on firm performance" (Foerstl et al., 2013, p. 689). In terms of talent management, "both talent management and performance management have a positive impact on cross-functional integration and functional coordination" (Foerstl et al., 2013, p. 689). In terms of marketing innovation,

> causal pathways leading to cross-functional coordination and marketing adaptiveness can be enhanced by resource dependency, cross-functional teams, multifunctional training, and management support. In particular,

management support is a crucial condition for cross-functional teams and multifunctional training. While resource dependency is an important internal factor for coordination, a high resource dependency can result in a negative effect on marketing adaptiveness.

(Mohsen and Eng, 2016, p. 5946)

In terms of supply chain management and HRM, the success of cross-functional teams contributes to job satisfaction (McAndrews and Ha-Brookshire, 2016). Furthermore, "cross-functional executive involvement and worker involvement positively affect the strategic alignment of the lean manufacturing statement and bundles (just-in-time, total quality management, total preventive maintenance, and human resources management) with environmental and social goals and practices" (Longoni and Cagliano, 2015, p. 1332). In terms of knowledge management, "knowledge integration in the context of cross-functional project implementation is in essence a process of engaging organizational members through the promotion of project benefits and the management of social networks" (Chuang and Newell, 2003, p. 167). In terms of resource management "across business processes, team working and greater cross-functional co-operation make it much easier to understand what is happening within the system" (Scapens and Jazayeri, 2003, p. 227).

The concise literature-based arguments of this section demonstrate that in order to optimise the effectiveness of strategic plans across different functional areas of total business management, the cross-functional business teams play a crucial role in the contemporary business environment. Such cross-functional teams of innovation management in business can be formed, based on the team members from the strategic management, HRM, marketing, research and development, stakeholder relationships management, corporate social responsibility, quality control and assurance, finance and accounting, environmental change and sustainability, supply chain management, e-commerce and other functional areas in business. Following the discussion of this chapter thus far, Chapter 2 to Chapter 11 of this book present diverse insights on strategic innovation management from various business functional areas. In relation to the definition of strategic innovation in business that is discussed in this chapter, the last chapter of this book, Chapter 12, develops and supports arguments, based on the different business functional areas-centred innovation management insights, in order to propose an integrated cross-functional model of strategic innovation management in business and its future research areas.

The need for further research on cross-functional business management

Although cross-functional business management is an established research domain, many areas of this field are either not completely explored or partially explored. For example, "despite substantial efforts to improve information and communication infrastructures or to bring departments in closer proximity with one another, structural investments often fail to produce the desired positive impact on cross-functional, R&D cooperation" (Stock et al., 2013, p. 924). In terms of new product development, "the literature on new product development (NPD) contains several studies of management practices involved in different types of innovation. However, few studies focus on how cross-functional integration affects incremental and radical innovation product projects" (Jugend et al., 2017, p. 1). Moreover, researchers argue that

> one of the key challenges that organizations face when trying to integrate knowledge across different functions is the need to overcome knowledge boundaries between team members. In cross-functional teams, these boundaries, associated with different knowledge backgrounds of people from various disciplines, create communication problems, necessitating team members to engage in complex cognitive processes when integrating knowledge toward a joint outcome.
>
> (Kotlarsky et al., 2012, p. 319)

In the purchasing and supply chain management field, more recently, it is argued that "in cross-functional sourcing teams, differences in goals and personality traits can lead to tensions and reduced effectiveness" (Kaufmann and Wagner, 2017, p. 5). "The limited duration and the high time constraints facing projects may pose challenges to the development of working relationships in project teams" (Buvik and Rolfsen, 2015, p. 1484), which is a concern for effective collaboration between different cross-cultural teams, who work together to pursue the deadline of multifaceted projects. In terms of the lack of research on cross-functional business management in relation to optimising the outcome of an organisation's marketing management, another recent study reveals that

> as the gap between accelerating rate of change and organizational capability in responding to it widens, managers face increasing challenges to coordinate and align diverse intra-firm functions. Although coordination across functions in an organization is necessary for integrating complex resources, little is known about the internal conditions of a firm in which cross-functional coordination influences marketing adaptiveness.
>
> (Mohsen and Eng, 2016, p. 5946)

In terms of innovation management in HRM from the context of cross-functional input, it is argued that "with low levels of intrinsic involvement among employees, a lack of task visibility from upper management and limited social interaction among group members, many organisations struggle to combat the issue of social loafing in cross functional working groups" (O'Leary et al., 2017, p. 1). These arguments from the contemporary literature on the significance of and need for further research demonstrate that we need ongoing research on cross-functional business management for strategic innovation management, with an aim to pursue the vision of "cross-functional innovation for homogeneous socio-economic development across the world".

Conclusion

Along with discussing the need for ongoing research on strategic innovation and cross-functional perspectives and its significance, this chapter provides a background to explore how a firm engages in and supports new ideas, novelty, experimentation and creative processes that may result in new products, services or technological processes, in order to plan, implement and monitor their strategic business innovation process for long-term success. Based on this definition and characteristics of business innovation, Chapter 2 to Chapter 11 of this book attempt to explore the different business function-specific issues, in order to develop insights on how a particular business function, such as HRM, marketing, entrepreneurship, business risks and strategies and so forth deploy their function-specific knowledge and capabilities for strategic innovation management in business. From this context, the following chapters of this book explore the strategic innovation perspectives, based on the following business function-specific issues:

- Chapter 2 – neuroscience and its impact on marketing;
- Chapter 3 – information and communication science and its impact on stakeholder relationships and engagement;
- Chapter 4 – international trade and export management for agri-business;
- Chapter 5 – entrepreneurship for knowledge management;
- Chapter 6 – financial management and profitability;
- Chapter 7 – persuasion science for business communication;
- Chapter 8 – strategic innovation management for customer satisfaction in the higher education industry;
- Chapter 9 – stakeholder relationship management and marketing for entrepreneurial innovation;
- Chapter 10 – business risks, strategies and environment, and
- Chapter 11 – cross-cultural issues for HRM and mergers and acquisitions.

In relation to the definition of innovation that is discussed in this chapter, the final chapter of this book, Chapter 12, overviews how the ten different business functional areas of Chapter 2 to Chapter 11 of this book develop strategic innovation management insights, based on their function-specific issues and arguments. Following this overview, Chapter 12 develops, justifies and proposes an integrated cross-functional model of strategic innovation management in business and its future research areas, in order to pursue the cross-functional

8 *S. M. Riad Shams et al.*

strategic innovation management vision, which is "cross-functional innovation for homogeneous socio-economic development across the world".

References

Bresciani, S., Thrassou, A. and Vrontis, D. (2012). Human resource management – Practices performance and strategy in the Italian hotel industry. *World Review of Entrepreneurship, Management and Sustainable Development*, 8 (4), 405–423.

Burton-Jones, A. (2001). *Knowledge Capitalism-Business, Work, and Learning in the New Economy*. Oxford: Oxford University Press.

Buvik, M. P. and Rolfsen, M. (2015). Prior ties and trust development in project teams – A case study from the construction industry. *International Journal of Project Management, 33*, 1484–1494.

Chesbrough, H. W. (2010). Business model innovation: opportunities and barriers. *Long Range Planning, 43*, 354–363.

Christofi, M., Vrontis, D., Kitchen, P. and Papasolomou, I. (2015). Innovation and cause-related marketing success: a Conceptual framework and propositions. *Journal of Services Marketing, 29* (5), 354–366.

Chuang, J. C. and Newell, S. (2003). Knowledge integration processes and dynamics within the context of cross-functional projects. *International Journal of Project Management, 21* (3), 167–176.

Clercq, D. D., Thongpapanl, N. T. and Dimov, D. (2011). A closer look at cross-functional collaboration and product innovativeness: Contingency effects of structural and relational context. *Journal of Product Innovation Management, 28* (5).

Conta, F., Fiore, M., Vrontis, D. and Silvestri, R. (2015). Innovative marketing behaviour determinants in wine SMEs: the case of an Italian wine region. *International Journal of Globalisation and Small Business, 7* (2), 107–124.

Edmondson, A. C. and Harvey, J. F. (2017). Cross-boundary teaming for innovation: Integrating research on teams and knowledge in organizations. *Human Resource Management Review* (published online ahead of print, DOI: https://doi.org/10.1016/j.hrmr.2017.03.002).

Foerstl, K., Hartmann, E., Wynstra, F. and Moser, R. (2013). Cross-functional integration and functional coordination in purchasing and supply management: Antecedents and effects on purchasing and firm performance. *International Journal of Operations & Production Management, 33* (6), 689–721.

Jugend, D., Araujo, T. R. D., Pimenta, M. L. P., Gobbo Jr., J. A. and Hilletofth, P. (2017). The role of cross-functional integration in new product development: differences between incremental and radical innovation projects. *Innovation, Organization & Management* (published online ahead of print, DOI: http://dx.doi.org/10.1080/14479338.2017.1364971).

Kaufmann, H. R., and Shams, S. M. R. (Eds.). (2015). *Entrepreneurial challenges in the 21st century: Creating stakeholder value co-creation*. Hampshire, UK: Palgrave Macmillan.

Kaufmann, L. and Wagner, C. M. (2017). Affective diversity and emotional intelligence in cross-functional sourcing teams. *Journal of Purchasing and Supply Management, 23* (1), 5–16.

Kotlarsky, J., Hooff, B. V. D. and Houtman, L. (2012). Are we on the same page? Knowledge boundaries and transactive memory system development in cross-functional teams. *Communication Research, 42* (3), 319–344.

Longoni, A. and Cagliano, R. (2015). Cross-functional executive involvement and worker involvement in lean manufacturing and sustainability alignment. *International Journal of Operations & Production Management, 35* (9),1332–1358.

Lumpkin, G.T. and Dess, G.G. (1996). Clarifying the entrepreneurial orientation construct and linking it to performance. *Academy of Management Review, 21* (1), 135–172.

McAndrews, L. E. and Ha-Brookshire, J. E. (2016). *Working Together is Success: Examining Cross-Functional Team Performance in the Global Apparel Supply Chain.* Retrieved from http://lib.dr.iastate.edu/cgi/viewcontent.cgi?article=1640&context=itaa_proceedings (accessed 18 October, 2017).

McDonough, E. F. (2000). Investigation of factors contributing to the success of cross-functional teams. *Journal of Product Innovation Management, 17* (3), 221–235.

Mohsen, K. and Eng, T. Y. (2016). The antecedents of cross-functional coordination and their implications for marketing adaptiveness. *Journal of Business Research, 69* (12), 5946–5955.

O'Leary, K., O'Reilly, P., Feller, J., Gleasure, R., Li, S. and Cristoforo, J. (2017). *Exploring the Application of Blockchain Technology to Combat the Effects of Social Loafing in Cross Functional Group Projects.* Retrieved from https://dl.acm.org/citation.cfm?id=3125464&CFID=821760462&CFTOKEN=46518150 (accessed 22 October, 2017).

Piercy, N., Phillips, W. and Lewis, M. (2013). Change management in the public sector: The use of cross-functional teams. *Production Planning & Control, 24* (10–11), 976–987.

Romer, P. M. (1990). Endogenous technological change. *Journal of Political Economy, 98* (5), 71–102.

Sanchez, B. D., Kaufmann, R. and Vrontis D. (2012). A new organisational memory for cross-cultural knowledge management. *Cross Cultural Management: An International Journal, 19*, (3), 336–351.

Santa, R., Bretherton, P., Ferrer, M., Soosay, C. and Hyland, P. (2011). The role of cross-functional teams on the alignment between technology innovation effectiveness and operational effectiveness. *International Journal of Technology Management, 55* (1–2), 122–137.

Santoro, G., Vrontis, D., Thrassou, A. and Dezi, L. (2017). The Internet of Things: Building knowledge management systems for open innovation and knowledge management capacity. *Technological Forecasting and Social Change,* (published online ahead of print, DOI: 10.1016/j.techfore.2017.02.034).

Scapens, R.W. and Jazayeri, M. (2003). ERP systems and management accounting change: opportunities or impacts? A research note. *European Accounting Review, 12* (1), 201–233.

Sethi, R., Smith, D. C. and Park, W. (2001). Cross-functional product development teams, creativity, and the innovativeness of new consumer products. *Journal of Marketing Research, 38* (1), 73–85.

Shams, S. M. R. (2011). A relationship marketing model to enable sustainable growth of the Bangladesh Cricket Board: A stakeholder causal scope analysis (Doctoral thesis), Central Queensland University, Rockhampton.

Shams, S. M. R. (2013a). Implications of relationship marketing indicators to enable organizational growth: A stakeholder causal scope analysis. In Kaufmann, H. R. and Panni, M. F. A. (Eds.), *Customer centric-marketing strategies: Tools for building organizational performance* (pp. 214–244). Hershey, PA, USA: IGI Global.

Shams, S. M. R. (2013b). Stakeholder causal scope centric market positioning: Implications of relationship marketing indicators. In Kaufmann, H. R. and Panni, M. F. A. (Eds.), *Customer centric-marketing strategies: Tools for building organizational performance* (pp. 224–264). Hershey, PA, USA: IGI Global.

Shams, S. M. R. (2015). Modernism to postmodernism: The transdisciplinary mode-2 knowledge production of relationship marketing. *International Journal of Customer Relationship Marketing and Management, 4*(3), 44–56.

Shams, S. M. R. (2016a). Capacity building for sustained competitive advantage: A conceptual framework. *Marketing Intelligence & Planning, 34* (5), 671–691.

Shams, S. M. R. (2016b). Sustainability issues in transnational education service: A conceptual framework and empirical insights. *Journal of Global Marketing, 29* (3), 139–155.

Shams, S. M. R. (2017). Transnational education and total quality management: A Stakeholder-centred model. *Journal of Management Development, 36* (3), 376–389.

Shams, S. M. R. and Belyaeva, Z. (2017). Quality assurance driving factors as antecedents of knowledge management: A stakeholder-focussed perspective in higher education. *Journal of the Knowledge Economy*, 1–14 (published online ahead of print, DOI: https://doi.org/10.1007/s13132-017-0472-2).

Shams, S. M. R. and Kaufmann, H. R. (2016). Entrepreneurial co-creation: a research vision to be materialised. *Management Decision, 54* (6), 1250–1268.

Shams, S. M. R., and Lombardi, R. (2016). Socio-economic value co-creation and sports tourism: Evidence from Tasmania. *World Review of Entrepreneurship. Management and Sustainable Development, 12*(2/3), 218–238.

Shams, S. M. R., Vrontis, D. and Czinkota, M. R. (2017). Innovation management and entrepreneurial development: The antecedent role of stakeholder engagement. *Journal of Business Research*. Retrieved from www.journals.elsevier.com/journal-of-business-research/call-for-papers/innovation-management-and-entrepreneurial-development-the-an (accessed 15 October, 2017).

Spietch, P., Schneckenberg, D. and Ricart, J. E. (2014). Business model innovation – State of the art and future challenges for the field. *R&D Management, 44* (3), 237–247.

Stock, R. M., Totzauer, F. and Zacharias, N. A. (2013). A closer look at cross-functional R&D cooperation for innovativeness: Innovation-oriented leadership and human resource practices as driving forces. *Journal of Product Innovation Management, 31* (5), 924–938.

Teece, D. J. (2010). Business models, business strategy and innovation. *Long Range Planning, 43*, 172–194.

Thrassou, A., Vrontis, D. and Bresciani, S. (2014). Strategic reflexivity in the hotel industry – A value-based analysis, *World Review of Entrepreneurship, Management & Sustainable Development, 10* (1–2), 352–371.

Vrontis, D., Tharassou, A., Chebbi, H. and Yahiaoui, D. (2012). Transcending innovativeness towards strategic reflexivity. *Qualitative Market Research: An International Journal, 15* (4), 420–437.

2 Neuromarketing applications of neuroprosthetic devices

An assessment of neural implants' capacities for gathering data and influencing behavior

Matthew E. Gladden

Introduction

Ongoing developments in the field of neuromarketing are being made possible by innovative applications of various technologies. For example, neuromarketing researchers and practitioners rely on instruments such as electroencephalography (EEG) and functional magnetic resonance imaging (fMRI) equipment to gather data about the ways in which potential consumers respond on a subconscious or unconscious level to the contents of advertisements or other stimuli. Once such insights have been developed, websites, email, and social media platforms and other technologies utilizing microtargeting approaches can be applied to deliver personalized advertising messages that are shaped to maximize their appeal to an individual recipient.

In this text, we argue that the emerging technologies of sensory, cognitive, and motor neuroprosthetics are creating powerful new tools that can potentially be used by neuromarketing professionals both for gathering data about the cognitive activity of potential consumers and for influencing their behavior. Rather than immediately developing an ethical, legal, or business analysis of the case for or against utilizing neuroprosthetic devices in such neuromarketing-related roles, our focus in this text is on the conceptually prior task of formulating a comprehensive framework for analyzing the technological and biocybernetic capacities of neuroprosthetic devices to be employed in such roles.

It is hoped that this conceptual framework can inform further investigations of the propriety and desirability of neuroprosthetically facilitated neuromarketing approaches from ethical, legal, and business perspectives. Such a framework can also facilitate the work of information security (InfoSec) professionals in two ways. First, InfoSec personnel must develop effective mechanisms for protecting neuroprosthetic devices against external actors' deployment of neuromarketing techniques that are considered unwelcome by the users of such devices or which are inherently unethical or illegal.

12 *Matthew E. Gladden*

Second, InfoSec personnel must ensure that those forms of neuromarketing conducted by means of neural implants that are acceptable to and authorized by the devices' users are performed in a way that suitably protects the confidentiality, integrity, and availability of information belonging to all of the stakeholders involved in those activities.

Developing and employing frameworks such as the one described in this text will become especially important as the number of human beings who possess neural implants continues to grow: while such devices are currently employed primarily to treat particular medical conditions, it is anticipated that their increasing use for purposes of human augmentation and elective enhancement will continually expand the portion of society that utilizes such technology. Moreover, due to the kinds of enhanced capacities that neuroprosthetic devices may grant and the great expense, surgical risks, and other obstacles involved with the acquisition of such devices, the groups of people who possess neuroprosthetic implants for medical or augmentative purposes may tend to disproportionately manifest particular cognitive, biological, professional, or socioeconomic characteristics (such as holding senior-level positions in business or government or possessing above-average levels of wealth) that make them especially attractive targets for particular kinds of neuromarketing. It is thus important to understand the full spectrum of ways in which neural implants might be employed for neuromarketing purposes.

Before our two-dimensional framework is presented, it will be helpful to briefly review the nature of neuromarketing and neuroprosthetic devices.

An overview of neuromarketing

The concept of 'neuromarketing' has been defined in various ways. Some definitions seek to position neuromarketing primarily as an academic discipline that analyzes consumer behavior through the lens of neuroscience. Lee, Broderick, & Chamberlain (2007, p. 200) emphasize the academic aspect, arguing that "neuromarketing as a field of study can simply be defined as the application of neuroscientific methods to analyze and understand human behaviour in relation to markets and marketing exchanges." Other definitions position neuromarketing primarily as a business practice; for example, for Fisher, Chin, & Klitzman (2010, p. 230), neuromarketing can be "defined as marketing designed on the basis of neuroscience research [...]." Still other definitions span both spheres, positioning neuromarketing as the applied branch of the academic field of 'consumer neuroscience' (Fisher et al., 2010).

In both its academic and applied forms, neuromarketing seeks to help businesses and other organizations understand how particular stimuli (such as the words or images used in TV advertisements or the background music played in retail stores) influence potential consumers' behavior; however, it does this not by asking individuals for their conscious reaction to stimuli but by directly monitoring biological activity in the brain or other organs in order to detect subconscious or unconscious cognitive responses that the individuals themselves cannot clearly describe or do not even realize that they are manifesting (Fisher et al., 2010). Such research might, for example, measure how consumers' 'willingness to pay' (WTP) for different products and services is influenced by the presentation of different stimuli (Ariely & Berns, 2010, p. 285). In order to gather such data, neuromarketing utilizes technologies such as electroencephalography (EEG), magnetoencephalography (MEG), functional magnetic resonance imaging (fMRI), Galvanic skin response (GSR), electrocardiography (EKG), electromyography (EMG), and eye tracking to detect responses to stimuli (Fisher et al., 2010; Lee et al., 2007; Morin, 2011; Ariely & Berns, 2010).

Applied forms of neuromarketing utilize the knowledge obtained by means of such technologies in order to craft designs for products and packaging, advertising messages, website content, and other goods, communications, or stimuli that are formulated to maximize the positive response on the part of potential consumers. Although accounts in the popular media sometimes focus on the perceived danger that neuromarketing techniques might allow businesses or other organizations to illicitly manipulate the brain and coerce consumers into taking actions against their own will, when used ethically neuromarketing practices can play a positive role in matching consumers with the goods and services that they most truly desire (Ariely & Berns, 2010). Neuromarketing techniques can be applied effectively in such diverse areas as the development of TV advertisements for food products, the architectural design of new buildings, and the management of political campaigns (Ariely & Berns, 2010).

An overview of neuroprosthetic devices

Neuroprosthetic devices are pieces of technology that are directly integrated into the human body's neural circuitry (Gladden, 2015b, p. 20; Gladden, 2016; Lebedev, 2014). At present, such neuroprostheses are typically invasive devices designed to be surgically implanted in the body of their human host (often, though not always, within the brain itself); while non-invasive technologies such as EEG and fMRI equipment may be utilized as brain-computer interface (BCI) technologies in a broader sense, they are not generally considered to be neuroprostheses insofar as they are not "integrated into" the neural circuitry of their human subject in a direct and long-term manner. While future technological advances may yield a growing range of non-invasive neuroprostheses that can be incorporated into an individual's neural circuitry without physically entering the brain, for purposes of this text the phrases 'neuroprosthetic device' and 'neural implant' can be considered roughly synonymous. Such neuroprostheses should not be confused with passive RFID tags or other kinds of implantable devices that may provide valuable information relating to their host's physical location or movements but which – because they are not integrated into a host's

14 *Matthew E. Gladden*

neural circuitry – do not directly gather information about or influence a host's cognitive activity.

Classification of neuroprostheses by function

Particular neural implants can be described as *sensory, cognitive,* or *motor* neuroprostheses; a neural implant may also combine more than one of these functions in a single device (Lebedev, 2014; Gladden, 2015b).

Sensory neuroprostheses provide sense data to the brain of their human host. Most existing sensory neuroprostheses are utilized for purposes of treating medical conditions; such devices already in use include cochlear implants and retinal prostheses (Koops & Leenes, 2012; Gladden, 2015b, pp. 22–24). However, the use of sensory neuroprostheses for purposes of human augmentation and enhancement has already begun on an experimental basis and is expected to grow in the coming years; such technologies might, for example, provide a human subject with telescopic or infrared vision or the ability to hear ultrasonic frequencies (Warwick, 2014; Gasson, Kosta, & Bowman, 2012; Merkel et al., 2007).

Cognitive neuroprostheses affect cognitive processes and phenomena internal to the brain of their human host (Gladden, 2015b, pp. 26–27), including imagination (Cosgrove, 2004; Gasson, 2012), emotion (Soussou & Berger, 2008), conscious alertness (Kourany, 2013, pp. 992–93), and the sense of personal identity (Van den Berg, 2012). While it is not possible to precisely edit the contents of memories within a human mind using existing cognitive neuroprosthetic technologies – and may never be possible, if the nature of memory storage within the brain is found to be sufficiently holographic or holistic (Levy, 2010, p. xv) – experimental technologies have, for example, already been developed that can create or erase simple memories in the brains of mice (Ramirez et al., 2013; Han et al., 2009).

Motor neuroprostheses, meanwhile, either detect motor instructions within the brain of their human host and convey them to some external system or generate motor instructions which the brain itself is not able to provide (Lebedev, 2014; Gladden, 2015b, pp. 24–26). Such devices allow their hosts to control robotic prosthetic limbs, motorized wheelchairs, or computers (Donchin & Arbel, 2009); are used to treat conditions such as bladder function disorders, swallowing disorders, and sleep apnea; provide a means of communication for paralyzed patients suffering from ALS, traumatic brain injury, or stroke (Taylor, 2008); and can potentially be used to treat conditions such as epilepsy (Fountas & Smith, 2007), Alzheimer's disease, anxiety disorders, bulimia, and addictions (Ansari, Chaudhri, & Al Moutaery, 2007) or to allow their users to control external networked systems such as drones or 3D printers (Gladden, 2015a).

Biocybernetic aspects of neuroprosthetic devices

The field of cybernetics offers a transdisciplinary theoretical framework and vocabulary that can translate insights between the diverse range of disciplines that study patterns of communication and control in machines, living organisms, or social systems (Wiener, 1961). In the case of neuroprosthetic devices, such processes of communication and control involve both the devices themselves and the biological organisms in which they are implanted. When neural implants are viewed from a biocybernetic perspective, one considers not only their internal physical components and behaviors but also the ways in which they interact with a host's organism through executing, sharing in, or being affected by processes of communication and control.

While the interaction between a neural implant and human host may be relatively simple and unidirectional (such as when a cochlear implant electrically stimulates the cochlear nerve to present auditory sense data to the mind of its human host), a growing number of neuroprosthetic devices create complex biocybernetic feedback loops that allow their human users to both manipulate some external physical or virtual environment and then sense the ways in which that environment has been altered as a result of their actions (Gladden, 2015a; Fairclough, 2010; Park, Goldman, Belknap, & Friehs, 2009).

A framework for analyzing neuroprostheses' neuromarketing applications

In addition to deploying specialized equipment (such as dedicated fMRI and EEG devices) to gather data about consumers' responses to stimuli and relying on customized tools such as microtargeting websites and TV advertisements to deliver the marketing messages that are developed as a result, we suggest that it will increasingly be possible for neuromarketing professionals to accomplish both tasks by utilizing neuroprosthetic devices that have already been implanted in members of the public for therapeutic or augmentative purposes and which possess direct access to the neural circuitry of their human hosts.

We would argue that such potential applications of neuroprosthetic devices for neuromarketing can be effectively identified and analyzed with the assistance of a two-dimensional conceptual framework that reflects: 1) the different functional types of neuroprosthetic technologies; and 2) the fact that a given technology can be employed either to gather data about consumers' cognitive activity or to influence consumers' behavior.

It should be noted that the conceptual framework presented in this text is intended to capture the full universe of potential neuromarketing applications of neuroprosthetic devices that are expected to become *technologically feasible* during the coming years; it is not, however, claimed that all (or even any) potential applications identified through use of this framework are *ethically meritorious or legally permissible*. Indeed, one of the anticipated uses of the proposed framework is to aid government policymakers, ethicists, neuroprosthetic device manufacturers, InfoSec professionals, and neuromarketing researchers and practitioners to identify new ethical questions and concerns that result from the increasing availability within the general population of implanted neuroprosthetic devices that can be exploited for neuromarketing purposes

16 *Matthew E. Gladden*

and to develop more robust legal and regulatory frameworks, industry best practices and ethics guidelines, and InfoSec controls and countermeasures to address such possibilities. We can now consider each of the framework's axes in more detail.

First axis: Functional types of neuroprosthetic devices

One axis of the framework delineates the main functional types of neuroprosthetic devices – namely, 1) sensory, 2) cognitive, and 3) motor neuroprostheses. There is not a separate category for hybrid neuroprosthetic devices that combine multiple types, such as a bidirectional sensorimotor neuroprosthesis in the form of a robotic prosthetic arm that allows a human amputee to both feel the pressure of an object held within the robotic fingers' grasp and to control the fingers' motion through his or her thoughts; such a hybrid device could be analyzed within this framework as though it were a set of separate sensory and motor neuroprostheses.

Second axis: The role of gathering data or influencing behavior

The second axis of our framework describes two critical roles that a particular technological device might play within the practice of neuromarketing: 1) gathering data about potential consumers' cognitive activity; or 2) influencing potential consumers' behavior.

At present, the more widely accepted and employed use of neuro-technologies in neuromarketing is in gathering data about the way in which the brain of a potential consumer responds to different kinds of stimuli (Lee et al., 2007; Fisher et al., 2010; Morin, 2011). For example, neuromarketing research has used EEG and MEG technologies to study how the brain reacts differently to various kinds of advertisements and which types of formats and elements can be employed to optimize the processes of attention, memory, and trust that are needed to cultivate brand recognition and loyalty in consumers who are exposed to such advertisements (Lee et al., 2007, p. 201).

A more controversial role that neurotechnologies might possibly play within the field of neuromarketing is that of influencing or even directly controlling the behavior of consumers. Certainly, the use of technological media such as TV advertisements to influence consumers' actions is a longstanding and widely accepted practice. However, neurotechnologies provide new and potentially vastly more powerful tools for attempting to shape consumers' behavior. Such influence can be created either indirectly (e.g., through the creation of cybernetic sensorimotor feedback loops that incentivize and 'train' consumers to behave in particular ways) or directly, through the immediate artificial stimulation of neurons within the brain. While it is not feasible to directly influence consumers' neural activity without their knowledge or consent employing current technologies like EEG and fMRI (Fisher et al.,

Neuromarketing of neuroprosthetic devices 17

2010; Murphy, Illes, & Reiner, 2008, pp. 297–98), such actions might be possible in the future if consumers' existing neuroprosthetic implants could be accessed and exploited (Bonaci, Calo, & Chizeck, 2015) by neuromarketing practitioners.

POTENTIAL NEUROMARKETING APPLICATION

	Gathering data on cognitive activity	Influencing behavior
Sensory	• Access to sense data received or transmitted by a device may reveal information about its host's focus of attention (e.g., direction of gaze) or biological processes (e.g., the sounds of breathing or heartbeat). • Altered or fabricated sense data may be supplied to the host via the device so that his or her reaction can be observed via the device or other means.	• 'Real' sense data may be replaced with altered or fabricated data intended to elicit a particular automatic biological response (e.g., physical discomfort, increased stress, or drowsiness). • Sense data may be altered or fabricated in order to create certain beliefs in the host's mind and elicit in response some conscious action that the host would not otherwise perform.
Cognitive	• Emotional states, the focus of the host's attention, and the general nature of a host's current thoughts may be discernible, even if not otherwise outwardly detectable. • The contents of existing memories and associations held within the host's mind may be detected (if only in a broad sense).	• A host's mood or emotional state may be altered in order to make particular behaviors more or less likely. • A host's conscious alertness may be increased or decreased. • Existing memories may be altered or new memories created in order to generate a desired conscious or unconscious response from the host when later exposed to specific stimuli.
Motor	• Access to motor instructions received by a device from a host's brain may reveal information about the host's thoughts, volitions, and physical state that is not otherwise detectable. • A device's motor behavior may be altered in a particular way in order to observe the host's response.	• A device may directly stimulate or control action of the eyes (e.g., shifting the host's gaze), heart (altering the heart rate), limbs and digits (e.g., to reach toward an object), or other organs. • Behavior of a device (e.g., a motorized wheelchair or robotic limb) may be altered in a way designed to elicit a particular conscious or unconscious response by the host.

TYPE OF NEUROPROSTHESIS

Figure 2.1 Examples of potential neuromarketing applications for neuroprostheses

18   *Matthew E. Gladden*

Completing the framework

When the two axes described above are combined, they yield a matrix of the sort depicted in Figure 2.1. For each of the six fields within the matrix, a description is shown of ways in which that type of neuroprosthetic device might fill the given type of neuromarketing role, based on the device's technological and biocybernetic characteristics.

An assessment of neuromarketing applications by neural implant type

Having formulated this two-dimensional framework, we can now use it to identify capacities possessed by particular types of neuroprosthetic devices that are already in use or whose development is being pursued that can allow them to be employed in the dual neuromarketing roles of gathering data about the cognitive activity of the devices' human hosts or influencing the hosts' behavior. As noted earlier, the analysis of sensory, cognitive, and motor neuroprostheses presented below is not an assessment of the ethical or legal propriety or commercial desirability of utilizing neuroprosthetic devices for such purposes but rather a technological and biocybernetic assessment of the capacity of neural implants to be employed in such ways by an organizational or individual actor who wishes to utilize them in such a manner.

Sensory neuroprostheses: Assessment of potential neuromarketing applications

The commercial utilization of BCIs to detect covert mental states in the devices' human hosts for purposes of carrying out neuromarketing activities is noted by Brunner, Bianchi, Guger, Cincotti, & Schalk (2011) as an emerging application for BCIs. One form that this activity might take is the exploitation of sensory neuroprosthetic devices that are already implanted in human hosts for medical or augmentative purposes in order to gain access to data about the hosts' cognitive processes. From a technological perspective, it is possible to perform such actions either with the knowledge and consent of a device's human host (e.g., if the individual 'opts in' to allowing a marketing firm or other company to have limited access to data contained in his or her sensory neuroprosthesis) or in a surreptitious and likely unlawful manner (e.g., by compromising or replacing the components of an already existing BCI device (Bonaci et al., 2015)). Data received or transmitted by a sensory neuroprosthesis and made available to neuromarketers might reveal information about its host's focus of attention (e.g., by decoding information from a retinal implant to detect the direction of its host's gaze) or biological processes (e.g., by filtering the audio data generated by a cochlear implant to detect its user's heart rate or breathing patterns). Moreover, altered or fabricated sense data representing particular stimuli might be supplied to a host's brain via the sensory neuroprosthesis so that the host's unconscious reaction could be observed using the device itself or another mechanism.

It is also technologically possible for various kinds of sensory neuroprostheses to be used legitimately or illicitly to influence the behavior of their human hosts. Daigle (2010, p. 40) notes that manipulation of the sensory signals reaching the brain can be used as a means of influencing or controlling the brain's behavior; for example, by hacking the artificial retinal implants of a human host and providing him or her with fabricated visual information that creates a particular (mistaken) belief about the host's environment or physical state, the host could be induced to enact certain conscious physical responses that he or she would not otherwise perform. (For example, a host who is artificially made to feel thirsty or to falsely perceive that all of the other patrons of a restaurant are greatly enjoying their beverages might himself or herself choose to order a drink.)

Bublitz (2011, pp. 111–12) distinguishes between 'indirect' and 'direct' interventions in an individual's cognitive processes: *indirect interventions* include the presentation of stimuli to sensory organs (e.g., in the form of music, spoken language, or TV advertisements) that are processed by the brain along with all other external environmental stimuli, while *direct interventions* include techniques such as deep brain stimulation (DBS) and transcranial magnetic stimulation (TMS) that use technological means to artificially and directly stimulate neurons within the brain. According to that schema, the use of sensory neuroprostheses to influence a host's behavior will typically constitute 'indirect' interventions, while 'direct' interventions might be performed more readily, for example, through the manipulation of cognitive neuroprostheses.

Cognitive neuroprostheses: Assessment of potential neuromarketing applications

There are numerous ways in which already-implanted cognitive neuroprostheses could potentially be utilized by neuromarketers to gather data about the cognitive activity of their human hosts. Through access to data contained in such devices, a host's emotional states, the focus of a host's attention, and the general nature of a host's current thoughts may be discernible, even if they are not otherwise outwardly detectable. While it might not be theoretically possible for a neuroprosthetic device to identify complex semantic content of specific memories, it may be possible for a cognitive neuroprosthesis to determine on the basis of neural signals that, for example, its human host is listening to a particular piece of music (Horgan, 2004). Even generalized access to the contents of cognitive processes might help accomplish neuromarketing goals such as that of identifying "the relationship between smells and colors of food products" (Lee et al., 2007, p. 200).

Influencing a host's behavior through the use of an implanted cognitive neuroprosthetic device is also quite feasible. For example, deep brain stimulation can be employed to alter a user's moods (Bublitz, 2011, p. 116). Kohno, Denning, & Matsuoka (2009) and Bublitz (2011, pp. 97–98) explicitly consider the possibility that hackers might illicitly access neural implants that have been installed in human hosts for legitimate therapeutic purposes (such as DBS) and use them to influence their hosts' thoughts, moods, and emotions in order to directly shape their behaviors as consumers – i.e., for purposes of neuromarketing. Analyzing the mind-altering effects of DBS that have already been demonstrated, Rowland, Breshears, & Chang (2013) similarly raise the question of whether brain-machine interface devices might be used for 'cognitive control.' It is also known that transcranial magnetic stimulation can affect the formation of volitions (Bublitz, 2011, p. 116). TMS devices induce an electric current in neurons in order to facilitate or inhibit synaptic activity; such tools have been used by researchers to temporarily take particular brain regions 'offline,' thereby allowing researchers to determine how the brain's performance of specific tasks is affected by impairing the functioning of those regions (Ariely & Berns, 2010). Having gained such knowledge through their use, the same or similar technologies could potentially be employed to elicit or block particular kinds of cognitive activity. It has also been shown that commercially available BCI technologies can already be used to develop 'brain spyware' or 'BCI-enabled malicious applications' which, for example, can electrically stimulate the brain to impede users' responses when they are lying (Bonaci et al., 2015, p. 35; Luber, Fisher, Appelbaum, Ploesser, & Lisanby, 2009).

Moreover, if neuroprosthetic implants can store memories – thus serving as a sort of 'supplemental memory' to the storage capacity of the brain's natural biological neural network (Daigle, 2010, p. 37; Gladden, 2015b, pp. 148–49) – then any mechanism that can manipulate or alter the contents of such devices could be used to influence future behaviors that are dependent on or affected by such memories. Noting researchers' assessment of DARPA's ongoing $40 million Restoring Active Memory (RAM) and Systems-Based Neurotechnology for Emerging Therapies (SUBNET) programs to develop next-generation implantable neuroprostheses for treating memory and cognitive disorders, Talan (2014, pp. 9–10) cites "a growing concern that the manipulation of brain networks" by means of such devices "could be used as a form of mind control." Similarly, Krishnan (2014, p. 10) notes the possibility that an actor might compromise an implanted neural device in order to influence or control the behavior of its human host; he distinguishes the application of such 'mind hacking' to exercise short-term control over its host's body versus using it to effect a permanent 'rewiring' of the host's memories or behavior (Krishnan, 2014, p. 10).

Motor neuroprostheses: Assessment of potential neuromarketing applications

There are various means by which conventional motor neuroprostheses already implanted in human hosts could potentially be utilized by neuromarketers to gather data about the cognitive activity of those hosts. For example, access to motor instructions received by a device from a host's brain may reveal information about the host's thoughts, volitions, and physical state that is not otherwise detectable (Gladden, 2015b, pp. 24–26). It may also be possible to disrupt, control, or otherwise alter a device's motor behavior in a particular way in order to observe the host's response to that unexpected stimulus.

A motor neuroprosthetic device could also be used to directly stimulate or control action of the eyes (e.g., shifting the host's gaze to a particular object), heart (e.g., artificially increasing or decreasing the heart rate), limbs and digits (e.g., extending an arm to reach for an object), or other organs. The behavior of a device such as a motorized wheelchair or robotic limb might also be altered in a way that is designed to elicit some desired conscious or unconscious response by the device's human user. Already, tens of thousands of people worldwide possess implanted neuroprosthetic devices used for deep brain stimulation, which is employed primarily to treat Parkinson's disease and other movement disorders but which has also been found to generate mood changes in patients (Daigle, 2010, pp. 35–36; Van den Berg, 2012); such neuroprostheses could potentially be used to alter the moods of their human hosts in a way that would make certain consumer activities more or less likely at a given point in time.

Conclusion

As we have seen, the kinds of neuroprosthetic devices that are utilized by a growing segment of the population for the treatment of medical conditions or for purposes of human enhancement constitute powerful new tools that can conceivably be used for the two key neuromarketing tasks of gathering data about the ways in which potential consumers' cognitive processes react to particular stimuli and delivering stimuli that can influence consumers' behavior in a desired fashion. While general questions have already been posed by ethicists and others regarding the use of neuroprosthetic devices to gather information about the cognitive activity of their human hosts – either surreptitiously or with the hosts' consent – and to influence the hosts' behavior, such issues have not yet been comprehensively explored from the perspective of the technological and biocybernetic capacity of neuroprosthetic devices to be employed for such purposes within the field of neuromarketing.

The conceptual framework proposed in this text represents one approach to developing such a framework; it is hoped that it can aid scholars and practitioners in identifying and exploring the practical, legal, and ethical issues that arise if neuroprosthetic devices that have been implanted in human hosts for other purposes are accessed and utilized by neuromarketing professionals for neuromarketing-related ends. Moreover, it is hoped that the schema presented in this text can assist InfoSec professionals in developing robust security practices and mechanisms both to safeguard the users of neuroprosthetic devices against undesired and illicit forms of neuromarketing and to ensure that legitimate forms of neuromarketing conducted by means of neural implants are carried out in a way that appropriately protects the confidentiality, integrity, and availability of the information of all stakeholders who participate in such activities.

References

Ansari, S., Chaudhri, K., & Al Moutaery, K. (2007). Vagus nerve stimulation: Indications and limitations. In D. E. Sakas & B. A. Simpson (Eds.), *Operative neuromodulation* (pp. 281–86). Springer Vienna.

Ariely, D., & Berns, G. S. (2010). Neuromarketing: The hope and hype of neuroimaging in business. *Nature Reviews Neuroscience, 11(4)*, 284–92.

Bonaci, T., Calo, R., & Chizeck, H. (2015). App stores for the brain. *IEEE Technology and Society Magazine*, 1932–4529(*15*), 32–39.

Brunner, P., Bianchi, L., Guger, C., Cincotti, F., & Schalk, G. (2011). Current trends in hardware and software for brain-computer interfaces (BCIs). *Journal of Neural Engineering, 8(2)*, 25001.

Bublitz, J. C. (2011). If man's true palace is his mind, what is its adequate protection? On a right to mental self-determination and limits of interventions into other minds. In B. Van Den Berg & L. Klaming (Eds.), *Technologies on the stand: Legal and ethical questions in neuroscience and robotics* (pp. 89–114). Nijmegen: Wolf Legal Publishers.

Cosgrove, G. R. (2004). *In Session 6: Neuroscience, brain, and behavior V: deep brain stimulation, a meeting of the President's Council on Bioethics*, Washington, DC, June 24–25, 2004. Retrieved from https://bioethicsarchive.georgetown.edu/pcbe/transcripts/june04/session6.html (accessed 8 May 2016).

Daigle, K. R. (2010). *Manipulating the mind: The ethics of cognitive enhancement* (M.A. thesis, Bioethics). Wake Forest University, Winston-Salem, NC. Retrieved from Z. Smith Reynolds Library, https://wakespace.lib.wfu.edu/handle/10339/30407 (accessed 8 May 2016).

Donchin, E., & Arbel, Y. (2009). P300 based brain computer interfaces: A progress report. In D. D. Schmorrow, I. V. Estabrooke, & M. Grootjen (Eds.), *Foundations of augmented cognition. Neuroergonomics and operational neuroscience* (pp. 724–31). Springer Berlin Heidelberg.

Fairclough, S. H. (2010). Physiological computing: Interfacing with the human nervous system. In J. Westerink, M. Krans, & M. Ouwerkerk (Eds.), *Sensing emotions* (pp. 1–20). Philips Research Book Series 12. Springer Netherlands.

Fisher, C. E., Chin, L., & Klitzman, R. (2010). Defining neuromarketing: Practices and professional challenges. *Harvard Review of Psychiatry, 18(4)*, 230–37.

Fountas, K. N., & Smith, J. R. (2007). A novel closed-loop stimulation system in the control of focal, medically refractory epilepsy. In D. E. Sakas & B. A. Simpson (Eds.), *Operative neuromodulation* (pp. 357–62). Springer Vienna.

Gasson, M. N. (2012). Human ICT implants: From restorative application to human enhancement. In M. N. Gasson, E. Kosta, & D. M. Bowman (Eds.), *Human ICT implants: Technical, legal and ethical considerations* (pp. 11–28). T. M. C. Asser Press.

Gasson, M. N., Kosta, E., & Bowman, D. M. (2012). Human ICT implants: From invasive to pervasive. In M. N. Gasson, E. Kosta, & D. M. Bowman (Eds.), *Human ICT implants: Technical, legal and ethical considerations* (pp. 1–8). T. M. C. Asser Press.

Gladden, M. E. (2015a). Cybershells, shapeshifting, and neuroprosthetics: Video games as tools for posthuman 'body schema (re)engineering,' keynote presentation at the Ogólnopolska Konferencja Naukowa Dyskursy Gier Wideo, Facta Ficta Research Centre / AGH, Kraków, June 6, 2015. Retrieved from www.youtube.com/watch?v=Ruu52x28jjg (accessed 4 April 2016).

Gladden, M. E. (2015b). *The handbook of information security for advanced neuroprosthetics*. Indianapolis: Synthypnion Academic.

Gladden, M. E. (2016). Neural implants as gateways to digital-physical ecosystems and posthuman socioeconomic interaction. In Ł. Jonak, N. Juchniewicz, & R. Włoch (Eds.), *Digital ecosystems: Society in the digital age* (pp. 85–98). Warsaw: Digital Economy Lab, University of Warsaw.

Han, J.-H., Kushner, S. A., Yiu, A. P., Hsiang, H.-W., Buch, T., Waisman, A., Bontempi, B., Neve, R. L., Frankland, P. W., & Josselyn, S. A. (2009). Selective erasure of a fear memory. *Science, 323*(5920), 1492–96.

Horgan, J. (2004). The myth of mind control. *Discover, 25*(10).

Kohno, T., Denning, T., & Matsuoka, Y. (2009). Security and privacy for neural devices. *Neurosurgical Focus, 27*, 1–4.

Koops, B.-J., & Leenes, R. (2012). Cheating with implants: Implications of the hidden information advantage of bionic ears and eyes. In M. N. Gasson, E. Kosta, & D. M. Bowman (Eds.), *Human ICT implants: Technical, legal and ethical considerations* (pp. 113–34). T. M. C. Asser Press.

Kourany, J. A. (2013). Human enhancement: Making the debate more productive. *Erkenntnis, 79*(5), 981–98.

Krishnan, A. (2014). From psyops to neurowar: What are the dangers?, presented at ISAC-ISSS 2014 Annual Conference on Security Studies, University of Texas, Austin, Texas, November 16, 2014. Retrieved from http://web.isanet.org/Web/Conferences/ISSS%20Austin%202014/Archive/b137347c-6281-466d-b9e7-ef7e0e5d363c.pdf (accessed 8 May 2016).

Lebedev, M. (2014). Brain-machine interfaces: An overview. *Translational Neuroscience, 5*(1), 99–110.

Lee N., Broderick, A. J., & Chamberlain, L. (2007). What is 'neuromarketing'? A discussion and agenda for future research. *International Journal of Psychophysiology, 63*, 199–204.

Levy, N. (2010). Preface. In J. J. Giordano & B. Gordijn (Eds.), *Scientific and Philosophical perspectives in neuroethics*. Cambridge: Cambridge University Press.

Luber, B., Fisher, C., Appelbaum, P. S., Ploesser, M., & Lisanby, S. H. (2009). Non-invasive brain stimulation in the detection of deception: Scientific challenges and ethical consequences. *Behavioral Sciences and the Law, 27*(2), 191–208.

Merkel, R., Boer, G., Fegert, J., Galert, T., Hartmann, D., Nuttin, B., & Rosahl, S. (2007). Central neural prostheses. In *Intervening in the brain: Changing psyche and society* (pp. 117–60). Springer Berlin Heidelberg.

Morin, C. (2011). Neuromarketing: The new science of consumer behavior. *Society, 48*(2), 131–35.

Murphy E. R., Illes, J., & P. B. Reiner (2008). Neuroethics of neuromarketing. *Journal of Consumer Behavior, 7*, 293–302.

Park, M. C., Goldman, M. A., Belknap, T. W., & Friehs, G. M. (2009). The future of neural interface technology. In A. M. Lozano, P. L. Gildenberg, & R. R. Tasker (Eds.), *Textbook of stereotactic and functional neurosurgery* (pp. 3185–200). Springer Berlin Heidelberg.

24 *Matthew E. Gladden*

Ramirez, S., Liu, X., Lin, P.-A., Suh, J., Pignatelli, M., Redondo, R. L., Ryan, T. J., & Tonegawa, S. (2013). Creating a false memory in the hippocampus. *Science, 341*(6144), 387–91.

Rowland, N. C., Breshears, J., & Chang, E. F. (2013). Neurosurgery and the dawning age of brain-machine interfaces. *Surgical Neurology International, 4.*

Soussou, W. V., & Berger, T. W. (2008). Cognitive and emotional neuroprostheses. In *Brain-computer interfaces* (pp. 109–23). Springer Netherlands.

Talan, J. (2014). DARPA: On the hunt for neuroprosthetics to enhance memory. *Neurology Today, 14*(20), 8–10.

Taylor, D. M. (2008). Functional electrical stimulation and rehabilitation applications of BCIs. In *Brain-computer interfaces* (pp. 81–94). Springer Netherlands.

Van den Berg, B. (2012). Pieces of me: On identity and information and communications technology implants. In M. N. Gasson, E. Kosta, & D. M. Bowman (Eds.), *Human ICT implants: Technical, legal and ethical considerations* (pp. 159–73). T. M. C. Asser Press.

Warwick, K. (2014). The cyborg revolution. *Nanoethics, 8,* 263–73.

Wiener, N. (1961). *Cybernetics: Or control and communication in the animal and the machine.* Second edition. Cambridge, MA: The MIT Press [Quid Pro ebook edition for Kindle, 2015].

3 The role of information sharing and communication strategies for improving stakeholder engagement

Francesco Caputo, Federica Evangelista and Giuseppe Russo

Introduction

The increasing complexity and competitiveness of social and economic configurations is pushing both researchers and practitioners to identify possible new ways to improve the capability of organizations to survive in a challenging scenario (Schoemaker, 1992; Payne and Frow, 2005). Traditional managerial models and organizational approaches based on the view of a company as an autonomous entity able to influence the market and encourage stakeholders towards specific behaviours and aims are proving increasingly inefficient (Birkinshaw, 1997; Reinartz *et al.*, 2004). The consequence of the old market approach is the increasing risk of many organizations being unable to understand the evolution of market, with negative effects on their chances of survival (Buysse and Verbeke, 2003; Freeman *et al.*, 2007; Barile *et al.*, 2012; Golinelli *et al.*, 2012; Saviano and Caputo, 2012, 2013).

In the last few years, to overcome the risks and failures of the old approach, different researchers and research streams have tried to identify possible new ways, focusing attention on the ability of an organization to forecast the evolution of consumers' behaviours and lifestyles (Vrontis and Thrassou, 2007; Solomon *et al.*, 2012); on the organizational setting and models on which organizations' strategies and vision are based (Cummings and Worley, 2014; Senge, 2014); and on the instruments needed to acquire more information on the evolution of context and how better to use them (Campanella *et al.*, 2013; Di Nauta *et al.*, 2015).

Building on the different contributions offered by literature on the ways to face the emerging social and economic challenges, it is possible to identify a common element: the increasing attention afforded to the role and the relevance of stakeholders as actors endowed by knowledge, competences and capabilities fundamental to the survival of every type of social and economic organization (Kandampully, 2002; Ayuso *et al.*, 2006; Vargo *et al.*, 2008; Hage *et al.*, 2010; Sanchez *et al.*, 2012).

Donaldson and Preston (1995) define stakeholders as persons or groups with interests characterized by legitimacy in both procedural and substantive aspects of corporate activity. Building on this more general classification, it is possible to affirm that the concept of a stakeholder includes all individuals and groups influencing or able to influence organizations' behaviours, actions and strategies. According to Freeman (1984), the concept of a stakeholder is an inclusive domain that refers to employees, customers, communities and government officials, among others. The state of knowledge on the concept of the stakeholder is principally based on stakeholder theory (Freeman, 1994; Donaldson and Preston, 1995) as the general framework that underlies the need for companies to understand and satisfy the needs of different actors involved in their field of action (Jensen, 2001; Friedman and Miles, 2002; Freeman *et al.*, 2004).

According to An *et al.* (2011), stakeholder theory enriches previous studies on companies' strategies, underlining the need to meet multiple goals related to a wide range of stakeholders. Building on this, the real challenge for every type of organization is to understand the needs of different stakeholders and to develop strategies able to satisfy them in efficient, effective and affordable ways (Cleland, 1999; Barile *et al.*, 2013). This challenge requires overcoming the traditional perspective of organizations as autonomous entities to adopt a vision in which companies need to interact with their stakeholders and, if possible, they need to collaborate with them and to include them in their actions and strategies to maximize the potential for organizations to survive (Shindler and Cheek, 1999; Iandolo *et al.,* 2013; Barile *et al.*, 2014).

Accordingly, stakeholder engagement can be considered an opportunity for companies to share their values and to generate and circulate trust and knowledge in order to build a stronger collaboration with their stakeholders (Healey, 1997; Caputo *et al.*, 2016a, Caputo, 2017). In such a vein, the chapter aims to investigate if information sharing and communication strategies can be considered useful pathways to build the preconditions required for the stakeholder engagement. It then proposes to investigate companies' approach to communication as the key pathway through which to act to improve the alignment between companies and stakeholders in order to build possible preconditions for stakeholder engagement. The contribution of companies' attention to information sharing and communication strategies to development of stronger relationships with stakeholders is verified via an empirical research oriented to investigate if there is a positive relationship among variables such as use of informal instruments of communication, publishing of social reports, number of years in which social reports are published, and availability of information on companies and companies' market value, measured by their market capitalization.

The rest of this chapter is structured as follows. In the section "Conceptual and theoretical framework" a brief literature review on the topics on which the reflections herein are based is presented. In the section "Methodology" the research design adopted with reference to empirical research is described. In the "Findings" section the results of empirical researches are presented, and in the Discussion they are analysed from both a theoretical and practical point of view. Finally, in the section "Final remarks and future lines of research" some conclusions are presented and possible future lines of research are identified.

Conceptual and theoretical framework

Stakeholder engagement

In the last few years, an interesting debate on the role of stakeholders in companies' strategies has involved an increasing number of researchers (Freeman, 1984; Atkinson *et al.*, 1997; Jensen, 2001; Buysse and Verbeke, 2003). They have tried to explain what are the potential contributions that stakeholders can offer to the survival of companies in the emerging challenging scenario (Clarkson, 1995; Donaldson and Preston, 1995; Hart and Milstein, 2003) and what are the better approaches to use stakeholders' contributions without increasing the complexity that affects the management of companies (Mitchell *et al.,* 1997; Bryson, 2004; Freeman, 2010). Building on the fundamental definition of the stakeholder proposed by Freeman (1984, p. 46) as "any group or individual who can affect or is affected by the achievement of the organization's objectives", an increasing number of contributions have focused attention on the concept of stakeholders, on their role, and on strategies to improve the relationship between companies and stakeholders (Carroll, 1989; Hill and Jones, 1992; Clarkson, 1994; Donaldson and Preston, 1995; Mitchell *et al.*, 1997; Olander, 2007)

Analysing the state of knowledge on the domain of stakeholders, it is possible to note how different contributors have tried to investigate this concept in order to identify possible instruments and guidelines to classify stakeholders with reference to their relevance in the achievement of companies' aims (Mitchell *et al.*, 1997; Agle *et al.,* 1999; Moneva *et al.*, 2007; Caputo, 2016). These contributions are supported by the awareness that the competitiveness of companies is related to their capacity to collaborate with stakeholders and to include them in their strategies and planning. However, at the same time, not all stakeholders can be engaged in companies' decisions, projects and governance without compromising the management and functions of companies (Hillman and Keim, 2001; Aaltonen, 2008; Saviano *et al.*, 2016).

According to Lawrence (2002), a possible solution requires the definition of a three step 'plan of engagement' for the stakeholders in which companies: 1) map stakeholders and their interests; 2) attempt to manage stakeholders and their social issues; and 3) actively engage stakeholders for long-term value creation. Following this indication, it is necessary to underline that different stakeholders have different perspectives: therefore, any possible effective strategy of engagement requires that companies are able to identify and satisfy several needs and expectations (Parasuraman *et al.*, 1991; Buttle, 2009; Santoro *et al.*, 2017) and to recognize the best route to engaging different relevant stakeholders (El-Gohary *et al.*, 2006).

28 *Francesco Caputo et al.*

To this end, companies can obtain stakeholders' support in decision processes (Starkey, 2009), and they have the opportunity to acquire the specific knowledge owned by stakeholders (Wenger *et al.*, 2002; Coff, 1999). Accordingly, stakeholder engagement involves a stance of mutual responsibility, information-sharing, open and respectful dialogue, and an ongoing commitment to joint problem-solving (Svendsen, 1998; Waddock, 2002). Then, to build an efficient, effective and sustainable strategy for stakeholder engagement, companies need to develop some preliminary conditions related to the information offered to stakeholders and to the ways in which they are transferred.

Information sharing

The existent literature on stakeholder engagement appears to be primarily focused on the definition of stakeholders' features and on the opportunities and challenges related to a stronger collaboration with stakeholders (Roome and Wijen, 2006). Few contributions and empirical researchers propose an investigation into the effects and opportunities for specific ways of engagement.

Among the studies on possible strategies to develop and improve stakeholders' engagement, some interesting advancements in knowledge are proposed with reference to the ability of companies to provide information on their pathways and decisions as strategies to improve the alignment between companies and stakeholders and, consequently, the opportunities for and advantages of stakeholder engagement (Keown *et al.*, 2008). Therefore, according to Roberts (1992), it is possible to affirm that the ability of companies to satisfy stakeholders' requests for information is relevant to build conditions for future collaboration and relationships between stakeholders and companies. Similarly, Deegan and Samkin (2009) assert that companies should provide to stakeholders all information related to their activities if they want to develop a condition of reciprocal understanding and loyalty. Therefore, building on these contributions, the chapter states that:

> H_1: There is a positive relationship between the publication of informal instruments of communication by the company and the companies' market capitalization (Market Cap).
>
> H_2: There is a positive relationship between the availability of information on companies and companies' market capitalization (Market Cap).

While recognizing the relevance of companies' ability to provide information on themselves as a strategy to build preconditions for stakeholder engagement, it is also necessary to underline that the ways in which information is transferred to the context can influence its impact on the opportunity for collaboration with stakeholders (Prahalad and Ramaswamy, 2004; Edvardsson *et al.*, 2011; Caputo *et al.*, 2017a, 2017b; Reynoso *et al.*, 2017). Accordingly, companies interested in developing a stakeholder engagement strategy should pay attention not only to the provision of information, but also to the ways in which it is communicated (Scholes and James, 1998; Morsing and Schultz, 2006).

Communication strategy

From a general viewpoint, the stakeholder engagement process can be considered in terms of pathways for companies to share with stakeholders the values, information and knowledge needed to build the preconditions required to develop a strong collaboration (Gray and Wood, 1991; Healey, 1997). To this end, as underlined in the previous section, companies that aim to attract stakeholders in an engagement process need to provide them with information on their actions and strategies (Perrini and Tencati, 2006; Cooper and Owen, 2007). The ways in which this information is provided to stakeholders can impact on the opportunities for alignment between companies and stakeholders (Cornelissen, 2014). Accordingly, companies should pay more attention to their communication strategies (Siano et al., 2011; Argenti, 2012).

Communication can be considered in terms of the pathways that connect a sender with a receiver by using a defined pathway to transfer a specific message (Jablin and Putnam, 2000; Van Riel and Fombrun, 2007). The planning and the management of communication strategies require verification of whether there are elements liable to affect the transfer of the message negatively and to ensure that the message received by the receiver has the same meaning as that planned by the sender (Shannon, 1949).

Different studies have investigated the domain of communication, focusing attention on the structure of communication flows (Hinds and Kiesler, 1995; Caputo et al., 2016c), on the best instruments to transfer a specific message (Marschan-Piekkari et al., 1999), and on the kinds of message to transfer (Fombrun, 2001).

Adopting the interpretative lens of stakeholder engagement, companies' communication strategies should be based on the prior identification of stakeholders that have a right to be informed, and of their needs (Gray, 2001). After this, companies should evaluate what kind of information they want to transfer and what kind of information they want to receive (Roberts, 1992). Accordingly, a useful contribution to a better understanding of what strategies companies can develop to transfer the right information in the best ways to their stakeholders is offered by studies on voluntary corporate disclosure (Healy and Palepu, 2001; Evangelista et al., 2016). These studies outline how social disclosures can be strategically used to manage relationships with stakeholders by influencing the external demands originating from a range of different stakeholders (Ullmann, 1985) and to involve them in the companies' pathways (Carayannis et al., 2014). They show that the more critical stakeholders are to the success of companies, the more likely it is the companies will satisfy their demand for information (Ullmann, 1985). Roberts (1992), building on the framework developed by Ullmann (1985), reveals that stakeholder power, strategic positioning and economic performance are

30 *Francesco Caputo et al.*

significantly related to levels of corporate social disclosure and that companies can use corporate social disclosure as a managerial instrument to engage stakeholders. In the same direction, Abdolmohammadi (2005) and Reid *et al.* (2005) show that there is a strong a positive relationship between companies' communication strategies and their market capitalization.

Similarly, Lindblom (1984) asserts that corporate social disclosure may be viewed as the result of a public desire for information to evaluate if the activities carried out by companies are 'appropriate' or 'right and proper'. To this end, voluntary corporate social disclosure, as a direct approach to inform stakeholders about organizational activities, outputs and goals which are not generally readily observable (Neu *et al.*, 1998), can be considered a relevant pathway on which to base corporate communication strategies to develop a strong stakeholder engagement (Donaldson and Preston, 1995; Dervitsiotis, 2003).

Among the studies on voluntary corporate disclosure, the topic of the social report is garnering attention in managerial and organizational discussion (Bell, 1969; Van der Laan, 2009). Its usage by companies to transfer voluntary information to stakeholders is facilitating a debate on the opportunities and implications for stakeholder engagement and for the development of strong collaboration between companies and stakeholders (Heww, 2008). More specifically, companies' provision of social reports on their activities becomes a strategic driver in developing conditions for a better reciprocal understanding between companies and stakeholders (Mellahi and Wood, 2003) and it could impact on stakeholders' perception of companies and, consequently, on companies' market value (Healy and Palepu, 2001; Polese *et al.*, 2016). Therefore, this chapter states that:

> H_3: There is a positive relationship between companies' publishing of social reports and companies' market capitalization (Market Cap).
>
> H_4: There is a positive relationship between the number of years in which social reports have been published by the companies and companies' market capitalization (Market Cap).

Methodology

Our sample was selected from a dataset of Italian companies provided by Thomson Reuters Datastream (https://financial.thomsonreuters.com). Among the 4,361,127 companies in Italy (ISTAT, 2016), a sample of 113 companies was extracted. Information on the extracted companies was acquired using the database offered by Thomson Reuters Datastream for companies' market capitalization; companies' websites were consulted to verify if they had published social reports between 2004 and 2014; and Google was consulted to verify the availability of information on companies.

The value of variables was established using the Datastream databases, companies' websites and Google.

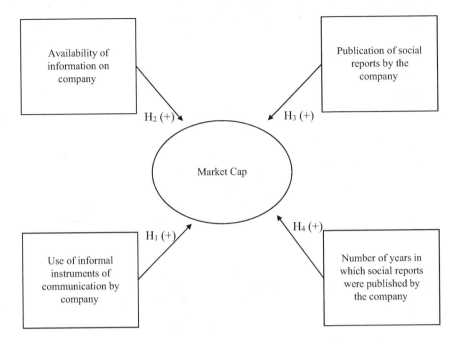

Figure 3.1 The conceptual model

As shown in Figure 3.1, the reliability of data was measured via Cronbach's alpha (Hinkin, 1995), discriminant validity was tested by comparing the square roots of the average variance extracted (AVEs) with the correlations between the constructs, and the hypotheses were tested via structural equation modelling (SEM).

To evaluate the fitting of the model some indexes were measured such as the Chi-square-to-degrees-of-freedom ratio (χ^2/df), goodness of fit index (GFI), the adjusted goodness-of-fit index (AGFI), and the parsimony goodness-of-fit index (PGFI).

Findings

Table 3.1 reports Cronbach's alpha (α) coefficients and square roots of the AVEs for each construct.

According to Nunnally (1978), the reliability of data is achieved with a α equal or greater than 0.7. Observing the results show in Table 3.1 it is possible to affirm that the reliability for all the constructs is achieved. Moreover, the discriminant validity is verified because the square roots of the AVEs were all greater than their respective relationships, providing solid evidence of discriminant validity.

The hypotheses were tested via SEM as shown in Table 3.2.

32   *Francesco Caputo et al.*

Table 3.1 Relationships among study constructs

Constructs	α	*(1)*	*(2)*	*(3)*	*(4)*	*(5)*
Publication of informal instruments of communication by the company	0.73	1				
Availability of information on the company	0.71	0.542*	1			
Publication of social report by the company	0.78	0.373*	0.214*	1		
Number of years in which social reports were published by the company	0.73	0.318*	0.203*	0.160*	1	
Market Cap	0.89	0.276*	0.178*	0.104*	0.12	1

* Correlation is significant at the 0.01 level (two-tailed).

Table 3.2 Results of SEM

Hypothesis	Standardized regression coefficient	P-value
H$_1$ (+): Publication of informal instruments of communication by the company → Market Cap	0.634	0.005
H$_2$ (+): Availability of information on company → Market Cap	0.583	***
H$_3$ (+): Publication of social report by the company → Market Cap	0.721	***
H$_4$ (+): Number of years in which social reports were published by the company → Market Cap	0.634	0.023

*** Standardized regression coefficient is significant at the 0.001 level (two-tailed)

All the hypotheses with a probability value (P-value) higher than 0.5 are considered confirmed.

The fitting of the conceptual model is verified by measuring some fitness indexes (Table 3.3).

As show by Tables 3.2 and 3.3 the model is verified and all the hypotheses are confirmed.

Discussion

The empirical results confirm the validity of the proposed reflections. More specifically, from the results of empirical research it emerges that companies'

Table 3.3 Fitness indexes

Index	Value	Cut-off value
Chi-square-to-degrees-of-freedom ratio ($\chi2/df$)	1.825	≤ 3 (Byrne, 2001)
Goodness of fit index (GFI)	0.915	> 0.90 (Hoe, 2008)
Adjusted goodness of fit index (AGFI)	0.912	> 0.90 (Li *et al.*, 2007)
Parsimony goodness of fit index (PGFI)	0.686	> 0.50 (Mulaik *et al.*, 1989)

market value, measured in terms of market capitalization, is influenced by the companies' attention to the adoption of extensive communication strategies. Accordingly, the results underline that a high degree of attention from companies on the transfer of information to stakeholders impacts on their market capitalization.

More specifically, with reference to H_1, the results of the research show that the use of informal instruments of communication is positively related to companies' market capitalization. This result is aligned with previous studies on the relevance of communication (Riel, 1995; Jo and Shim, 2005) and with empirical researches on the contributions that informal instruments of communication such as blogs, social networks and mailing lists, among others, can offer to the improvement of the companies' image as perceived by stakeholders (Schmidt, 2007; Kietzmann *et al.*, 2011). Therefore, the evidence of the research enriches previous managerial studies and proposes the need to use informal instruments of communication better as relevant key drivers in the definition of companies' strategies.

Considering H_2, the empirical evidence shows that the availability of information on companies is positively associated with companies' market capitalization. This evidence is also aligned with previous studies on the topic of communication (Morley *et al.*, 1997; Lodhia, 2006) and stakeholder engagement (Foster and Jonker, 2005; Greenwood, 2007). More specifically, this result underlines how an improvement in possible stakeholder engagement strategy requires that companies share with stakeholders an adequate amount of information (Perrini and Tencati, 2006; Succar, 2009). The transfer and the sharing of information, in fact, represents the first step to develop a pathway of alignment between companies and stakeholders and, consequently, a first step of the direct pathway to building a strong collaboration between companies and stakeholders (Donaldson and Preston, 1995; Bourne, 2012; Del Giudice *et al.*, 2012).

With reference to H_3, the empirical evidence shows the positive relationship that exists between the publication of social reports and the companies' market capitalization. This result is aligned with the evidence proposed by previous studies on the topic of corporate social disclosure (Gray *et al.*, 1997) and on social reports (Schaltegger and Wagner, 2006). It

34   *Francesco Caputo et al.*

underlines the relevance that voluntary information offered by companies to stakeholders can have in terms of its impact on companies' market value (Healy and Palepu, 2001). Accordingly, the social report could be considered a relevant instrument in the implementation of a stakeholder engagement strategy because it supports the transfer of information from companies to stakeholders and offers stakeholders tangible evidence of the will of companies to develop a transparent relationship with them (Dervitsiotis, 2003; Di Fatta *et al.*, 2016).

Finally, with reference to H_4, the empirical evidence underlines that there is a positive relationship between the number of years during which companies have published social reports and their market value in terms of market capitalization. This result highlights the relevance of companies' voluntary corporate disclosure from the perspective of stakeholders (Lev, 1992). It shows that if the companies' attention to transferring and sharing information with stakeholders over time is continuous, stakeholders tend to develop a more positive perception of the companies. They have the opportunity to identify more common elements on which to develop possible synergies, and they are more inclined to support companies in their market strategies with their resources and efforts (Post *et al.*, 2002; Hess, 2008).

Final remarks and future lines of research

The challenging scenario in which social and economic organizations act every day requires the development of new models, instruments and approaches to better support decision makers in understanding the dynamics (Prahalad and Ramaswamy, 2004; Wright *et al.*, 2005; Christofi *et al.*, 2015a, 2015b; Tronvoll *et al.*, 2017; Calabrese *et al.*, 2017; Del Giudice *et al.*, 2017). The new challenge for any organization that aims to survive in the modern era is to better understand stakeholders' needs in order to improve strategies and better align behaviour with their perspectives (Miles *et al.*, 2006; Barile *et al.*, 2014, 2015; Del Giudice *et al.*, 2016).

This emerging challenge requires companies to overcome the traditional boundaries of their activities and to open themselves to the possible new opportunities offered by collaboration, information sharing and their relationship with stakeholders (Freeman and Gilbert, 1987; Vrontis and Thrassou, 2007; Vrontis *et al.*, 2010; Del Giudice and Maggioni, 2014; Caputo *et al.*, 2016b). Therefore, the new aim for proactive companies that want to improve their competitiveness and their market position is to develop an effective, efficient and suitable stakeholder engagement strategy (Head, 2007; Hartzler *et al.*, 2013).

To this end, this chapter shows that the development of a stakeholder engagement strategy requires some preliminary conditions related to the capabilities of companies to offer the right information in the correct way to stakeholders. Accordingly, building on the contributions offered by the literature on the topic of information sharing and communication strategy, this

Information sharing and communication   35

chapter investigates possible key variables that impact on the relationships between companies and stakeholders.

With the aim to define possible guidelines for the implementation of preconditions required for an effective collaborative strategy between companies and stakeholders, the chapter investigates the impact that information sharing and transfer in different configurations have on companies' market value.

Through empirical evidence there emerges a positive relationship among the identified variables and the market capitalization of the analysed companies. This evidence shows that stakeholders' perception of companies' attention to transferring and sharing information with them affects their economic behaviours and choices and, consequently, affects the companies' economic performance. As a consequence of information received from companies, stakeholders have the opportunities to evaluate whether a company is aligned with their perspective of life and, eventually, to support it by buying its products/services and/or offering information, suggestions and evaluation. Only after these steps will companies have the opportunity to develop an affordable stakeholder engagement strategy.

The reflections and empirical evidence herein offer some contributions from both a theoretical and a practical point of view. In fact, from the first perspective, they underline the need for:

- In-depth analysis of elements and variables that affect the will of stakeholders to improve their collaboration with companies.
- The development of models that are better able to link stakeholders' behaviours and decisions to companies' competitiveness and position.
- Widening of the perspective in the studies on stakeholder engagement to overcome the simple phase of interaction between companies and stakeholders.

From a practical viewpoint, it is underlined that:

- Companies that want to develop stakeholder engagement strategies need to offer more information to the market on their activities, strategies and aims.
- Stakeholder engagement strategies are not limited to the interaction between companies and stakeholders, but refer rather to the perception that the market and social context have of the company.
- If companies aim to acquire affordable information on stakeholders, they need to proactively create conditions of reciprocal understanding, offering information on their activities, strategies and aims.

In summary, this chapter traces first reflections on the need to widen the perspective of study in the domain of stakeholder engagement to identify more

36 *Francesco Caputo et al.*

affordable, effective and efficient strategic pathways in creating preconditions for a collaborative relationship between companies and stakeholders. Therefore, the reflections and empirical evidence herein cannot be considered exhaustive, but they are a first step on a long pathway of research aimed at identifying possible relationships between companies' attention to information sharing and their implications in the light of stakeholder engagement. The final aim is to develop a toolkit able to support decision makers in evaluating the better behaviours to improve collaboration and relationships with their stakeholders.

References

Aaltonen, K., Jaakko, K. and Tuomas, O. (2008). Stakeholder salience in global projects. *International Journal of Project Management*, 26(5), 509–516.

Abdolmohammadi, M.J. (2005). Intellectual capital disclosure and market capitalization. *Journal of Intellectual Capital*, 6(3), 397–416.

Agle, B.R., Mitchell, R.K. and Sonnenfeld, J.A. (1999). Who matters to CEOs? An investigation of stakeholder attributes and salience, corporate performance, and CEO values. *Academy of Management Journal*, 42(5), 507-525.

An, Y., Davey, H. and Eggleton, I.R. (2011). Towards a comprehensive theoretical framework for voluntary IC disclosure. *Journal of Intellectual Capital*, 12(4), 571–585.

Argenti, P. (2012). *Corporate communication*. London, UK: McGraw-Hill Higher Education.

Atkinson, A.A., Waterhouse, J.H. and Wells, R.B. (1997). A stakeholder approach to strategic performance measurement. *MIT Sloan Management Review*, 38(3), 25–37.

Ayuso, S., Rodriguez, M.A. and Ricart, J.E. (2006). Responsible competitiveness at the 'micro' level of the firm: Using stakeholder dialogue as a source for new ideas: A dynamic capability underlying sustainable innovation. *Corporate Governance*, 6(4), 475–490.

Barile, S., Saviano, M. and Caputo, F. (2015). How are markets changing? The emergence of consumers market systems. In G. Dominici (Ed.), *The 3rd International Symposium Advances in Business Management. "Towards Systemic Approach"* (pp. 203–207). Avellino: Busyness Systems. E-book Series.

Barile, S., Carrubbo, L., Iandolo, F. and Caputo, F. (2013). From 'EGO' to 'ECO' in B2B relationships. *Journal of Business Market Management*, 6(4), 228–253.

Barile, S., Pels, J., Polese, F. and Saviano, M. (2012). An introduction to the viable systems approach and its contribution to marketing. *Journal of Business Market Management*, 5(2), 54–78.

Barile, S., Saviano, M. and Caputo, F. (2014). A systems view of customer satisfaction. In *National Conference "Excellence in quality, statistical quality control and customer satisfaction"*, University Campus "Luigi Einaudi", University of Turin, September 18–19, Turin.

Barile, S., Saviano, M. and Polese, F. (2014). Information asymmetry and co-creation in health care services. *Australasian Marketing Journal (AMJ)*, 22(3), 205–217.

Bell, D. (1969). The idea of a social report. *The Public Interest*, 15, 72–84.

Birkinshaw, J. (1997). Entrepreneurship in multinational corporations: The characteristics of subsidiary initiatives. *Strategic Management Journal*, 18(3), 207–229.

Bourne, L. (2012). *Stakeholder relationship management: a maturity model for organisational implementation*. Aldershot, UK: Gower Publishing Ltd.

Buttle, F. (2009), *Customer relationship management: concepts and technologies*. Burlington, MA: Routledge.

Buysse, K. and Verbeke, A. (2003). Proactive environmental strategies: A stakeholder management perspective. *Strategic Management Journal*, *24*(5), 453–470.

Byrne, B.M. (2001). Structural equation modelling with AMOS, EQS, and LISREL: Comparative approaches to testing for the factorial validity of a measuring instrument. *International Journal of Testing*, *1*(1), 55–86.

Calabrese, M., Iandolo F., Caputo. F., and Sarno, D. (2017). From mechanical to cognitive view: The changes of decision making in business environment. In S. Barile, M. Pellicano and F. Polese (Eds.) *Social Dynamics in a System Perspective*. New York: Springer.

Campanella, F., Del Giudice, M. and Della Peruta, M.R. (2013). The role of information in the credit relationship. *Journal of Innovation and Entrepreneurship*, *2*(1), 1–16.

Caputo F., Del Giudice M., Evangelista F. and Russo G. (2016a). Corporate disclosure and intellectual capital. The light side of information asymmetry. *International Journal of Managerial and Financial Accounting*, *8*(1), 75–96.

Caputo, F. (2016). A focus on company-stakeholder relationships in the light of the Stakeholder Engagement framework. In D. Vrontis, Y. Weber and E. Tsoukatos (Eds.) *Innovation, Entrepreneurship and Digital Ecosystems* (pp. 455–470). Cyprus: EuroMed press.

Caputo, F. (2017). Reflecting upon Knowledge Management studies: insights from Systems thinking. *International Journal of Knowledge Management Studies*, 8(3/4), 177–190.

Caputo, F., Evangelista, F. and Russo, G. (2016b). Information sharing and communication strategies: a stakeholder engagement view. In D. Vrontis, Y. Weber and E. Tsoukatos (Eds.) *Innovation, Entrepreneurship and Digital Ecosystems* (pp. 436–442). Cyprus: EuroMed press.

Caputo, F., Formisano, V., Buronova, B., Walletzky, L. (2016c). Beyond the digital ecosystems view: insights from Smart Communities. In D. Vrontis, Y. Weber and E. Tsoukatos (Eds.) Innovation, Entrepreneurship and Digital Ecosystems (pp. 443–454), EuroMed press, Cyprus.

Caputo, F., Ge, M. and Walletzky, L. (2017a). Modelling the service value process for smart cities. In *Interdisciplinary Information Management Talks*. Poděbrady, Czech Republic, September 6–8.

Caputo, F., Walletzky, L., Ge, M. and Carrubbo, L. (2017b). Combining the pillars of the Naples forum on Service: a multi-dimensional constructive tool. In E. Gummesson, C. Mele and F. Polese (Eds.), *Service Dominant Logic, Network and Systems Theory and Service Science: Integrating three Perspectives for a New Service Agenda*. Giannini: Napoli.

Carayannis, E., Del Giudice, M. and Della Peruta, M.R. (2014). Managing the intellectual capital within government-university-industry R&D partnerships: A framework for the engineering research centers. *Journal of Intellectual Capital*, *15*(4), 611–630.

Carroll, A.B. (1989). *Business and society: Ethics and stakeholder management*. Cincinnati, OH: South-Western.

Clarkson, M. (1994). A risk based model of stakeholder theory. In *Proceedings of the Second Toronto Conference on Stakeholder Theory in Toronto: Centre for*

38 *Francesco Caputo et al.*

Corporate Social Performance & Ethics, Toronto, July 1994. Toronto: University of Toronto Press.

Clarkson, M.E. (1995). A stakeholder framework for analyzing and evaluating corporate social performance. *Academy of Management Review*, *20*(1), 92–117.

Cleland, D.I. (1999). *Project Management – Strategic Design and Implementation.* New York, NY: McGraw-Hill.

Christofi, C., Leonidou, E. and Vrontis, D. (2015a). Cause-related marketing, product innovation and extraordinary sustainable leadership: the root towards sustainability. *Global Business and Economics Review, 17*(1), 93–111.

Christofi, M., Vrontis, D., Kitchen, P. and Papasolomou, I. (2015b). Innovation and cause-related marketing success: a conceptual framework and propositions. *Journal of Services Marketing*, *29*(5), 354–366.

Coff, R.W. (1999). When competitive advantage doesn't lead to performance: The resource-based view and stakeholder bargaining power. *Organization Science*, *10*(2), 119–133.

Cooper, S.M. and Owen, D.L. (2007). Corporate social reporting and stakeholder accountability: The missing link. Accounting. *Organizations and Society*, *32*(7), 649–667.

Cornelissen, J. (2014). *Corporate communication: A guide to theory and practice.* London, UK: Sage.

Cummings, T. and Worley, C. (2014). *Organization development and change.* Stamford, CT: Cengage learning.

Del Giudice, M., Ahmad, A., Scuotto, V. and Caputo, F. (2017). Influences of cognitive dimensions on the collaborative entry mode choice of small and medium-sized enterprises. *International Marketing Review*, *34*(5), 582–605.

Del Giudice, M., Caputo, F. and Evangelista, F. (2016). How decision systems are changing? The contribution of social media to the management decisional liquefaction. *Journal of Decision Systems*, *25*(3), 214–226.

Del Giudice, M. and Maggioni, V. (2014). Managerial practices and operative directions of knowledge management within inter-firm networks: a global view. *Journal of Knowledge Management*, *18*(5), 841–846.

Del Giudice, M., Carayannis, E.G. and Della Peruta, M.R. (2012). Culture and cooperative strategies: knowledge management perspectives. In M. Del Giudice, E.G. Carayannis and M.R. Della Peruta (Eds.), *Cross-cultural knowledge management* (pp. 49–62). New York, NY: Springer.

Dervitsiotis, K.N. (2003). Beyond stakeholder satisfaction: aiming for a new frontier of sustainable stakeholder trust. *Total Quality Management and Business Excellence*, *14*(5), 515–528.

Di Fatta, D., Caputo, F., Evangelista, F. and Dominici, G. (2016). Small world theory and the World Wide Web: Linking small world properties and website centrality. *International Journal of Markets and Business Systems*, *2*(2), DOI: 10.1504/IJMABS.2016.080237.

Di Nauta, P., Merola, B., Caputo, F. and Evangelista, F. (2015). Reflections on the role of university to face the challenges of knowledge society for the local economic development. *Journal of the Knowledge Economy*, 1–19.

Donaldson, T. and Preston, L.E. (1995). The stakeholder theory of the corporation: Concepts, evidence, and implications. *Academy of Management Review*, *20*(1), 65–91.

Edvardsson, B., Tronvoll, B. and Gruber, T. (2011). Expanding understanding of service exchange and value co-creation: a social construction approach. *Journal of the Academy of Marketing Science, 39*(2), 327–339.

El-Gohary, N.M., Osman, H. and El-Diraby, T.E. (2006). Stakeholder management for public private partnerships. *International Journal of Project Management, 24*(7), 595–604.

Evangelista, F., Caputo, F., Russo, G. and Buhnova, B. (2016). Voluntary corporate disclosure in the era of social media. In F. Caputo (Ed.), *The 4th International Symposium Advances in Business Management. "Towards Systemic Approach"* (pp. 124–128). Avellino: Business Systems. E-book series.

Fombrun, C.J. (2001). Corporate reputations as economic assets. In M.A. Hitt, E.R. Freeman and J.S. Harrison (Eds.), *The Blackwell handbook of strategic management* (pp. 289–312). Oxford, UK: Blackwell Publishers.

Foster, D. and Jonker, J. (2005). Stakeholder relationships: the dialogue of engagement. *Corporate Governance, 5*(5), 51–57.

Freeman, R.E. (1984). *Strategic management: a stakeholder approach.* Boston, MA: Pitman.

Freeman, R.E. (1994). The politics of stakeholder theory: Some future directions. *Business Ethics Quarterly, 4*(4), 409–421.

Freeman, R.E. (2010). *Strategic management: A stakeholder approach.* New York, NY: Cambridge University Press.

Freeman, R.E. and Gilbert, D.R. (1987). Managing stakeholder relationships. In S.P. Sethi and C.M. Falbe (Eds.), *Business and society: Dimensions of conflict and cooperation* (pp. 397–423). Lexington, MA: Lexington Books.

Freeman, R.E., Harrison, J.S. and Wicks, A.C. (2007). *Managing for stakeholders: Survival, reputation, and success.* New Haven and London: Yale University Press.

Freeman, R.E., Wicks, A.C. and Parmar, B. (2004). Stakeholder theory and "the corporate objective revisited". *Organization Science, 15*(3), 364–369.

Friedman, A.L. and Miles, S. (2002). Developing stakeholder theory. *Journal of Management Studies, 39*(1), 1–21.

Golinelli, G.M., Barile, S., Saviano, M. and Polese, F. (2012). Perspective shifts in marketing: toward a paradigm change? *Service Science, 4*(2), 121–134.

Gray, B. and Wood, D.J. (1991). Collaborative alliances: Moving from practice to theory. *The Journal of Applied Behavioral Science, 27*(1), 3–22.

Gray, R. (2001). Thirty years of social accounting, reporting and auditing: what (if anything) have we learnt? *Business Ethics: A European Review, 10*(1), 9–15.

Gray, R., Dey, C., Owen, D., Evans, R. and Zadek, S. (1997). Struggling with the praxis of social accounting – stakeholders, accountability, audits and procedures. *Accounting, Auditing & Accountability Journal, 10*(3), 325–364.

Greenwood, M. (2007). Stakeholder engagement: beyond the myth of corporate responsibility. *Journal of Business Ethics, 74*(4), 315–327.

Hage, M., Leroy, P. and Petersen, A.C. (2010). Stakeholder participation in environmental knowledge production. *Futures, 42*(3), 254–264.

Hart, S.L. and Milstein, M.B. (2003). Creating sustainable value. *The Academy of Management Executive, 17*(2), 56–67.

Hartzler, A., McCarty, C.A., Rasmussen, L.V., Williams, M.S., Brilliant, M., Bowton, E.A. and Fullerton, S.M. (2013). Stakeholder engagement: a key component of integrating genomic information into electronic health records. *Genetics in Medicine*, *15*(10), 792–801.

Head, B.W. (2007). Community engagement: participation on whose terms? *Australian Journal of Political Science*, *42*(3), 441–454.

Healey, P. (1997). *Collaborative Planning: Shaping Places in Fragmented Societies*. Basingstoke, UK: Macmillan.

Healy, P.M. and Palepu, K.G. (2001). Information asymmetry, corporate disclosure, and the capital markets: A review of the empirical disclosure literature. *Journal of Accounting and Economics, 31*(1), 405–440.

Hess, D. (2008). The three pillars of corporate social reporting as new governance regulation: Disclosure, dialogue, and development. *Business Ethics Quarterly*, *18*(4), 447–482.

Hill, C.W.L. and Jones, T.M. (1992). Stakeholder-agency theory. *Journal of Management Studies*, *29*(2), 131–154.

Hillman, A.J. and Keim, G.D. (2001). Shareholder value, stakeholder management, and social issues: what's the bottom line? *Strategic Management Journal*, *22*(2), 125–139.

Hinds, P. and Kiesler, S. (1995). Communication across boundaries: Work, structure, and use of communication technologies in a large organization. *Organization Science*, *6*(4), 373–393.

Hinkin, T.R. (1995). A review of scale development practices in the study of organizations. *Journal of Management*, *21*(5), 967–988.

Hoe, S.L. (2008). Issues and procedures in adopting structural equation modelling technique. *Journal of Applied Quantitative Methods*, *3*(1), 76–83.

Iandolo, F., Calabrese, M., Antonucci, E. and Caputo, F. (2013). Towards a value co-creation based healthcare system. In E. Gummesson, C. Mele and F. Polese (Eds.), *Service dominant logic, network and systems theory and service science: integrating three perspectives for a new service agenda* (pp. 61–83). Napoli: Giannini.

ISTAT (2016), *Noi Italia*, Istat, Roma.

Jablin, F.M. and Putnam, L.L. (2000). *The new handbook of organizational communication: Advances in theory, research, and methods*. Thousand Oaks, CA: Sage Publications.

Jensen, M.C. (2001). Value maximization, stakeholder theory, and the corporate objective function. *Journal of Applied Corporate Finance*, *14*(3), 8–21.

Jo, S., and Shim, S.W. (2005). Paradigm shift of employee communication: The effect of management communication on trusting relationships. *Public Relations Review*, *31*(2), 277–280.

Kandampully, J. (2002). Innovation as the core competency of a service organisation: the role of technology, knowledge and networks, *European Journal of Innovation Management*, *5*(1), 18–26.

Keown, K., Van Eerd, D. and Irvin, E. (2008). Stakeholder engagement opportunities in systematic reviews: knowledge transfer for policy and practice. *Journal of Continuing Education in the Health Professions*, *28*(2), 67–72.

Kietzmann, J.H., Hermkens, K., McCarthy, I.P. and Silvestre, B.S. (2011). Social media? Get serious! Understanding the functional building blocks of social media. *Business Horizons*, *54*(3), 241–251.

Lawrence, A.T. (2002). The drivers of stakeholder engagement. *Journal of Corporate Citizenship*, *2*(6), 71–85.

Lev, B. (1992). Information disclosure strategy. *California Management Review*, *34*(4), 9–32.

Li, Y.F., Lake, E.T., Sales, A.E., Sharp, N.D., Greiner, G.T., Lowy, E., Liu, C.F., Mitchell, P.H. and Sochalski, J.A. (2007). Measuring nurses' practice environments with the revised nursing work index: Evidence from registered nurses in the Veterans Health Administration. *Research in Nursing & Health*, *30*(1), 31–44.

Lindblom, C.K. (1984). The implications of organizational legitimacy for corporate social performance and disclosure. In *Conference Proceedings, Critical Perspectives on Accounting Conference, New York*. New York, NY: Free Press.

Lodhia, S.K. (2006). Corporate perceptions of web-based environmental communication: an exploratory study into companies in the Australian minerals industry. *Journal of Accounting & Organizational Change*, *2*(1), 74–88.

Mellahi, K. and Wood, G, (2003). The role and potential of stakeholders in 'hollow participation': conventional stakeholder theory and institutional alternatives. *Business and Society Review*, *108*(2), 183–202.

Miles, M.P., Munilla, L.S. and Darroch, J. (2006). The role of strategic conversations with stakeholders in the formation of corporate social responsibility strategy. *Journal of Business Ethics*, *69*(2), 195–205.

Mitchell, R.K., Agle, B.R. and Wood, D.J. (1997). Toward a theory of stakeholder identification and salience: Defining the principle of who and what really counts. *Academy of Management Review*, *22*(4), 853–886.

Moneva, J.M., Rivera-Lirio, J.M. and Muñoz-Torres, M.J. (2007). The corporate stakeholder commitment and social and financial performance. *Industrial Management & Data Systems*, *107*(1), 84–102.

Morley, D.D., Shockley-Zalabak, P. and Cesaria, R. (1997). Organizational communication and culture: A study of 10 Italian high-technology companies. *Journal of Business Communication*, *34*(3), 253–268.

Morsing, M. and Schultz, M. (2006). Corporate social responsibility communication: stakeholder information, response and involvement strategies. *Business Ethics: A European Review*, *15*(4), 32-338.

Mulaik, S.A., James, L.R., Van Alstine, J., Bennet, N., Lind, S. and Stilwell, C.D. (1989). Evaluation of goodness-of-fit indices for structural equation models. *Psychological Bulletin*, *105*(3), 430–445.

Neu, D., Warsame, H. and Pedwell, K. (1998). Managing public impressions: environmental disclosures in annual reports. *Accounting, Organizations and Society*, *23*(3), 265–282.

Nunnally, J. (1978). *Psychometric methods*. New York, NY: McGraw-Hill.

Olander, S. (2007). Stakeholder impact analysis in construction project management. *Construction Management and Economics*, *25*(3), 277–287.

Parasuraman, A., Berry, L.L. and Zeithaml, V.A. (1991). Understanding customer expectations of service. *Sloan Management Review*, *32*(3), 39–48.

Payne, A. and Frow, P. (2005). A strategic framework for customer relationship management. *Journal of Marketing*, *69*(4), 167–176.

Perrini, F. and Tencati, A. (2006). Sustainability and stakeholder management: the need for new corporate performance evaluation and reporting systems. *Business Strategy and the Environment*, *15*(5), 296–308.

Polese, F., Caputo, F., Carrubbo, L. and Sarno, D. (2016). The value (co)creation as peak of social pyramid. In T. Russo-Spena and C. Mele (Eds.), Proceedings 26th Annual RESER Conference, "What's ahead in service research: new perspectives for business and society" (pp. 1232–1248). RESER, University of Naples "Federico II".

42 *Francesco Caputo et al.*

Post, J.E., Preston, L.E. and Sauter-Sachs, S. (2002). *Redefining the corporation: Stakeholder management and organizational wealth.* Stanford, CA: Stanford University Press.

Prahalad, C.K. and Ramaswamy, V. (2004). Co-creation experiences: The next practice in value creation. *Journal of Interactive Marketing, 18*(3), 5–14.

Reid, M., Luxton, S. and Mavondo, F. (2005). The relationship between integrated marketing communication, market orientation, and brand orientation. *Journal of Advertising, 34*(4), 11–23.

Reinartz, W., Krafft, M. and Hoyer, W.D. (2004). The customer relationship management process: Its measurement and impact on performance. *Journal of Marketing Research, 41*(3), 293–305.

Reynoso, J., Barile, S., Saviano, M., Caputo, F. and La Sala, A. (2017). Envisioning future scenarios for service research. In E. Gummesson, C. Mele and F. Polese (Eds.), *Service dominant logic, network and systems theory and service science: integrating three perspectives for a new service agenda.* Giannini: Napoli.

Riel, C.V. (1995). *Principles of corporate communication.* Hemel Hempstead, UK: Prentice-Hall.

Roberts, R.W. (1992). Determinants of corporate social responsibility disclosure: an application of stakeholder theory. *Accounting, Organizations and Society, 17*(6), 595–612.

Sanchez, B.D., Kaufmann, R. and Vrontis, D. (2012). A new organisational memory for cross-cultural knowledge management. *Cross Cultural Management: An International Journal, 19*(3), 336–351.

Santoro, G., Vrontis, D. and Thrassou, Dezi, L. (2017). The Internet of Things: Building knowledge management systems for open innovation and knowledge management capacity. *Technological Forecasting and Social Change,* DOI: 10.1016/j.techfore.2017.02.034.

Saviano, M., Caputo, F., Formisano, V. and Walletzký, L. (2016). From theory to practice: applying systems thinking to Smart Cities. In F. Caputo (Ed.), *The 4th International Symposium Advances in Business Management. "Towards Systemic Approach"* (pp. 35–40). Avellino: Business Systems. E-book series.

Saviano, M. and Caputo, F. (2012). Le scelte manageriali tra sistemi, conoscenza e vitalità. Management senza confini. Gli studi di management: tradizione e paradigmi emergent. In *XXXV Convegno annuale AIDEA*, University of Salerno,4–5 October, pp. 1–21.

Saviano, M. and Caputo, F. (2013). Managerial choices between systems, knowledge and viability. In S. Barile (Ed.), *Contributions to theoretical and practical advances in management. A viable systems approach (VSA)* (pp. 219–242). Roma: Aracne.

Schaltegger, S. and Wagner, M. (2006). Integrative management of sustainability performance, measurement and reporting. *International Journal of Accounting, Auditing and Performance Evaluation, 3*(3), 1–19.

Schmidt, J. (2007). Blogging practices: An analytical framework. *Journal of Computer-Mediated Communication, 12*(4), 1409–1427.

Schoemaker, P.J. (1992). How to link strategic vision to core capabilities. *Sloan Management Review, 34*(1), 67–81.

Scholes, E. and James, D. (1998). Planning stakeholder communication. *Journal of Communication Management, 2*(3), 277–285.

Senge, P.M. (2014). *The fifth discipline fieldbook: Strategies and tools for building a learning organization.* New York, NY: Crown Business.

Shannon, C.E. (1949). Communication in the presence of noise. *Proceedings of the IRE, 37*(1), 10–21.

Shindler, B. and Cheek, K.A. (1999). Integrating citizens in adaptive management: a propositional analysis. *Conservation Ecology, 3*(1), 9–23.

Siano, A., Confetto, A.V., Vollero, A. and Siglioccolo, M. (2011). A framework based on the structure-system paradigm for governance and management of corporate communication. In S. Barile, C. Bassano, M. Calabrese, M. Confetto, P. Di Nauta, P. Piciocchi, F. Polese, M. Saviano, A. Siano, M. Siglioccolo and A. Vollero (Eds.), *Contributions to theoretical and practical advances in management: a viable systems approach (VSA)* (pp. 175–198). Avellino: International Printing.

Solomon, M., Russell-Bennett, R. and Previte, J. (2012). *Consumer behaviour.* Australia, AU: Pearson Higher Education.

Starkey, K., Hatchuel, A. and Tempest, S. (2009). Management research and the new logics of discovery and engagement. *Journal of Management Studies, 46*(3), 547–558.

Succar, B. (2009). Building information modelling framework: A research and delivery foundation for industry stakeholders. *Automation in Construction, 18*(3), 357–375.

Svendsen, A. (1998). *The stakeholder strategy: profiting from collaborative business relationships.* San Francisco, CA: Berrett-Koehler.

Tronvoll, B., Barile, S. and Caputo. F. (2017). A systems approach to understanding the philosophical foundation of marketing studies. In S. Barile, M. Pellicano and F. Polese (Eds.) *Social dynamics in a system perspective.* New York: Springer.

Ullmann, A.A. (1985). Data in search of a theory: a critical examination of the relationships among social performance, social disclosure, and economic performance of U.S. firms. *Academy of Management Review, 10*(3), 540–547.

Van der Laan, S. (2009). The role of theory in explaining motivation for corporate social disclosures: Voluntary disclosures vs 'solicited' disclosures. *Australasian Accounting Business & Finance Journal, 3*(4), 15–29.

Van Riel, C.B. and Fombrun, C.J. (2007). *Essentials of corporate communication: Implementing practices for effective reputation management.* London: Routledge.

Vargo, S.L., Maglio, P.P. and Akaka, M.A. (2008). On value and value co-creation: A service systems and service logic perspective. *European Management Journal, 26*(3) 145–152.

Vrontis, D., & Thrassou, A. (2007). A new conceptual framework for business-consumer relationships. *Marketing Intelligence & Planning, 25*(7), 789–806.

Vrontis, D., Thrassou, A., and Zin, R.M. (2010). Internal marketing as an agent of change–implementing a new human resource information system for Malaysian Airlines. *Journal of General Management, 36*(1), 21–41.

Waddock, S. (2002). *Leading corporate citizens: vision, values, value added.* New York, NY: McGraw-Hill.

Wenger, E., McDermott, R.A. and Snyder, W. (2002). *Cultivating communities of practice: A guide to managing knowledge.* Boston, MA: Harvard Business Press.

Wright, M., Filatotchev, I., Hoskisson, R.E. and Peng, M.W. (2005). Strategy research in emerging economies: Challenging the conventional wisdom. *Journal of Management Studies, 42*(1), 1–33.

4 Assessing the dynamic of agri-food export trends before and after the EU Eastern Enlargement

Antonino Galati, Marcella Giacomarra and Maria Crescimanno

Introduction

One of the most important political and economic challenges faced by the European Union (EU) in the last decade has been the enlargement to the Central and Eastern European Countries (CEECs). Two historical events marked this process: first, in 2004, during which the biggest enlargement took place with the entry of Czech Republic, Cyprus, Estonia, Hungary, Latvia, Lithuania, Malta, Poland, Slovakia and Slovenia; and second, after three years, in 2007, with the accession of Romania and Bulgaria.

In the enlargement process as well as in the framework of the EU's bilateral relations with third countries (Crescimanno et al., 2013a, 2013b, 2014), the agricultural sector has played a central role, owing to its importance at the EU level and its strategic role in the economic and political life of the Eastern candidate countries (European Commission, Directorate-General for Agriculture, 2002). For these reasons, the bilateral European agreements signed since 1991 between the EU and the candidate countries, as part of the EU's pre-accession strategy, were aimed at eliminating barriers to trade, initially including only part of the agri-foods that would be subject to reciprocal tariff concessions. Later, owing to the double-zero agreement in force since 2000, there has been more intense trade liberalization, which affected, at that time, about two-thirds of agricultural products traditionally traded (European Commission, Directorate-General for Agriculture, 2002), to achieve total elimination of tariff protection in 2004.

Numerous studies have attempted to assess the impact of the EU enlargement on the dynamics and changes that occurred in the agri-food trade structure, primarily focusing on the pre-accession period. Results reveal an overall increase in trade between the Old and New Member States, which has strengthened the economic role of the EU in the world agri-food market (Gavrilescu, 2013). However, there exists a significant asymmetry of the dynamics individually recorded by each New Member State, with regard to their initial conditions. This study contributes to the enrichment of the existing literature on the impact of EU enlargement on agri-food exports of the New Members States in the European common market, by extending the reference period to twelve years, in order to detect variations in the economic efficiency of agri-food exports during the enlargement process. In particular, it aims to assess the economic gains/losses resulting from the EU adhesion, by comparing the efficiency scores of CEECs during the period 2000–2011.

Literature review

Research on the impact of EU enlargement to the CEECs primarily focused on the pre-accession period. Results suggest that this process has largely been beneficial for the economies of the New Member States (NMSs), due to the comparative advantage of candidate countries related to low labor costs and the gradual increase in price level (Rollo, 1995; Forslid et al., 2002; Halkos and Tzeremes, 2009). In particular, as suggested by Bartošová et al. (2008), NMSs have gained from free access to the EU market, increasing the exports of dairy products and sugar up to four and eight times, respectively, although the net effect (exports minus imports) has been much lower, particularly for these products. Melewar et al. (2008) examine whether or not EU enlargement would cause companies to standardize their brand portfolios and the brands they offer. They found that external factors, which are market-based and product-based elements, seem to encourage standardization. However, as emphasized by the same authors, the main obstacles are endogenous to corporations and pertain to company structure, strategy and historic resistance to standardization.

The impact of EU enlargement has also been studied in relation to the direct effects of the preferential treatments granted to the candidate countries during the pre-accession period. In this regard, results reveal that the process of integration and trade liberalization has contributed to the growing of the agri-food trade between the Old and New Member States. On the other hand, this process has had a negative impact, owing to a permanent and significant resistance to the agri-food exports from the CEECs in the European market (Bartošová et al., 2008; Chevassus-Lozza et al., 2008); the unsatisfactory level of export quality, insufficient sanitary and phytosanitary arrangements, lack of competitiveness in the food processing industry, insufficient export surplus availability and insufficient marketing are the main constraints to export growth (Frohberg and Hartmann, 1997; Duponcel, 1998; Chevassus-Lozza et al., 2008). As can be seen, a substantial literature exists on the impact of the EU enlargement in the pre-accession phase. However, little attention has been paid to the changes registered during the entire enlargement process (pre- and post-accession phases).

With reference to the agricultural sector, some studies show a significant impact of the enlargement on agricultural dynamics (Zemeckis and Drozdz, 2009; Csaki and Jambor, 2013). While on one hand, the integration process has led to a reduction in both the contribution of the agricultural sector to GDP and the rate of employment in agriculture, on the other hand, this process has brought about an increase in the income of farmers – related to the increase in prices, production, the EU direct payments, and the financial support of EU structural funds- and agri-food trade. Results, however, show significantly different behaviors of the NMSs in relation to the pre-accession conditions and the policies adopted in the post-accession phase (Csaki and Jambor, 2013).

With specific reference to the dynamics and changes in the agri-food trade structure, Bojnec and Fertő (2009a) analyze the effects of EU enlargement in the pre- and post-accession phases on the level, composition and differences in the advantages/disadvantages of agri-food trade for eight central European and Balkan countries in the EU market and their implications for food policy. They found that the enlargement has had an overall negative impact on these countries, but this is different in relation to the countries' characteristics among which natural factor endowments and agricultural structures, labor input costs for horticultural products, food processing and food supply marketing chains represent relevant elements (Bojnec and Fertő, 2009a). In a more recent study, the same authors (Bojnec and Fertő, 2012) analyze the impact of EU enlargement on the agri-food exports of 12 NMSs during the period 1999–2007 and confirm that these countries stood to gain from the EU eastward enlargement, with an increase in exports of primarily higher value-added, consumer-ready and more competitive niche agri-food products. However, Fogarasi (2008), referring to the dynamics of agri-food exports to Hungary and Romania from the EU market, shows that the improvement in performance should not be viewed in terms of competitiveness, but from the EU market demand side, in this manner, explaining the improvement in competitiveness of some sectors (meat, fruit, vegetables and beverages, in particular).

This brief literature review represents the starting point of the present work, where the main hypothesis to be verified is whether all the new Member States experienced a growth in their exports of agricultural and food products. If so, in what terms did this growth occur? Namely, did all NMSs follow the same trade pattern during the pre-accession and post-adhesion periods? Did specific past trade agreements affect internal dynamics?

Data and methods

Data

With the final aim to investigate the performance of CEECs, which entered the EU during the enlargement process that occurred in 2004 and 2007, we implemented a DEA (data envelopment analysis) window analysis. As reported in Table 4.1, data originate from different sources and socio-economic indicators chosen to measure the economic efficiency of agri-food exports. Countries included in the analysis are Bulgaria (BL), Czech Republic (CZ), Estonia (EE), Hungary (HU), Latvia (LV), Lithuania (LT), Poland (PL), Romania (RO), Slovakia (SK), and Slovenia (SI). Cyprus and Malta have been excluded from the sample because of missing data.

Table 4.1 Indicators used in the analysis

Indicator	Unit of measure	Source
Mean labour cost levels (including business economy, industry (except construction), services of the business economy)	Units of currency, Euro	EUROSTAT – [lc_lci_lev]
Percentage of graduates from tertiary education graduating from agriculture programs, social sciences, business and law programs, engineering, manufacturing and construction programs (both sexes)	Percentage (%)	UNESCO – Institute for Statistics – Education (ISCED)
Employment by sex, age and economic activity (1983–2008, NACE Rev. 1 and from 2008 onwards, NACE Rev. 2). From 15 to 64 years. Agriculture, forestry and fishing Manufacturing	1,000	EUROSTAT – [lfsa_egan2]
Employment by sex, age and economic activity (1983–2008, NACE Rev. 1.1 and from 2008 onwards, NACE Rev. 2). From 15 to 64 years All NACE sectors	1,000	EUROSTAT – [lfsa_egana]
Export flows – n. 24 Commodities	Dollar ($)	United Nations – Department of Economic and Social Affairs – Statistics Division – Trade Statistics

The time period (2000–2011) was motivated by the need to accurately capture the starting points of each country as well as any consequences that occurred after the EU adhesion.

Some preliminary specifications regarding the indicators are necessary. As for labor cost levels, the average values of three sectors have been included in the analysis, such as: business economy, industry (except construction), and services of the business economy. This classification prevented the exclusion of important information, making the context description more complete. The same procedure was followed for the three International Standard Classification of Education indicators (ISCED) and for the employment levels. Moreover, as for employment, after calculating the average values of the three economic sectors of interest, by using the total employment value of each country (that includes all NACE sectors), the percentage of employees in

48 *Antonino Galati et al.*

agriculture and manufacturing sectors in the total number of employees has been calculated. All these modifications were made to collect a good level of features of the export economic branch, including any satellite activities/skills.

Regarding export commodities, the classification of the UN Comtrade database has been considered, using the codes related to the agri-food products. According to the trade partners of the sample, data on export flows were collected after examining the exports towards the 27 EU partners (excluding Croatia, as it is too recent to adhesion).

The labor cost input represents a strategic indicator characterizing the labor market of Eastern countries, in particular, since the adhesion moment, as these countries had the lowest labor costs in Europe, such that even if these costs increased during the twelve-year period, they certainly did not reach the average of those of Old Member States (OMSs).

Method

To evaluate the efficiency scores of ten NMSs during the period 2000–2011, a DEA window analysis has been applied. DEA is a non-parametric technique, measuring the relative efficiency of decision-making units (DMUs), with multiple inputs and outputs, assuming neither a specific functional form for the production function nor the inefficiency distribution. The method, first proposed by Charnes et al. (1978), aims at measuring the relative efficiency of DMUs that are similar to each other in terms of products and services. As originally developed by Debreu (1951) and Farrell (1957), this method is based on the concept of productivity, defined as the ratio between a single output and a single input. Assuming n DMUs, each with m inputs and s outputs, the efficiency score of a test DMU p is obtained by solving the following model (Charnes et al., 1978):

$$\max ho = \frac{\sum_{k=1}^{S} v_k y_{ki}}{\sum_{j=1}^{m} u_j x_{ji}} \quad k = 1, \ldots, s; \ j = 1, \ldots, m; \ i = 1, \ldots, n$$

$$\frac{\sum_{k=1}^{S} v_k y_{ki}}{\sum_{j=1}^{m} u_j x_{ji}} \leq 1 \forall i \ and$$

$$u_j, v_k \geq \forall k,$$

Where y_{ki} is the amount of output k of DMU i and x_{ki} is the amount of j-*th* inputs by the DMU i; u_j, $v_k \geq 0$ are the weights that are applied to inputs and outputs to maximize the efficiency ratio.

Dynamics of agri-food export trends 49

Differently from the DEA basic approach, through which it is possible to carry out analysis by including observations only from one time period, the Window formulation (Charnes and Cooper, 1985) is able to measure efficiency in cross-sectional and time-varying data, allowing a dynamic effects study (Hartman and Storbeck, 1996; Webb, 2003; Asmild et al., 2004; Cooper et al., 2007; Halkos and Tzeremes, 2008; Tsolas, 2011; Halkos and Tzeremes, 2009; Adler and Golany, 2011; Halkos and Tzeremes, 2011; Bono and Giacomarra, 2014; Kirkulak and Erdem, 2014).

This approach can indicate efficiency trends over a specified period of time, while simultaneously examining the stability and other properties of the efficiency evaluations within the specified windows. It operates on the principle of moving averages (Charnes et al., 1985; Yue, 1992; Charnes et al., 1994) and establishes efficiency measures by treating each DMU in different years as a separate unit. The performance of a DMU in a period can be compared against its own performance in other periods as well as against the performance of other DMUs (Asmild et al., 2004) through a sequence of overlapping windows (Webb, 2003; Hartman and Storbeck, 1996). Once the window is defined, the observations within that window are viewed in an inter-temporal manner, and therefore, the analysis is better referred to as locally inter-temporal (Tulkens and Vanden Eeckaut, 1995). Adopting the formulation of Asmild et al. (2004), let us consider n DMUs ($n=1,2,...,N$) observed in T periods of time ($t=1, 2,...,T$) producing m outputs and using s inputs. We create a sample of observations, where an observation n in period t () has an s-dimensional input vector and an m-dimensional output vector. Then a window with observations is denoted starting at time k, $1<k<T$ with width w. So the matrix of inputs is given as:

$$X_{kw} = \left(X_k^1, X_k^2,...,X_k^N, X_{k+1}^1 X_{k+1}^2,...,X_{k+1}^N, \; ... \; X_{k+w}^1, X_{k+w}^2, \; ..., \; X_{k+w}^N \right)$$

and the matrix of outputs is given as

$$Y_{kw} = \left(Y_k^1, Y_k^2,...,Y_k^N, Y_{k+1}^1 Y_{k+1}^2, \; ..., \; Y_{k+1}^N, \; ... \; Y_{k+w}^1, Y_{k+w}^2, \; ..., \; Y_{k+w}^N \right)$$

In our case, the DMUs represent the ten NMS (n = 10) over a twelve-year period (p = 12), producing m output (export flows in \$), using s inputs (labour cost, ISCED, and employment level). DEA window analysis implicitly assumes that there are no technical changes during the period under analysis within each window (Zhang et al., 2011). Similar to other scientific contributions in this methodological field (Halkos and Tzeremes, 2009; Zhang et al., 2011; Wang et al., 2013), a window width of three years (w = 3) has been decided. Starting from the year 2000, it has been possible to include the years 2004 and 2007 in separate windows, respectively, representing the two EU accession years.

Results and discussion

Table 4.2 reports the DEA window results implemented using Frontier Analyst software.

The performance of each DMU during the twelve-year period considered has been quite stable and, on average, characterized by high efficiency scores. This indicates that the EU enlargement to the CEECs has not led to an overall improvement in the latter's economic efficiency of the agri-food exports, despite an increase in absolute value, as already estimated in previous studies (Bartošová et al., 2008; Chevassus-Lozza et al., 2008; Fogarasi, 2008). Through the DEA window analysis, a country-wise comparison is possible, allowing the interpretation of data in terms of the efficiency of a DMU against itself (column view) or against other DMUs (row view). As other studies emphasize (Bojnec and Fertő, 2009a; Bojnec and Fertő, 2009b; Csaki and Jambor, 2013), the performances vary among the NMSs, owing to their pre-accession conditions and post-accession policies. The sample has been therefore divided into three different groups (Table 4.3), characterized by different levels of performance (ranged between 93 and 100 per cent) and dissimilar variation coefficients (ranged between 0.0 and 7.5 per cent).

Overall, results suggest that NMSs recorded high performance scores during the period 2000–2011, some of them followed a more constant growth pace (Group 2), while others experienced transition in their trade relationships, translating in wide alternation of peaks and troughs on their exports flows (Groups 1 and 3). An in-depth analysis through case studies of specific countries belonging to the first and third groups allows a further interpretation.

Table 4.2 DEA Window results (%)

%	BG	RO	CZ	SK	SI	HU	EE	LV	LT	PL
2000	79.7	85.3	100.0	100.0	100.0	100.0	100.0	100.0	100.0	100.0
2001	100.0	100.0	100.0	100.0	100.0	100.0	99.1	100.0	100.0	100.0
2002	100.0	100.0	100.0	100.0	100.0	96.4	100.0	100.0	99.6	100.0
2003	94.8	96.3	92.0	95.5	100.0	94.7	100.0	100.0	96.0	100.0
2004	87.5	100.0	100.0	100.0	100.0	100.0	100.0	100.0	100.0	100.0
2005	89.0	88.6	96.0	100.0	100.0	83.0	100.0	100.0	100.0	100.0
2006	100.0	91.7	91.2	100.0	100.0	100.0	100.0	100.0	100.0	100.0
2007	94.9	78.6	97.8	100.0	100.0	100.0	95.3	87.3	90.9	100.0
2008	84.7	91.2	100.0	92.7	100.0	100.0	100.0	98.6	100.0	100.0
2009	91.8	90.0	100.0	100.0	100.0	100.0	100.0	97.8	100.0	100.0
2010	100.0	94.6	96.6	100.0	100.0	100.0	100.0	100.0	100.0	100.0
2011	100.0	100.0	100.0	100.0	100.0	100.0	100.0	100.0	100.0	100.0

Table 4.3 Groups of countries according to their average efficiency scores

	Countries (DMUs)	Average values of efficiency scores (%)	Variation coefficient (%)
	BG	93.5	7.5
Group 1	RO	93.0	7.3
	CZ	97.8	3.3
	HU	97.8	5.1
	PL	100.0	0.0
Group 2	SI	100.0	0.0
	LT	98.9	2.8
	SK	99.0	2.4
	EE	99.5	1.4
Group 3	LV	98.6	3.7

Bulgaria case study (Group 1)

Bulgaria, during the pre-accession phase (2004–2007), registered a decline in the share of its agri-food exports on the total products exported by NMSs in the European market, with a recovery after the adhesion. As emphasized by Antimiani et al. (2012), NMSs belonging to other trade agreements, like the Central European Free Trade Agreement (CEFTA), registered a positive trend in the post-accession period, with an agri-food export-oriented preference towards goods whose sophistication is decreasing due to their re-localization of production process and export flows towards countries with a lower GDP per capita. Figure 4.1 confirms this finding, providing more interesting insights:

In fact, Bulgaria, immediately after the EU accession, maintained an almost stable agri-food export flow with historical trade partners, such as: Hungary, Czech Republic, Slovakia and Slovenia. This was due to the CEFTA trade agreement (lasting from 1997 to 2003) that facilitated the increase in trade flows among partner countries. Indeed, in 2004, with the accession to the EU, Czech Republic, Poland, Hungary, Slovenia and Slovakia left CEFTA, but the existing trade relations were preserved. As regards the relationship with Romania, the country increased its export flow towards this country, doubling and tripling its economic value (almost nonexistent during the 2000–2006 period). In 2007, when Romania and Bulgaria joined the EU, they also left CEFTA. As regards the Baltic Region, a very particular attitude characterized Bulgaria, above all with respect to the trade relations with Estonia that, after the Bulgarian adhesion, have been widely reduced, together with unstable trade paths with Lithuania and Latvia.

An interesting export dynamic has also been recorded as regards OMSs (Figure 4.2).

52 *Antonino Galati et al.*

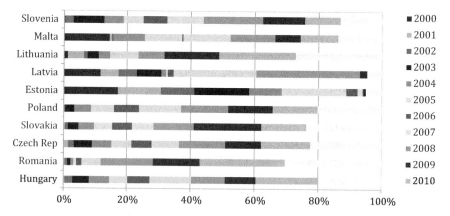

Figure 4.1 Bulgaria. Agri-food export dynamic towards NMS (2000–2011 period)

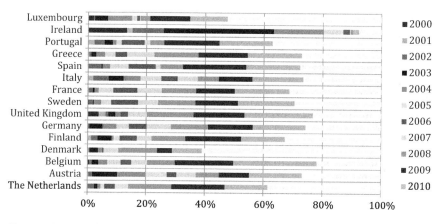

Figure 4.2 Bulgaria. Agri-food export dynamic towards OMS (2000–2011 period)

Since 2007, Bulgaria increased economic relations (following a stable and growing path) with the majority of NMSs. In particular, the trade relations with Denmark, Belgium and The Netherlands experienced a significant increase. This has been translated into a relevant reduction in the agri-food exports recorded from Bulgaria to Estonia. Indeed, the two countries characterized by historically intense agri-food flows, almost stopped this trend near the adhesion period, with a timid recovery only from 2011.

Latvia case study (Group 3)

From Group 3, and with the lowest efficiency score of the sample (98.6 per cent), Latvia showed a general and growing trend of its export flows immediately after the adhesion, towards almost all of the NMSs (Figure 4.3).

Dynamics of agri-food export trends 53

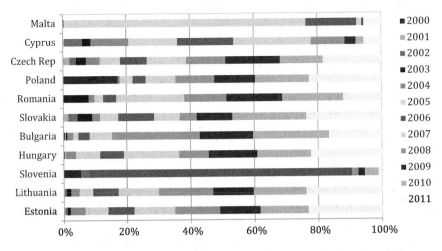

Figure 4.3 Latvia. Agri-food export dynamic towards NMS (2000–2011 period)

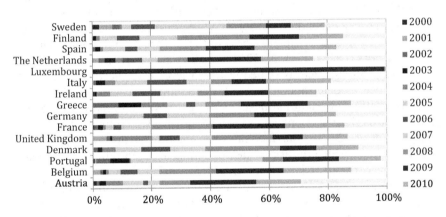

Figure 4.4 Latvia. Agri-food export dynamic towards OMS (2000–2011 period)

This growing trend was only interrupted by the unstable flow towards Slovenia and Malta. A similar growing trend has been identified for Latvian agri-food exports towards the OMSs (Figure 4.4), with the exception of Luxembourg that has not seemed to be so interested in the adhesion added value.

Conclusion

This paper provides new insights into the trade dynamics analysis of the agri-food sector for the enlarged EU by expanding the time period to include both pre- and post-accession phases. Results emphasize that, apart from an overall positive performance, NMSs have significantly differed in their approach in

54 *Antonino Galati et al.*

utilizing the opportunity of entry into the EU enlarged market, as outlined in the country studies for Bulgaria and Latvia.

Many countries show differences because they preferred to strengthen established trade relations with a past group of partner countries, as defined by agreements that are already in force (such as Bulgaria with CEFTA). This was partially due to their initial conditions, particularly referring to the structure of the agricultural sector and food industry of each single NMS, as well as to the speed of reaction to pre-accession policies and post-adhesion strategies.

In particular, many countries have not had the ability to take a net advantage from EU entry. This was mainly due to the pre-accession EU financial support that was specifically addressed to restructure the farming sector and would have made the sector even more competitive through investments in agricultural holdings and in the improvements to the processing and marketing of agricultural and fishery products. Financial support was intended to support the creation of greater synergies between the production and processing systems of the EU Member States, contributing, at the same time, to provide growing opportunities in an enlarged market.

In the future, the increase in the export flows of quality products together with the ability to enter new end-markets within the EU common framework will largely depend on the agri-food sector units' abilities to efficiently compete and sustain competitiveness in the European and global markets. Some authors (De Salvo et al., 2017; Galati et al., 2017) emphasize the role of human factors, such as the educational level, and the type of agriculture practice as determinants of industry competitiveness. In addition, a prerequisite for international business success is strictly related to the attitude towards sharing the precious resource of diverse employees' knowledge (Sanchez et al., 2012). This facilitates the creation of open and collaborative ecosystems which in turn create a sustainable organization and increase innovation capacity (Christofi et al., 2015a, 2015b; Santoro et al., 2017). In the coming years, NMSs' overall performance could be improved by strengthening the quality side of exported goods, to better comply with EU quality standards and to acquire a more competitive advantage in the single market. This is a challenge that NMSs are able to deal with thanks to the recent increase in employment and education levels.

Future research must focus on an in-depth analysis, with specific reference to country studies, to investigate changes in the different segments of products marketed, analyzing the trend achieved as regards quality certifications (both voluntary and regulated), as well as specific country-to-country trade internal arrangements.

References

Adler, N., & Golany, B. (2001). Evaluation of deregulated airline networks using data envelopment analysis combined with principal component analysis with an application to Western Europe. *European Journal of Operational Research, 132*, 260–273. https://doi.org/10.1016/S0377-2217(00)00150-8

Antimiani, A., Carbone, A., Costantini, V., & Henke, R. (2012). Agri-food export in the enlarged European Union. *Agricultural Economics (Czech Republic)*, 58(8), 354–366.

Asmild, M., Paradi, J., Aggarwal, V., & Schaffnit, C. (2004). Combining DEA window analysis with the Malmquist index approach in a study of the Canadian banking industry. *Journal of Productivity Analysis*, 21(1), 67–89. doi:10.1023/B:PROD.0000012453.91326.ec

Bartošová, D., Bartová, Ľ., & Fidrmuc, J. (2008). EU enlargement implications on the New Member States agri-food trade. *Proceeding of 12th Congress of the European Association of Agricultural Economists – EAAE* (pp. 26–29). Belgium.

Bojnec Š., & Fertő I. (2009b). Determinants of agro-food trade competition of Central European countries with the European Union. *China Economic Review*, 20(2), 327–337. https://doi.org/10.1016/j.chieco.2008.10.002

Bojnec, Š., & Fertő I. (2012). EU Enlargement and Agro-Food Export Performance on EU Market Segments (Discussion Paper MT-DP – 2012/6). Budapest: Institute of Economics, Research Centre for Economic and Regional Studies, Hungarian Academy of Science Budapest.

Bojnec, Š., and Fertő, I. (2009a). Agro-food trade competitiveness of Central European and Balkan countries. *Food Policy*, 34(5), 417–425. https://doi.org/10.1016/j.foodpol.2009.01.003

Bono, F., & Giacomarra, M. (2014). The effect of support schemes on Photovoltaic installed capacity in Europe: a WDEA-STATIS analysis. Proceeding of XLVII Scientific Meeting of the Italian Statistical Society. Cagliari.

Charnes, A., & Cooper, W.W. (1985). Preface to topics in data envelopment analysis. *Annals of Operation Research*, 2(1), 59–94. doi:10.1007/BF01874733

Charnes, A., Clark, C.T., Cooper, W.W., & Golany, B. (1985). A developmental study of data envelopment analysis in measuring the efficiency of maintenance units in the U.S. Air Forces. *Annals of Operations Research*, 2(1–4), 95–112. doi:10.1007/BF01874734

Charnes, A., Cooper, W.W., & Rhodes, E. (1978). Measuring the efficiency of decision making units. *European Journal of Operational Research*, 2(6), 429–444. https://doi.org/10.1016/0377-2217(78)90138-8

Charnes, A., Cooper, W.W., & Seiford, L.M. (1994). Extension to DEA models. In A. Charnes, W.W Cooper, A.Y. Lewin, & L.M. Seiford (Eds.), *Data envelopment analysis: Theory, methodology and applications* (pp. 49–61). Boston: Kluwer Academic Publishers.

Chevassus-Lozza, E., Latouche, K., Majkovič, D., & Unguru, M. (2008). The importance of EU-15 borders for CEECs agri-food exports: The role of tariffs and non-tariff measures in the pre-accession period. *Food Policy*, 33(6), 595–606. https://doi.org/10.1016/j.foodpol.2008.07.005

Christofi, C., Leonidou, E., & Vrontis, D. (2015b). Cause-related marketing, product innovation and extraordinary sustainable leadership: the root towards sustainability. *Global Business and Economics Review*, 17(1), 93–111. https://doi.org/10.1504/GBER.2015.066533

Christofi, M., Vrontis, D., Kitchen, P., & Papasolomou, I. (2015a). Innovation and cause-related marketing success: a conceptual framework and propositions. *Journal of Services Marketing*, 29(5), 354–366. https://doi.org/10.1108/JSM-04-2014-0114

Cooper, W.W., Seiford, L.M., & Tone, K. (2007). *Data envelopment analysis: A comprehensive text with models, applications, references and DEA-solver software.* New York, NY: Springer Science, Business Media.

Crescimanno, M., Galati, A., & Yahiaoui, D. (2013b). Determinants of Italian agrifood export in non-EU Mediterranean partners countries: an empirical investigation through a gravity model approach. *New Medit*, 7(4), 46–54.

Crescimanno, M., Galati, A., & Bal, T. (2014). The role of the economic crisis on the competitiveness of the agri-food sector in the main Mediterranean countries. *Agricultural Economics – Czeck*, 60(2), 49–64.

Crescimanno, M., Galati, A., Siggia, D., & Farruggia, D. (2013a). Intensity of Italy's agri-food trade with countries outside the EU Mediterranean. *International Journal of Business and Globalisation*, 10(1), 31–38. https.//doi.org/10.1504/IJBG.2013.051801

Csaki, C., & Jambor, A. (2013). Impact of the EU enlargements on the new member states agriculture. *Acta Oeconomica et Informatica*, 16(1), 35–50.

De Salvo, M., Begalli, D., Capitello, R., Agnoli, L., & Tabouratzi, E. (2017). Determinants of winegrowers' profitability: evidence from an Eastern Europe wine region. *EuroMed Journal of Business*, 12(3), 300–315. https://doi.org/10.1108/EMJB-12-2016-0043

Debreu, G. (1951). The coefficient of resource utilization. Econometrica, 19, 273–292.

Duponcel, M. (1998). The poor impacts of the liberalisation of EU agricultural imports from central and eastern Europe. Failure of the preferences, or failure of the associated countries? *Food Policy*, 23(2), 187–198. https://doi.org/10.1016/S0306-9192(98)00032-3

European Commission, Directorate-General for Agriculture (2002). EU agriculture and enlargement. Retrieved from https://ec.europa.eu/agriculture/publi/fact/enlarge/2002_en.pdf

Farrell, M.J. (1957). The measurement of productive efficiency. Journal of the Royal Statistical Society. Series A (General), 120(3), 253–281.

Fogarasi, J. (2008). Hungarian and Romanian agri-food trade in the European Union. *Management*, 3(1), 3–13.

Forslid, R., Haaland, J.I., Knarvik, K.H.M., & Mæstad, O. (2002). Integration and transition. Scenarios for the location of production and trade in Europe. *Economics of Transition*, 10, 93–117. doi: 10.1111/1468-0351.00104

Frohberg, K., & Hartmann, M. (1997). Promoting CEA Agricultural Exports through Association Agreements with the EU – Why it is not Working (Discussion paper No. 1). Halle (Saale), Germany: IAMO.

Galati, A., Crescimanno, M., Tinervia, S., Iliopoulos, C., & Theodorakopoulou, I. (2017). Internal resources as tools to increase the global competition: the Italian wine industry case. *British Food Journal*. https://doi.org/10.1108/BFJ-02-2017-0092

Gavrilescu, C. (2013). Romania's position in the EU extra-European agrifood trade (Working paper No 53261). Munich (Germany): MPRA.

Halkos, G.E., & Tzeremes, N.G. (2008). Trade efficiency and economic development: evidence from a cross country comparison. *Applied Economics*, 40(21), 2749–2764. http://dx.doi.org/10.1080/00036840600970302

Halkos, G.E., & Tzeremes, N.G. (2009). Economic efficiency and growth in the EU enlargement. *Journal of Policy Modeling*, 31(6), 847–862. https://doi.org/10.1016/j.jpolmod.2009.08.003

Halkos, G.E., & Tzeremes, N.G. (2011). Oil consumption and economic efficiency: A comparative analysis of advanced, developing and emerging economies. *Ecological Economics*, 70(7), 1354–1362. https://doi.org/10.1016/j.ecolecon.2011.02.010

Hartman, T.E., & Storbeck, J.E. (1996). Input congestion in loan operations. *International Journal of Production Economics*, 46, 413–421. https://doi.org/10.1016/S0925-5273(96)00076-X

Kirkulak, B., & Erdem, S. (2014). Market value chain efficiency in Turkey: application of DEA to the pre- and post-2001 financial crisis. *EuroMed Journal of Business*, 9(1), 2–17. https://doi.org/10.1108/EMJB-01-2013-0001

Melewar, T.C., Hayday, D., Gupta, S., & Cohen, G. (2008). EU enlargement: a case study of branding standardisation. *EuroMed Journal of Business*, 3(2), 179–201. https://doi.org/10.1108/14502190810891227

Sanchez, B.D., Kaufmann, R., & Vrontis, D. (2012). A new organisational memory for cross-cultural knowledge management. *Cross Cultural Management: An International Journal*, 19(3), 336–351. https://doi.org/10.1108/13527601211247080

Santoro, G., Vrontis, D., Thrassou, A. & Dezi, L. (2017). The Internet of Things: building knowledge management systems for open innovation and knowledge management capacity. *Technological Forecasting and Social Change*. https://doi.org/10.1016/j.techfore.2017.02.034

Tsolas, I.E. (2011). Bank branch-level DEA to assess overall efficiency. *EuroMed Journal of Business*, 6(3), 359–377. https://doi.org/10.1108/14502191111170178

Tulkens, H., & Vanden Eeckaut, P. (1995). Non-parametric efficiency. Progress and regress measures for panel data: Methodological aspects. *European Journal of Operational Research*, 80, 474–499. https://doi.org/10.1016/0377-2217(94)00132-V

Wang, K., Shiwei, Y., & Zhang. W. (2013). China's regional energy and environmental efficiency: A DEA window analysis based dynamic evaluation. *Mathematical and Computer Modeling*, 58(5–6), 1117–1127. https://doi.org/10.1016/j.mcm.2011.11.067

Webb, R. (2003). Levels of efficiency in UK retail banks: a DEA window analysis. *International Journal of Economics and Business*, 10(3), 305–322. http://dx.doi.org/10.1080/1357151032000126256

Yue, P. (1992). Data envelopment analysis and commercial bank performance. Federal Reserve Bank of St. Louis Review, 74, 31–45.

Zemeckis, R., & Drozdz, J. (2009). Evaluation of the EU accession impact for the agriculture and agrifood sector on the Baltic states. *Management Theory and Studies for Rural Business and Infrastructure Development*, 17(2), 1–9.

Zhang, X.P., Cheng, X.M., Yuan, J.H., & Gao, X.J. (2011). Total-factor energy efficiency in developing countries. *Energy Policy*, 39(2), 644–650.

5 How does entrepreneurial orientation influence knowledge exploitation?

Orlando Lima Rua and Alexandra França

Introduction

Turbulent business environments are forcing firms to be fierce competitors and to produce innovative solutions on a regular basis. The ability to be innovative, react promptly to competitors' newness and to answer the demands of partners, suppliers, clients and other stakeholders, is significantly influenced by the firms' talent to capture value from external knowledge (Stulova and Rungi, 2017).

Entrepreneurial orientation (EO) as a managerial attitude encompasses three key dimensions: innovation, proactive decisions and high risk taking. SMEs are believed to face greater uncertainty as a result of the external environment than large firms and, thus, they have a greater tendency to take risks and innovate in order to attain success (Stoll and Ha-Brookshire, 2012). SMEs are therefore encouraged to implement an entrepreneurial mind-set to recognize the threats and opportunities in the environment of the firm in order to ensure firms perpetuate and thrive (Kraus, Rigtering, Hughes, and Hosman, 2012).

Literature in the field of strategic management has been focusing on dynamic capabilities (for a review see Barreto, 2010). The firm's success depends not only on its resources and capabilities, but also the ability to adapt itself to the industry contingencies and the markets in which it operates. Firms may possess resources but must display dynamic capabilities otherwise shareholder value will be destroyed (Bowman and Ambrosini, 2003). It is in this context that emerges the Dynamic Capabilities View (DCV) (Amit and Schoemaker, 1993; Teece, Pisano, and Shuen, 1997) to support the adjustment to environmental change.

DCV is not divergent but rather an important stream of the Resource-Based View (RBV) to gain competitive advantage in increasingly demanding environments (Ambrosini and Bowman, 2009; Barreto, 2010; Eisenhardt and Martin, 2000; Wang and Ahmed, 2007). Monteiro, Soares and Rua (2017) defend that in versatile markets the firms' capabilities should be dynamic and managers must display the ability to ensure consistency between the business environment and strategy in order to continuously renew skills.

Dynamic capabilities as a mind-set constantly integrate, reconfigure, renew and recreate core capabilities in response to the ever changing environment in order to achieve and sustain competitive advantage (Wang and Ahmed, 2007). Moreover, these capabilities sense and shape opportunities and threats, seize opportunities, and maintain competitiveness by enhancing, combining, protecting and reconfiguring the businesses' intangible and tangible resources (Teece, 2007).

Absorptive capacity (ACAP) has become one of the most significant constructs in the last twenty years. Absorptive capacity is the dynamic capability that allows firms to gain and sustain a competitive advantage through the management of the external knowledge (Camisón and Forés, 2010).

Building on well-established theories, our research aims at exploring the influence of entrepreneurial orientation in exploitation of knowledge of Portuguese SMEs exporting footwear, by analysing the contributions of this capability in such a construct.

Theoretical framework

Entrepreneurial orientation

Entrepreneurial orientation emerged from the entrepreneurship definition which suggests that a company's entrepreneurial degree can be measured by how it takes risks, innovates and acts proactively (Miller, 1983). Entrepreneurship is connected to new business, and entrepreneurial orientation relates to the process of undertaking, namely, methods, practices and decision-making styles used to act entrepreneurially. Thus, the focus is not on the person but on the process (Wiklund, 1999).

Firms can be regarded as entrepreneurial entities and entrepreneurial behaviour can be part of its activities (Covin and Slevin, 1991). Entrepreneurial orientation emerges from a deliberate strategic choice, where new business opportunities can be successfully undertaken (Lumpkin and Dess, 1996). Thus, there is an entrepreneurial attitude mediating the vision and operations of an organization (Covin and Miles, 1999).

Several empirical studies indicate a positive correlation between entrepreneurial orientation and organizational growth (e.g. Miller, 1983; Covin and Slevin, 1991; Lumpkin and Dess, 1996; Wiklund, 2006; Davis, Bell, Payne and Kreiser, 2010; Frank, Kessler and Fink, 2010). Similarly, other studies also confirm that entrepreneurial orientation has a positive correlation with export performance, enhancing business growth (e.g. Zahra and Garvis, 2000; Okpara, 2009).

The underlying theory of entrepreneurial orientation scale is based on the assumption that the entrepreneurial companies are different from the remaining companies (Kreiser, Marino and Weaver, 2002), since they are likely to take more risks and act more proactively in seeking new businesses and opportunities (Khandwalla, 1977; Mintzberg, 1973).

Entrepreneurial orientation has been characterized by certain constructs that represent organizations' behaviour. Starting from the Miller (1983) definition, three dimensions were identified, innovation, proactiveness and risk-taking, which collectively increase companies' capacity to recognize and exploit market opportunities well ahead of competitors (Zahra and Garvis, 2000). However, Lumpkin and Dess (1996) propose two more dimensions to characterize and distinguish the entrepreneurial process: competitive aggressiveness and autonomy. In this study only innovation, risk-taking and proactiveness will be considered, as they are the most consensual and most used dimensions to measure entrepreneurial orientation (e.g. Covin and Miller, 2014; Covin and Slevin, 1989, 1991; Davis et al., 2010; Frank et al., 2010; Kreiser et al., 2002; Lisboa, Skarmeas and Lages, 2011; Miller, 1983; Okpara, 2009; Wiklund and Shepherd, 2005; Zahra and Covin, 1995; Zahra and Garvis, 2000).

Absorptive capabilities of knowledge exploitation

In order to survive certain pressures, companies need to recognize, assimilate and apply new external knowledge for commercial purposes (Jansen, Van Den Bosch and Volberda, 2005). This ability, known as absorptive capacity (Cohen and Levinthal, 1990), emerges as an underlying theme in the organizational strategy research (Jansen et al., 2005). Cohen and Levinthal (1990) conceptualize ACAP as the firms' ability to identify, assimilate and exploit knowledge acquired from external sources. As such, ACAP facilitates knowledge accumulation and its subsequent use. Thus, this ability to access and use new external knowledge, regarded as an intangible asset, is critical to success and depends mainly on prior knowledge level, since it is this knowledge that will facilitate the identification and processing of new knowledge. This prior knowledge not only includes the basic capabilities, such as shared language, but also recent technological and scientific data or learning skills. By analysing this definition it is found that absorptive capacity of knowledge only has three dimensions: the ability to acquire external knowledge; the ability to assimilate it inside; and the ability to apply it (Cohen and Levinthal, 1990). Zahra and George (2002) broaden the concept of ACAP from the original three dimensions (identify, assimilate and exploit) to four dimensions (acquire, assimilate, transform and exploit).

ACAP is a good example of a dynamic capability since it is embedded in a firm's routines. It combines the firm's resources and capabilities in such a way that together they influence "the firm's ability to create and deploy the knowledge necessary to build other organizational capabilities" (Zahra and George, 2002, p. 188).

According to Zahra and George (2002) ACAP is divided into potential absorptive capacity (PACAP), including knowledge acquisition and assimilation, and realized absorptive capacity (RACAP) that focuses on transformation and exploitation of that knowledge. PACAP reflects the companies' ability to

Entrepreneurial orientation and knowledge 61

acquire and assimilate knowledge that is vital for their activities. Knowledge acquisition and assimilation is related to routines and processes that permit the company to analyse, process, interpret and understand the external information. RACAP includes knowledge transformation and exploitation, where transformation is the ability to develop and perfect routines that facilitate the integration of newly acquired knowledge into existing knowledge; and exploitation means routines which enhance existing skills or create new ones by incorporating acquired and transformed knowledge internally.

Jansen et al. (2005) defend that a company's exposure to new knowledge is not a sufficient condition to successfully incorporate it, as it needs to develop organizational mechanisms which enable it to synthesize and apply newly acquired knowledge in order to cope with and enhance each ACAP dimension. Thus, there are coordination mechanisms that increase the exchange of knowledge between sectors and hierarchies, such as multitasking teams, participation in decision-making and job rotation. These mechanisms bring together different sources of expertise and increase lateral interaction between functional areas. The system mechanisms are behaviour programmes that reduce established deviations, such as routines and formalization. Socialization mechanisms create a broad and tacit understanding of appropriate rules of action, contributing to a common code of communication.

Studying absorptive capacity offers fascinating insights for the strategic management literature and provides new information regarding how firms may develop important sources of sustainable competitive advantages (Jansen et al., 2005). In this chapter the focus is on the exploitation of knowledge.

Hypothesis

Dynamic capabilities refer to "the firm's ability to integrate, build, and reconfigure internal and external competences to address rapidly changing environments" (Teece et al., 1997, p. 516).

Barreto (2010, p. 271) argued that a "dynamic capability is the firm's potential to systematically solve problems, formed by its propensity to sense opportunities and threats, to make timely and market-oriented decisions, and to change its resource base". On the other hand, dynamic capabilities enable companies to create, develop and protect resources allowing them to attain superior performance in the long run, are constructed (not acquired in the market), dependent on experience and are embedded in the company's organizational processes (Ambrosini and Bowman, 2009), not directly affecting the outputs, but contributing through the impact they have on operational capabilities (Teece et al., 1997). These capabilities refer to a firm's capacity to deploy resources, usually in combination, using both explicit and tacit elements (such as know-how and leadership). For this reason, capabilities are often firm-specific and are developed over time through complex interactions between the firm's resources (Amit and Schoemaker, 1993). Maintaining these capabilities requires a management that is able to

62 *Orlando Lima Rua and Alexandra França*

recognize adversity and trends, configure and reconfigure resources, adapt processes and organizational structures in order to create and seize opportunities, while remaining aligned with customer preferences. Indeed, dynamic capabilities allow businesses to achieve superior long-term performance (Teece, 2007).

Firms, therefore, need to continually analyse and interpret changing market trends and quickly recognize new opportunities in order to create competitive products (Tzokas, Kim, Akbar and Al-Dajani, 2015). The ACAP construct encompasses an outward-looking perspective that deals with the identification and generation of useful external knowledge and information and an inward-looking component that is related to how this knowledge is analysed, combined with existing knowledge, and implemented in new products, new technological approaches, or new organizational capabilities (Cohen and Levinthal, 1990). Ultimately, the following hypothesis is tested:

H1: Entrepreneurial orientation positively influences knowledge exploitation.

Methodology

Setting and data collection

To test the hypothesis a sample of Portuguese footwear companies was used, which meet the following criteria: companies in which at least 50% of income comes from export of goods, or companies in which at least 10% of income comes from export of goods and the export value is higher than €150,000 (INE, 2011).

Data collection was implemented through electronic questionnaire, with a link to the survey that was online. To reduce misunderstandings, the questionnaire was validated by the research department of Portuguese Footwear, Components and Leather Goods Association (APICCAPS).

We were provided with a database of 231 companies (company name, telephone contact, email, economic activity classification, export markets, export intensity and capital origin). Only 167 companies fulfilled the parameters, and were contacted by email by APICCAPS to respond to the questionnaire. Subsequently, all companies were contacted by the authors via email and telephone, to ensure a higher rate of valid responses. The questionnaires began on April 22, 2014 and ended on July 22, 2014. After finishing the data collection period, 42 valid questionnaires were received, representing a 25% response rate (Table 5.1). This response rate is considered quite satisfactory, given that the average of top management survey response rates are in the range of 15–20% (Menon and Bharadwaj, 1999).

In this investigation we chose a non-probabilistic and convenient sample since the respondents were chosen for being members of APICCAPS.

Table 5.1 Data summary

Universe of analysis – Portuguese footwear SMEs
Sample – non-probabilistic and convenient
Population – 367 firms
Sample – 167 firms
Response rate – 25%
Valid responses – 42
Time period – 22 April to 22 July 2014

Measures

For assessment of entrepreneurial orientation Covin and Slevin's scale (1989) was used, which consists of nine items: three for innovation, three for proactiveness and three for risk-taking; a five point Likert scale was used, where 1 means "strongly disagree" and 5 "strongly agree".

To measure exploitation of knowledge, and based on Jansen et al. (2005), the firm's ability to explore new external knowledge into their current operations was investigated through six questions (e.g. Jansen et al., 2005; Zahra and George, 2002). A five point Likert scale was used to measure each item, where 1 means "strongly disagree" and 5 "strongly agree".

Results

Reliability analysis

In order to verify the reliability of overall variables we estimated the stability and internal consistency through Cronbach's alpha (α). Generally, an instrument or test is classified with appropriate reliability when α is higher or equal to 0.70 (Nunnally, 1978). However, in some research scenarios in social sciences an α of 0.60 is considered acceptable, as long as the results are interpreted with caution and the context is taken into account (DeVellis, 2012). For the present study we used the scale proposed by Pestana and Gageiro (2008).

The result of 0.855 achieved for all variables is considered very good, confirming the sample's internal consistency. An internal consistency test was also conducted for all variables in each construct to assess their reliability (Table 5.2).

We found that entrepreneurial orientation has good consistency and that exploitation of knowledge presents very good reliability.

Exploratory factor analysis

We performed a factor analysis, with Varimax rotation, of entrepreneurial orientation construct items that comprise the scale, with the purpose of finding

64   Orlando Lima Rua and Alexandra França

Table 5.2 Internal consistency test by construct (Cronbach's alpha)

Construct	Cronbach's α	Items No.	N	Analysis
Entrepreneurial orientation	.739	9	42	Good
Exploitation of knowledge	.897	6	42	Very good

a solution that was more easily interpretable. Three factors were extracted and there was no need to delete items. Thus, we obtained a scale composed of nine items, distributed over three factors that explain 77.09% of total variance, with 35.52% of variance explained by the first factor, *Proactiveness*, 27.48% for the second factor, *Innovation*, and 14.09% by the third factor, *Risktaking*. Analysing the internal consistency of the three factors, we found that Cronbach's alphas have a good internal consistency. The Kaiser-Meyer-Olkin (KMO) test indicates that there is a reasonable correlation between the variables (0.695). Bartlett's sphericity test registered a value of $\chi^2(36, n = 42) = 171.176$, $p < 0.05$, therefore it is confirmed that $\chi^2 > \chi_{0.95}^2$, so the null hypothesis is rejected, i.e. the variables are correlated.

In the factor analysis, with Varimax rotation, of exploitation of knowledge we obtained a scale with six items, distributed by one factor that explained 69.17% of total variance, whose saturations range between 0.804 and 0.578. The internal consistency of the factor is $\alpha = 0.897$, this value indicating that these dimensions presented a very good internal consistency. The KMO test confirmed a good correlation between the variables (0.831). Bartlett's sphericity test registered a value of $\chi^2(10, n = 42) = 114.439$, $p < 0.05$, therefore it is confirmed that $\chi^2 > \chi_{0.95}^2$, so the null hypothesis is rejected and the variables are correlated.

Multiple regression analysis

Multiple regression analysis is a statistical technique that is used to analyse the relationship between a single dependent (criterion) variable and several independent (predictor) variables. The objective of multiple regression analysis is to use the independent variables whose values are known to predict the single dependent value selected by the researcher. Each independent variable is weighted by the regression analysis procedure to ensure maximal prediction from the set of independent variables.

The most commonly used measure of predictive accuracy for the regression model is the coefficient of determination (R^2). This coefficient measures the proportion of total variability that can be explained by regression ($0 \leq R \leq 1$), measuring the effect of independent variables on the dependent variable. When $R^2 = 0$ the model clearly does not adjust to data and when $R^2 = 1$ the adjustment is perfect. In social sciences when $R^2 > 0.500$ the adjustment is considered acceptable (Marôco, 2011). In Table 5.3 we present the results of the multiple regression analysis of our model.

Entrepreneurial orientation and knowledge 65

Table 5.3 Summary and ANOVA of multiple regression analysis[b]

Model	R	R^2	Adj. R^2	Standard error	F	Sig.
1	.556[a]	.309	.254	.86350080	5.662	.003*

a. Predictors: (constant), entrepreneurial orientation
b. Dependent variable: knowledge exploitation
* $p<0.05$

Table 5.4 Standardized beta coefficient[a]

Variables	Beta	Sig.
Entrepreneurial orientation		
Proactiveness	.076	n.s.
Innovation	.445	.002*
Risk-taking	.325	.021*

* $p<0.05$
n.s. – non significant
a. Dependent variable: Knowledge exploitation

The previous table presents for model 1 a value of F = 5.662, with p-*value* < 0.05 (Sig.), so H0 is rejected in favour of H1. Thus, this hypothesis is supported.

A mere comparison of the regression coefficients is not valid to evaluate the importance of each independent variable model, since these variables have different magnitudes. Thus, it is essential to use standard variables, known as beta (β) coefficients, in the model adjustment so that the independent variables can be compared.

The beta coefficient allows a direct comparison between coefficients with respect to their relative explanatory power of the dependent variable. Table 5.4 shows that the variables that have higher contribution to knowledge exploitation are *Innovation* (β = 0.445) and *Risk-taking* (β = 0.325).

Discussion and conclusion

The main purpose of this study was to analyse the influence of entrepreneurial orientation on knowledge exploitation. We conducted empirical research based on a sample of 42 companies, which completed a questionnaire in order to exploit data to test hypotheses, using statistical techniques. It is important to note that companies evaluated entrepreneurial orientation and exploitation of knowledge relative to their major competitors in the export market(s), so the results should be interpreted based on these two aspects.

The Portuguese footwear industry faces considerable challenges, not only concerning the international markets crisis, but also regarding consumption patterns. The reduction of shoe design lifecycles has consequences for the offer. On one hand, the products have to be adapted to different segment-specific needs and tastes (custom design, new models in small series, etc.), on the other hand, manufacturing processes must be increasingly flexible, adopt just-in-time production, and invest in the brand, qualified personnel, technology and innovation (APICCAPS, 2013).

This study demonstrated that the company's innovation and risk-taking have a positive and significant influence on knowledge exploitation. The analysed companies are able to exploit knowledge through informal knowledge gathering, clear definition of tasks, analysis and discussion of market trends and new product development, among others.

Dynamic capabilities can take a variety of forms and be involved in different functions, but the most important common characteristics are that they are higher level capabilities which provide opportunities for knowledge gathering and sharing, constant updating of the operational processes, interaction with the environment, and decision-making evaluations (Easterby-Smith, Lyles and Peteraf, 2009). However, the existence of common features does not imply that any particular dynamic capability is exactly alike across firms, rather they could be developed from different starting points and take unique paths (Eisenhardt and Martin, 2000).

In fact, according to the industrial organization, a company should find a favourable position in its industry from which it can better defend against competitive forces, or influence them in its favour through strategic actions such as raising barriers to entry, etc. (Porter, 1980). This perspective is consistent with Eisenhardt and Martin (2000) regarding the uniqueness of paths. The results of this study confirm that exploitation of knowledge enables firms to achieve superior long-term performance (Teece, 2007).

Theoretical and practical implications

It is known that strategy includes deliberate and emergent initiatives adopted by management, comprising resource and capabilities use to improve business performance (Nag, Hambrick and Chen, 2007). The findings are a contribution to clarify the influence of entrepreneurial orientation on the company's knowledge exploitation. This study also enabled a thorough analysis of a highly important industry for national exports, such as the footwear industry, allowing understanding that entrepreneurial orientation, as an industry strategic determinant, enhances exploitation of knowledge.

Jansen et al. (2005) maintain that companies need to develop organizational mechanisms to combine and apply newly acquired knowledge in order to deal with and enhance each absorptive capacity dimension. This study highlights the importance of knowledge absorptive capacity to business performance. It is essential that business owners are able to interpret, integrate and apply external knowledge in order to systematically analyse change in the target market and to incorporate this knowledge in their processes to enhance performance.

In addition, the results provide guidance to business practitioners because they indicate entrepreneurial orientation as a predictor for exploitation of knowledge. Companies are a bundle of resources and capabilities (Peteraf, 1993); it is essential to understand and identify which resources are relevant to gain competitive advantage and superior performance. In this study the importance of entrepreneurial orientation to the firms' exploitation of knowledge is obvious. Managers must be particularly sensitive to the identification of present and future needs and market trends, in order to anticipate changes in demand and seek new business opportunities.

By building on the literature of entrepreneurial orientation, absorptive capacity and exploitation of knowledge, this study aims to support the strategic development of business management policies designed to increase firms' performance in foreign markets and add value to the current context of change.

Research limitations

The main limitation of this study is related to the sample size, since it was difficult to find companies with the willingness to collaborate in this type of research. The sample is non-probabilistic and convenient and cannot be used to extrapolate to the general population. The study findings should therefore be analysed with caution.

The fact that the research does not consider the effect of control variables such as size, age, location and target market of the respondents can be seen as a limitation.

Finally, the fact that this study considered only exploitation of knowledge as an absorptive capacity can also be appointed as a limitation.

Future lines of research

In future work, we suggest that the model is used in a sample with a higher number of observations to confirm these results.

We further suggest pursuing the investigation of strategic management in Portugal, focusing on other sectors of the national economy, so that in the future one can make a comparison with similar studies, allowing the identification of new factors that enhance absorptive capacity.

Finally, the moderating effect of strategic variables (e.g. competitive advantage) in the relationship between entrepreneurial orientation and exploitation of knowledge should be studied.

References

Ambrosini, V., & Bowman, C. (2009). What are dynamic capabilities and are they a useful construct in strategic management? *International Journal of Management Reviews, 11*(1), 29–49. http://doi.org/10.1111/j.1468-2370.2008.00251.x

68　*Orlando Lima Rua and Alexandra França*

Amit, R., & Schoemaker, P. (1993). Strategic assets and organizational rent. *Strategic Management Journal, 14*(1), 33–46.

APICCAPS. (2013). Footure – Plano Estratégico – Cluster do Calçado (APICCAPS).

Barreto, I. (2010). Dynamic capabilities: a review of past research and an agenda for the future. *Journal of Management, 36*(1), 256–280. http://doi.org/10.1177/0149206309350776

Bowman, C., & Ambrosini, V. (2003). How the resource based and the dynamic capability views of the firm inform corporate level strategy. *British Journal of Management, 14*(4), 289–303. http://doi.org/10.1111/j.1467-8551.2003.00380.x

Camisón, C., & Forés, B. (2010). Knowledge absorptive capacity: New insights for its conceptualization and measurement. *Journal of Business Research, 63*(7), 707–715. http://doi.org/10.1016/j.jbusres.2009.04.022

Cohen, W., & Levinthal, D. (1990). Absorptive capacity: a new perspective on learning and innovation. *Administrative Science Quarterly, 35*(1), 128. http://doi.org/10.2307/2393553

Covin, J., & Miles, M. (1999). Corporate entrepreneurship and the pursuit of competitive advantage. *Entrepreneurship: Theory & Practice, 23*(3), 47–63.

Covin, J., & Miller, D. (2014). International entrepreneurial orientation: conceptual considerations, research themes, measurement issues, and future research directions. *Entrepreneurship Theory and Practice, 38*(1), 11–44. http://doi.org/10.1111/etap.12027

Covin, J., & Slevin, D. (1989). Strategic management of small firms in hostile and benign environments. *Strategic Management Journal, 10*(1), 75–87. http://doi.org/10.1002/smj.4250100107

Covin, J., & Slevin, D. (1991). A conceptual model of entrepreneurship as firm behavior. *Entrepreneurship: Theory & Practice, 16*, 7–25.

Davis, J. L., Bell, R. G., Payne, G. T., & Kreiser, P. M. (2010). Entrepreneurial orientation and firm performance: the moderating role of managerial power. *American Journal of Business, 25*(2), 41–54. http://doi.org/10.1108/19355181201000009

DeVellis, R. F. (2012). *Scale Development – Theory and Applications* (3ª). SAGE Publications, Inc.

Easterby-Smith, M., Lyles, M. A., & Peteraf, M. A. (2009). Dynamic capabilities: current debates and future directions. *British Journal of Management, 20*, S1–S8. http://doi.org/10.1111/j.1467-8551.2008.00609.x

Eisenhardt, K. M., & Martin, J. A. (2000). Dynamic capabilities: what are they? *Strategic Management Journal, 21*(10–11), 1105–1121. http://doi.org/10.1002/1097-0266(200010/11)21:10/11<1105::AID-SMJ133>3.0.CO;2-E

Frank, H., Kessler, A., & Fink, M. (2010). Entrepreneurial orientation and business performance: a replication study. *Schmalenbach Business Review*, (April), 175–199.

Jansen, J. J. P., Van Den Bosch, F. A. J., & Volberda, H. W. (2005). Managing Potential and realized absorptive capacity: how do organizational antecedents matter? *Academy of Management Journal, 48*(6), 999–1015. http://doi.org/10.5465/AMJ.2005.19573106

Khandwalla, P. N. (1977). Some top management styles, their context and performance. *Organization & Administrative Sciences, 7*(4), 21–51.

Kraus, S., Rigtering, J. P. C., Hughes, M., & Hosman, V. (2012). Entrepreneurial orientation and the business performance of SMEs: A quantitative study from the Netherlands. *Review of Managerial Science, 6*(2), 161–182. http://doi.org/10.1007/s11846-011-0062-9

Kreiser, P., Marino, L., & Weaver, K. (2002). Assessing the psychometric properties of the entrepreneurial orientation scale: A multi-country analysis. *Entrepreneurship Theory and Practice*, (1989), 71–95.

Lisboa, A., Skarmeas, D., & Lages, C. (2011). Entrepreneurial orientation, exploitative and explorative capabilities, and performance outcomes in export markets: A resource-based approach. *Industrial Marketing Management*, *40*(8), 1274–1284. http://doi.org/10.1016/j.indmarman.2011.10.013

Lumpkin, G., & Dess, G. (1996). Clarifying the entrepreneurial orientation construct and linking it to performance. *Academy of Management Review*, *21*(1), 135–172. Retrieved from http://amr.aom.org/content/21/1/135.short

Marôco, J. (2011). *Análise estatística com o SPSS Statistics* (5ª). Report Number, Lda.

Menon, A., & Bharadwaj, S. (1999). Antecedents and consequences of marketing strategy making: A model and a test. *Journal of Marketing*, *63*(April), 18–40.

Miller, D. (1983). The correlates of entrepreneurship in three types of firms. *Management Science*, *29*(7), 770–791.

Mintzberg, H. (1973). Strategy-making in three modes. *California Management Review*, *16*(2), 44–53.

Monteiro, A., Soares, A. M., & Rua, O. L. (2017). Entrepreneurial orientation and export performance: the mediating effect of organisational resources and dynamic capabilities. *Journal of International Business and Entrepreneurship Development*, 10(1).

Nag, R., Hambrick, D., & Chen, M. (2007). What is strategic management, really? Inductive derivation of a consensus definition of the field. *Strategic Management Journal*, *955*(October 2006), 935–955. http://doi.org/10.1002/smj

Nunnally, J. C. (1978). *Psychometric theory*. New York: McGraw-Hill.

Okpara, J. (2009). Entrepreneurial orientation and export performance: evidence from an emerging economy. *International Review of Business Research Papers*, *5*(6), 195–211.

Pestana, M. H., & Gageiro, J. N. (2008). *Análise de Dados para Ciências Sociais – A complementaridade do SPSS* (5ª). Edições Silabo.

Peteraf, M. (1993). The cornerstones of competitive advantage: A resource-based view. *Strategic Management Journal*, *14*(3), 179–191.

Porter, M. (1980). *Competitive Strategy*. New York: Free Press.

Stoll, E. E., & Ha-Brookshire, J. E. (2012). Motivations for success: case of U.S. textile and apparel small- and medium-sized enterprises. *Clothing and Textiles Research Journal*, *30*(2), 149–163. http://doi.org/10.1177/0887302X11429740

Stulova, V., & Rungi, M. (2017). Untangling the mystery of absorptive capacity: A process or a set of success factors? *Journal of High Technology Management Research*, *28*(1), 110–123. http://doi.org/10.1016/j.hitech.2017.04.008

Teece, D. J. (2007). Explicating dynamic capabilities: the nature and microfoundations of (sustainable) enterprise performance. *Strategic Management Journal*, *28*(13), 1319–1350. http://doi.org/10.1002/smj

Teece, D. J., Pisano, G., & Shuen, A. (1997). Dynamic capabilities and strategic management. *Strategic Management Journal*, *18*(7), 509–533. http://doi.org/10.1002/(SICI)1097-0266(199708)18:7<509::AID-SMJ882>3.0.CO;2-Z

Tzokas, N., Kim, Y. A., Akbar, H., & Al-Dajani, H. (2015). Absorptive capacity and performance: The role of customer relationship and technological capabilities in high-tech SMEs. *Industrial Marketing Management*, *47*, 134–142. http://doi.org/10.1016/j.indmarman.2015.02.033

Wang, C., & Ahmed, P. K. (2007). Dynamic capabilities: A review and research agenda. *International Journal of Management Reviews, 9*(1), 31–51. http://doi.org/10.1111/j.1468-2370.2007.00201.x

Wiklund, J. (1999). The sustainability of the entrepreneurial orientation performance relationship. *Entrepreneurship: Theory & Practice, 24*(1), 39–50. http://doi.org/Article

Wiklund, J., & Shepherd, D. (2005). Entrepreneurial orientation and small business performance: a configurational approach. *Journal of Business Venturing, 20*(1), 71–91. http://doi.org/10.1016/j.jbusvent.2004.01.001

Zahra, S., & Covin, J. G. (1995). Contextual influences on the corporate entrepreneurship-performance relationship: A longitudinal analysis. *Journal of Business Venturing, 10*(1), 43–58. http://doi.org/10.1016/0883-9026(94)00004-E

Zahra, S., & Garvis, D. (2000). International corporate entrepreneurship and firm performance: The moderating effect of international environmental hostility. *Journal of Business Venturing, 15*, 469–492.

Zahra, S., & George, G. (2002). Absorptive capacity: A review, reconceptualization, and extension. *Academy of Management Review, 27*(2), 185–203.

6 Profitability of the Italian credit cooperative banks

Giovanni Ossola, Guido Giovando and Chiara Crovini

Introduction

The banking system of the Credit Cooperatives in Italy finds its origins in the last quarter of 1800. Since their inception these credit cooperative institutions have been closely linked to the local communities in which they were established.

The earliest forms of credit cooperative in Italy were represented by the rural population and artisans, who, inspired by Christian values, played a key role in stimulating humble groups of rural people, especially farmers and craftsmen, to obtain loans on terms more favourable than those applied to traditional banks.

Since then, Rural and Artisan banks have maintained a very close relationship with the local territory, weaving their own story with that of the communities. The rural banks were also called upon to fulfil a social function, as well as financial income. In other words, the aim was not to maximize profits, but rather to support the local economy. Their role was, in fact, to carry out lending activities against people belonging to certain occupational groups such as farmers and artisans, members themselves of the cooperative bank, within a given territory in order to promote social and economic development of the community.

The rural banks were able to grow in number and spread over time, supporting the socio-economic development of their local areas. In 1993, the Banking Act laid down a radical change as the name changed from "Rural and Artisan banks" to the current "mutual banks".

This research fits into this framework as it concentrates on Italian credit cooperative banks (BCCs). We considered a sample of 264 Italian BCCs banks, which represented more than 72% of all Italian BCCs in 2015. In addition, the research focuses on the period between 2009 and 2014. Moreover, a sophisticated statistical model was not implemented in order to pursue the effectiveness of the results and to concentrate on the real relationship between the items considered to strengthen the role of these banks for the growth and value-creation of the local territory. Therefore, to do that we tried to find a relation between net assets and net banking income and profit/loss of the banks of the sample.

72 *Giovanni Ossola et al.*

The general approach is balance-sheet and income statement based, as this preliminary analysis starts from the data extracted from the Bankscope database and consequently from the financial statements of banks. However, despite the limits of the research, thanks to this analysis and the results obtained, we may consider the opportunities for growth and development of this analysis.

In conclusion, one of the aims of this research is to improve the existing literature by using a quantitative empirical approach. However it might be useful to analyse this reality with large listed banks through a multiple-case study.

The remainder of this study is organized as follows. First, the Literature review and Theoretical background are presented. Second, we define the methodology. Third, we present the findings of our study. Finally, discussions and conclusions are presented in the last part of the research.

Literature review and theoretical background

The structure and functioning of banks has been studied in its entirety by many scholars (Vasiliadis, 2009; Koch and MacDonald, 2007; Ossola, 2005; Giovando and Gianoglio, 1999; Giovando, 1996). Several researchers have studied the bank account (Bocchino et al., 2013; Ossola, 2005), its performance (Barros et al., 2007; Berger, 2005; Boubakri et al., 2005; Tsolas, 2011; Schiniotakis, 2012) and its financial analysis (Hartvigsen, 1992). Recent studies concentrated on the accounting policy of banks, focusing on the application of the International Accounting Standards (Dezzani et al., 2014), and other specific studies focused on the analysis of the assets and liabilities of the balance sheets (Ossola, 2000).

In addition other researchers have recently analysed the impact of the new capital requirements under Basel III on bank lending rates and loan growth (Kahlert and Wagner, 2015; Kosmidis and Terzidis, 2011). As a result higher capital requirements, raising the marginal cost of bank funding, have led to higher rates (Cosimano and Hakura, 2011; Elliott, 2009; Laeven and Valencia, 2008).

Some studies focused on the way some financial entities have addressed this moment of global crisis (Crowley, 2015; Costa and Thegeia, 2013; Avdjie et al. 2012; Caprio et al., 2005; Mihai Yiannaki, 2011). Others concentrated on this period of financial crisis (Kapan and Minoiu, 2015; Calvo, 2012), highlighting the crucial role played by the liquidity risk in the stability of a bank, and, more generally, in the financial system (Borio, 2008; Dell'Ariccia et al., 2008). Some have tried to locate the perimeter within which to identify the financial risk and study methods for good management, in accordance with the requirements of Basel (Álvarez and Rossignolo, 2015; Angelini et al., 2011).

An important study analysed, by means of alternative techniques, both cost and profit efficiency in a sample of ten countries of the European Union for the period 1993–1996, again obtaining profit efficiency levels lower than cost efficiency levels (Maudos et al., 2002).

Profitability of credit cooperative banks 73

For many years, a comparison of accounting ratios in the banking sector has shown the existence of remarkable differences in average costs. Wide ranges of return on equity (ROE) are found, although these results are more difficult to evaluate due to their greater instability.

Other studies focused on the effect of banks' capitalization on banks' ROE (Blaga, 2015). A debate emerged on the costs for banks of the increase in capital requirements under Basel III (Camara et al., 2015).

Some researchers analysed the performance of banks belonging to individual countries (Faisal et al., 2015; Rauf and Fu, 2014; Iqbal and Raza, 2009; Ali and Ansari, 2007; Barros Ferreira and Williams, 2007). Iannotta et al. (2007) as well as Illueca et al. (2008) documented that bank ownership is an important determinant of lending behaviour, risk taking and performance.

With reference to the Italian context the importance of local small banks, such as BCCs, was emphasized in a few studies (Usai and Vannini, 2005; Ferri and Messori, 2000). In particular several researchers concentrated on this kind of bank, in terms of characteristics and role within the Italian banking sector, by emphasizing their importance (Bonfante, 2010; Agostini, 2009; Costa, 2007; Capriglione 2005; Bonfante, 2004; Vella, 2004; Appio, 1996). Zago and Dongili (2014) examined in depth the impact of the financial crisis on the Italian credit cooperative banks and the technical efficiency of the Italian BCCs for the period 2003 to 2012. They also discussed and tested different specifications and objective functions for BCCs.

A credit cooperative bank is a member-owned financial cooperative, democratically controlled by its members and it operates for the purpose of promoting thrift, providing credit at competitive rates and providing other financial services to its members (Ossola et al., 2017).

More than 50% of total Italian banks are credit cooperative banks (BCCs). They are usually small banks (according to the classification of Banca d'Italia) and their total weight on the loan market is 8%. In addition, they are particularly relevant for small and medium enterprises (SMEs). In the Italian context, credit cooperative banks base their organization and mission on mutualism and localism (Zago and Dongili, 2014). In 2015 there were 364 credit cooperative banks, 4,400 branches and 37,000 employees. In total there are more than 1,200,000 members of the mutual banks and mutual banks consist of more than 6 million customers. The main characteristics of these banks are:

- Widespread ownership: as cooperatives, BCCs have a variable share capital and consequently there is the so-called "open-door policy". This policy give the directors significant powers related to the possibility of choosing and excluding new members. The choice of excluding new members in these banks obviously has to be motivated adequately.
- Those who have accounts in the credit cooperative bank are its members and owners and they elect their board of directors in a one-person-one-vote system, regardless of their amount invested.
- Link with the territory: members must live and/or operate where their bank operates.

74 *Giovanni Ossola et al.*

- Mutualism: BCCs' activities must be prevalently towards members because they are "not-for-profit" oriented. In fact, their purpose is to serve their members rather than to maximize profits.
- Very limited profit-seeking nature: credit cooperative banks must allocate most of their annual profits to legal reserves (at least 70%) and to specific funds for the development of cooperation (at least 3%).

As mentioned above, the mission of the BCCs, defined by statute and law, is to pursue the spirit of mutual benefit, to promote value for members and social cohesion and sustainable development of the territory where their members operate. This mission can be carried out and represented in two phases:

- Production phase: consists in providing services at favourable conditions to their members, in terms of low interest rates on loans and high interest rates on deposits. It also consists in choosing an efficient management style, capable of maintaining the BCCs' intertemporal sustainability and competitiveness, and in expanding the access to credit to otherwise excluded groups of clients.
- Distribution phase: consists in distributing resources to the territory and the social context in which they operate, through support and sponsorship of meritorious initiatives.

The importance of local small banks was also emphasized by Ferri and Messori (2000), who stressed that a close and long-lasting customer relationship between small banks and firms can promote a favourable allocation of credit for economic growth. Usai and Vannini (2005) distinguished among various types of banks while studying the finance-growth nexus in Italian regions. Good capitalization, stable funds availability and liquidity have given BCCs the ability to provide credit even during the recent financial crisis, when they have replaced other banks suffering more from the credit crunch. These elements positively affect the local community in which the BCC operates, by supporting families and the development of businesses. In 2007–2008, the financial crisis caused significant new problems in risk assessment and management. As a consequence, some researchers tried to locate the perimeter within which to identify the financial risk and study methods for good management, in accordance with the requirements of Basel (Álvarez and Rossignolo, 2015; Angelini et al., 2011).

This theoretical contribution in the field of credit cooperative banks has the aim to show that the BCCs are relevant in the Italian banking sector and that they enhance growth and value-creation for the local community in which they operate thanks to their activities.

Methodology

This research represents a theoretical contribution and a preliminary quantitative analysis in the field of Credit cooperative banks, seen as key drivers for sustainable value-creation and growth, not only of the specific financial sector, but in particular with regard to the local community of companies and families to whom the BCC provides credit (Ossola et al., 2017). This study follows a methodology that aims to formulate research questions by problematizing some dominant assumptions in existing research (Davis, 1971). Successful problematization is a matter of creativity, intuition, reading inspiring texts that offer critical insights (but without being accepted as a new fixed framework), talking to other people, having specific experiences, or making observations that may trigger new thinking (Alvesson and Sandberg, 2013; Alvesson and Sandberg, 2011). This methodology also has the advantage of facilitating focus, working as a support for a research identity around being a problematizer and facilitating description of what one has accomplished.

As regards the philosophical approach, constructivism implies that the new knowledge is built not only on the basis of what has been gained in past experiences but also through sharing and negotiation of meanings expressed by a "community of interpreters". The "construction" is therefore based on cognitive maps that serve to individuals to orient themselves and build their own interpretations. The following sub-sections describe the sample and the phases of analysis followed to conduct this research.

The sample and the data

This analysis focuses on the Italian BCCs. Our sample represents 264 BCCs of a total of 364 BCCs in Italian territory, for the period 2009–2014. We decided to exclude the banks for which financial statements were not available for all the years considered.

This study can help us understand the context and the main business in which banks operate. Data were extracted from Bankscope, which is a database containing comprehensive information on financial companies (banks and insurance companies) in Italy. In the first part of Phase 2, we focused on information about net assets, net banking income and profit/loss.

It should be noted that data provided in our figures all refer to the mean of the single element analysed. In the second part of Phase 2, we concentrated on some ratios, such as profit/loss on equity to total assets and net banking income on profit/loss, provided by Bankscope.

Research questions and phases of analysis

The present research is based on the following hypotheses:

- *H1*: The BCCs represent a significant banking institution in the Italian territory.
- *H2*: The net banking income is the profitability linked to the core business of banking. In the sample of BCCs examined the net banking income is preponderant.

76 *Giovanni Ossola et al.*

To reach the goals of this study, we need to formulate three research questions:

> *RQ1*: What is the trend during the period monitored between the net banking income and the profit/loss?
> *RQ2*: What is the trend in the period between 2009 and 2014 between the profit margin and ROE?
> *RQ3*: Is there a correlation between the net banking income and the profit/loss?

The research methodology follows three phases:

> *Phase 1*: the BCCs system and its characteristic features.
> *Phase 2*: Empirical analysis and findings. This involves an analysis of the information derived from the sample. The research methodology only uses the information provided in the financial statements because it is sufficient to answer the research questions.

With reference to *RQ1*, we want to show that the BCCs are relevant in the Italian banking sector and also demonstrate that the sample is particularly significant as an indicator of the Italian banking sector.

Referring to *RQ2,* we have appropriately calculated two indicators, the profit margin and ROE, and we compared them to see how they changed over the years. We concentrated on the analysis of the Profit margin ratio and ROE because we based our research on the Dupont analysis. It also called the Dupont model and is a financial ratio based on the return on equity ratio that is used to analyse a company's ability to increase its return on equity. In other words, this model breaks down the return on equity ratio to explain how companies can increase their return for investors. The Dupont analysis looks at three main components of the ROE ratio:

- profit margin;
- total asset turnover;
- financial leverage.

Based on these three performance measures the model concludes that a company can raise its ROE by maintaining a high profit margin, increasing asset turnover or leveraging assets more effectively. The Dupont Corporation developed this analysis in the 1920s. The name has stuck with it ever since.

With reference to *RQ3*, we calculate the Pearson correlation ratio between profit/loss and net banking income of each year. Thanks to this relationship, we are able to analyse the possible correlation of net banking income with the profitability of the banks, in order to assess the effects of a policy that is carried out by corporate governance to face the difficulties that the banking world has been experiencing.

As mentioned above, the correlation ratio of Pearson (p) is used to identify a positive or negative correlation between the profit/loss and net banking income. Therefore, it is necessary to emphasize the following conditions:

- if $p > 0$ there is a direct correlation;
- if $p = 0$ there is no correlation;
- if $p < 0$ there is an indirect correlation;
- if $0 < p < 0.3$ the correlation is weak;
- if $0.3 < p < 0.7$ the correlation is moderate;
- if $p > 0.7$ the correlation is strong.

    Phase 3: Conclusions and limitations of the research.

Findings

First of all, before analysing the data obtained, it is important to provide further details and definitions.

The profit margin ratio is an index that is created as the ratio of profit/loss and net banking income. This index shows the impact of different management from the net banking income on the operating result. ROE is calculated as the ratio between net income and shareholders' equity. It represents the net return for the shareholder. Phase 2 concerns the stages of analysis of results and the related comments.

Starting with *H1*, every BCC is a structured system on a network of approximately 364 cooperative banks. The main feature of the BCC is to be widely spread throughout Italy, for over 130 years BCCs have played their role of local banks, performing a specific function, to promote development and to address the economic and social needs of local communities. In Italian territory BCCs have 4,414 branches (14.8%), with 1,248,724 members and 36,500 employees. The total funding (including deposits from banks, customer deposits and bonds) amounted to €196.7 billion and customer deposits with bonds represented €161.8 billion.

The market share of customer deposits including bonds is 7.7%. Economic loans amounted to €134 billion. The market share of lending for mutual banks is 7.2%; loans amounted to €149 billion. On the basis of the data and the considerations above it can be argued that H1 is confirmed and BCCs are important banking institutions in Italy. In order to proceed with the analysis, Table 6.1 presents the descriptive statistics of the data collected for the selected sample over the period 2009–2014.

The trend of the selected items are shown in Figure 6.1 and Figure 6.2. In particular, with reference to RQ 1, Figure 6.1 shows the trend of net banking income and profit/loss in the period between 2009 and 2014. The data refer to the mean of the sample for each year.

Figure 6.1 confirms the first hypothesis. Therefore, in the sample of banking firms considered, it can be noted that the net banking income substantially grows, while profit steadily decreases over the period. Moreover, H2 cannot

Table 6.1 Main items considered in the financial statement analysis

		2009	2010	2011	2012	2013	2014
Net assets	Mean	€53,248,775	€54,146,355	€51,875,244	€58,385,757	€59,852,789	€62,900,690
	Median	€38,887,792	€37,894,855	€36,578,651	€42,534,866	€42,651,894	€44,934,293
	Max	€574,282,677	€581,983,976	€563,434,911	€644,165,552	€706,866,923	€747,322,795
	Min	€2,806,597	€2,310,158	€2,102,883	€3,071,128	€2,608,013	€1,234,285
	Std. dev.	€58,023,361	€59,627,273	€58,253,290	€64,450,364	€67,170,376	€71,058,513
Net banking income	Mean	€15,271,042	€14,654,857	€15,829,806	€18,808,016	€19,202,108	€22,360,217
	Median	€11,032,347	€10,384,311	€11,501,707	€13,211,618	€14,155,574	€16,069,505
	Max	€219,821,974	€96,943,712	€190,368,842	€250,573,032	€217,946,906	€248,110,914
	Min	€302,681	€902,261	€1,148,809	€1,248,021	€1,353,727	€1,715,234
	Std. dev.	€18,024,387	€16,826,969	€17,151,888	€21,322,259	€21,372,301	€25,148,830
Profit/ loss	Mean	€2,159,771	€1,370,879	€1,323,646	€1,428,378	€512,429	€1,203,610
	Median	€1,302,454	€894,464	€916,636	€1,115,313	€767,636	€917,666
	Max	€33,638,627	€30,257,871	€18,106,653	€20,144,982	€21,140,332	€25,913,278
	Min	–€3,511,339	€13,770,862	–€14,483,137	–€23,517,128	–€25,747,756	–€13,979,750
	Std. dev.	€3,202,692	€3,309,409	€2,536,456,97	€3,437,043	€3,979,242	€3,795,589
Profit margin ratio	Mean	13.98%	7.18%	8.83%	8.61%	0.67%	5.23%
	Median	13.58%	9.48%	9.20%	9.49%	2.17%	6.23%
	Max	191.02%	40.95%	38.56%	44.74%	12.32%	42.04%
	Min	–52.64%	–87.98%	–63.03%	–93.18%	–36.10%	–110.23%
	Std. dev.	14.70%	15.74%	10.79%	14.70%	6.62%	16.42%
ROE	Mean	3.96%	2.00%	2.76%	2.57%	0.67%	1.60%
	Median	3.90%	2.69%	2.92%	3.10%	2.17%	2.32%
	Max	13.38%	14.56%	14.25%	16.93%	12.32%	27.51%
	Min	–11.64%	–36.91%	–19.77%	–76.27%	–36.10%	–52.20%
	Std. dev.	2.94%	4.54%	3.78%	6.62%	6.62%	6.42%

Profitability of credit cooperative banks 79

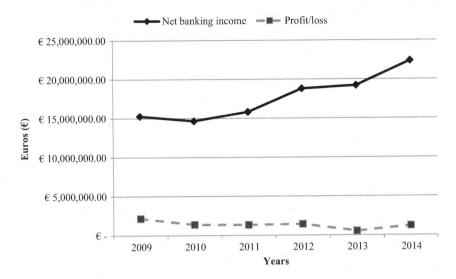

Figure 6.1 The trend of net banking income and profit/loss of BCCs in the period between 2009 and 2014

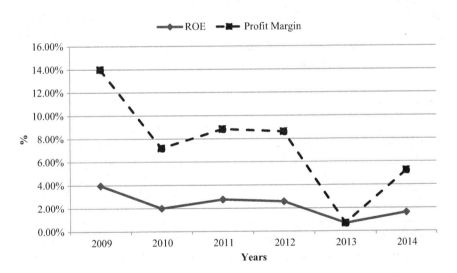

Figure 6.2 The trend of ROE and the profit margin ratio of BCCs in the period between 2009 and 2014

be confirmed in all the years considered. Continuing the analysis in order to answer *RQ2*, Figure 6.2 compares the profit margin ratio, which is an index that is created as the ratio of profit/loss and net banking income, and ROE, which is calculated as the ratio between net income and shareholders' equity.

80   *Giovanni Ossola et al.*

Table 6.2 The Pearson correlation ratio between profit/loss and net banking income

Net banking income	Profit/loss					
	2009	2010	2011	2012	2013	2014
2009	0.87					
2010		0.70				
2011			0.56			
2012				0.48		
2013					0.29	
2014						0.55

In Figure 6.2 it can be noted that the two ratios do not have the same trend. This tendency shows that in the sample ROE is almost stable over the period analysed but its composition is different because the net margin varies significantly. In order to answer *RQ3*, we calculated the Pearson correlation ratio between profit/loss and net banking income of each year between 2009 and 2014. Table 6.2 shows the results deriving from the Pearson correlation ratio calculated.

Table 6.2 confirms that there is a strong correlation between the profit/loss and the net banking income in 2009 and 2010. However, the correlation started decreasing from 2011 to 2013. In fact in 2013, the Pearson ratio is 0.29. In 2014, the ratio recovered. Therefore, we can affirm that *RQ3* cannot be confirmed for all the years considered, especially in recent years, in which the correlation is very low.

Discussion

This research and its results confirm what many previous studies have stated: the credit cooperative banking system in Italy is an important reality. In the world of Italian banking BCCs are definitely relevant. Our H1 was confirmed by the analysis of data for the whole Italian BCC system giving ample confirmation of the initial hypothesis. As regards H2 and *RQ1*, the net banking income trend was positive. But the value of the net banking income between 2009 and 2011 was not as significant, while the profit/loss trend declined significantly between 2009 and 2010, remained constant until 2012 and then, again, decreased in 2013. In 2014, the profit started growing again.

This is certainly due to the financial and economic crisis, which had a negative effect both on the net banking income and on the profit. The decrease in the profit in 2013 is linked to the negative impact of the extraordinary management activities. As regards *RQ2* the answer is less convincing. The analysis carried out on the sample indicates that although in the early years (2009 and 2010) there is a substantial correlation, that is not the case in recent years.

Consequently in 2009 and 2010, the profit/loss was influenced by the net banking income. In the following years this correlation is lower, in fact, in

2013 the Pearson index is 0.29. This may mean that in these years the BCCs have diversified their activities and expanded their business. Those activities that affect our income statement therefore do not always represent the core business of banking. So *RQ2* is not verified and we can deduce that the banking business over the years has evolved in areas that do not always represent the banks' core business. That can also be explained by the crisis of the banking business, which forced the governance of those banks to change their business objectives.

Conclusions

This study focuses on Italian credit cooperative banks and on their relevance in the financial system in Italy. This study helps us to understand the context and the main business in which these banks operate. The sample analysed includes 264 Italian BCCs and data were extracted from Bankscope, which is a database containing comprehensive information on financial companies in Italy.

The aim is to show that the BCCs are a fundamental reality in the Italian banking sector as they enhance growth and value-creation for the local community in which they operate thanks to their activities. To do that, two indicators (the profit margin and ROE) were compared to see how they have changed over the years. Furthermore, by calculating the Pearson correlation ratio between profit/loss and net banking income of each year, this research analyses the possible correlation of net banking income with the profitability of the banks, in order to assess the effects of a policy carried out by corporate governance to face the difficulties that the banking system has been experiencing.

This research raises important issues regarding the BCCs' role in Italy and the evolution of their business in recent years.

But more importantly, this study raises important considerations for the role of these BCCs in the development of local companies, in terms of financial support for their growth, innovation, sustainability and possibility to open up to new markets (Sanchez et al., 2012; Santoro et al., 2017; Christofi et al., 2015a; Christofi et al., 2015b). This element helps introduce the limitations of this research. First of all this study represents the first step of a much deeper analysis that can take into account other variables, financial indicators and margins. An extremely complex model was not implemented because the aim was to achieve effective results and focus on the true relationship between the factors taken into account. One of the future developments is to extend both the years under consideration and the same analysis to other banks that do not belong to the world of BCCs in order to compare and contrast the situation between different realities.

References

Agostini, S. (2009). *Le banche di credito cooperativo*, Cooperativa e consorzi, n.10, Milano: Ipsoa.

Ali, A. & Ansari, I. A. (2007). Financial sector reforms and soundness of banks operating in Pakistan. *Journal of Management and Social Sciences*, 3(2), 63–69.

Álvarez, V. A., & Rossignolo A. F. (2015). Análisis Comparativo De Técnicas (IMA) Para Determinar Capitales Mínimos Regulados Por Basilea, Ante Crisis En Mercados Emergentes (Comparative analysis of techniques (IMA) for determining minimum capital regulated by Basel, facing crises in emerging markets, Social Science Research Network. *ODEON* (8), 13–14.

Alvesson, M. & Sandberg, J. (2011). Generating research questions through problematization. *Academy of Management Review*, 36, 247–271.

Alvesson, M. & Sandberg, J. (2013). *Constructing Research Questions: Doing Interesting Research*. London: Sage.

Angelini, P., Clerc, L., Cúrdia, V., Gambacorta, L., Gerali, A., Locarno, A., Motto, R., Roeger, W., Van den Heuvel, S. & Vlček, J. (2011). Basel III: Long-Term Impact on Economic Performance and Fluctuations. Federal Reserve Bank of New York Staff Report, 485.

Appio, C. L. (1996). Le banche di credito cooperativo tra Testo Unico e disciplina del diritto comune. *Dir. banc. merc. Fin.*

Avdjie, S., Zsolt, K., & Előd, T. (2012). *The Euro area crisis and cross-border bank lending to emerging markets*. BIS Quarterly Review, 10, December 2012. www.bis.org/publ/qtrpdf/r_qt1212f.pdf [last accessed: 15 January 2017].

Barros Ferreira, P. C., & Williams, J. (2007). Analyzing the determinants of performance of best and worst European banks. *Journal of Banking and Finance*, 31 (7), 2189–2203.

Berger, A. N. (2005). Corporate governance and bank performance: A joint analysis of the static, selection, and dynamic effects of domestic, foreign, and state ownership. *Journal of Banking and Finance*, 29(8–9), 2179–2221.

Blaga, L. (2015). The influence of the endogenous and exogenous factors on credit institutions' return on equity. *Arad – Economics Series*, 25(1), 16–25, DOI: 10.1515/sues-2015-0002.

Bocchino, U., Ossola, G., Giovando, G., & Venuti, F. (2013). *Il bilancio delle banche*. Milano: Giuffrè

Bonfante, G. (2004). Commento all'art. 2538 c.c.. *Il nuovo diritto societario*.

Bonfante, G. (2010). *La nuova società cooperativa*. Bologna: Zanichelli.

Borio, C. (2008). *The financial turmoil of 2007. A preliminary assessment and some policy considerations*, BIS Working Papers No. 251. www.bis.org/publ/qtrpdf/r_qt0903e.pdf

Calvo, G. (2012). Financial crises and liquidity shocks: a bank-run perspective. *European Economic Review*, 56(3), 317–326.

Camara, B., Castellani, F.-D., Fraisse, H., Frey, L., Héam, C., Labonne, L., & Martin, V. (2015). Does the capital structure affect banks' profitability? Pre- and post-financial crisis evidence from significant banks in France. Paris: Banque de France. Retrieved from https://acpr.banque-france.fr/fileadmin/user_upload/acp/publications/Debats_economiques_et_financiers/201403-Does-the-capital-structure-affect-banks-profitability.pdf [last accessed 20 January 2017].

Capriglione, F. (2005). Le banche cooperative e il nuovo diritto societario. Problematiche e prospettive. *Banca Borsa Titoli di Credito*.

Caprio, G. D., Klingebiel, Laeven L., & Noguera. G. (2005). Appendix: Banking Crisis Database. In P. Honohan and L. Laeven (Eds.). *Systemic Financial Crises: Containment and Resolution*, Cambridge, UK: Cambridge University Press.

Christofi, M., Vrontis, D., Kitchen, P. & Papasolomou, I. (2015a). Innovation and cause-related marketing success: a conceptual framework and propositions. *Journal of Services Marketing*, 29(5), 354–366.

Christofi, C., Leonidou, E. & Vrontis, D. (2015b). Cause-related marketing, product innovation and extraordinary sustainable leadership: the root towards sustainability. *Global Business and Economics Review*, 17(1), 93–111.

Cosimano, T. F. & Hakura, D. (2011). Bank Behaviour in Response to Basel III: A Cross-Country Analysis. IMF Working Paper No. 11/119. http://dx.doi.org/10.2139/ssrn.1860182

Costa Navajas, M. & Thegeya , A. (2013). Financial Soundness Indicators and Banking Crises. IMF Working Paper WP/13/XX.

Costa, C. (2007). La riforma delle società e le banche cooperative. *Il nuovo diritto delle società: Liber amicorum Gian Franco Campobasso, Torino.*

Crowley, J. (2015). *Central and Commercial Bank Balance Sheet Risk Before, During and After the Global Financial Crisis.* Washington, D.C.: International Monetary Fund.

Davis, M. S. (1971). That's interesting! Towards a phenomenology of sociology and a sociology of phenomenology. *Philosophy of Social Sciences*, 1, 309–44.

Dell'Ariccia, G., Igan, D., & Laeven, L. (2008). Credit booms and lending standards: evidence from the subprime mortgage market. IMF Working Papers, 08/106.

Dezzani, F., Biancone, P. P. & Busso, D. (2014). *IAS/IFRS*. Milano: IPSOA.

Elliott, D. J. (2009). *Quantifying the Effects on Lending of Increased Capital Requirements*, Brookings Briefing Paper. Washington, D.C.: Brookings Institution.

Faisal, S., Tariq , M. & Farzand, A. J. (2015). Financial performance of banks in Pakistan: a comparative analysis of public and private sectors. *Vfast Transactions On Education And Social Sciences*, 6(2), 2309–3951.

Ferri, G. & Messori, M. (2000). Bank–firm relationships and allocative efficiency in Northeastern and Central Italy and in the South. *Journal of Banking and Finance* 24, 1067–1095.

Giovando, G. (1996). La banca. In *Lezioni di Economia Aziendale*, Milano: Giuffrè.

Giovando, G., & Gianoglio, G. (1999). Le banche. In *Euro ed Economia Aziendale*. Milano: Giuffrè.

Hartvigsen, G. (1992). Limitations of knowledge-based systems for financial analysis in banking. *Expert Systems with Applications*, 4(1),19–32.

Iannotta, G., Nocera, G., & Sironi, A. (2007). Ownership structure, risk and performance in the European banking industry. *Journal of Banking and Finance*, 31(7), 2127–2149.

Illueca, M., Norden, L., & Udell, G. (2008). *Liberalization, Corporate Governance, and Savings Banks*. EFA 2008 Athens Meetings Paper.

Iqbal, J. & Raza, G. (2009). *Building global banks: A comparative analysis of European banks over time*, Cambridge, U.K.: Cambridge University Press.

Kahlert D., & Wagner N. (2015). Are Eurozone Banks Undercapitalized? A Stress Testing Approach to Financial Stability. A Stress Testing Approach to Financial Stability, Working Paper, http://dx.doi.org/10.2139/ssrn.2568614

Kapan, T., & Minoiu, C. (2015). Balance Sheet Strength and Bank Lending During the Global Financial Crisis. http: //dx.doi.org / 10.2139/ ssrn.2247185

Koch, T., & MacDonald, S. (2007). *Bank Management*, Marson, Ohio: South–Western Cengage Learning, 7th ed.

Kosmidis, K., & Terzidis, K. (2011). Manipulating an IRB model: considerations about the Basel II framework. *EuroMed Journal of Business*, 6(2), 174–191, https://doi.org/10.1108/14502191111151250

84 *Giovanni Ossola et al.*

Laeven, L., & Valencia, F. (2008). *Systemic Banking Crisis: A New Database*. IMF Working Paper 8–224. Washington, D.C.: International Monetary Fund.

Maudos, J., Pastor, J. M., Pérez, F., & Quesada, J. (2002). Cost and profit efficiency in European banks. *Journal of International Financial Markets, Institutions and Money*, 12(1), 33–58.

Mihai Yiannaki, S. (2011). Bank bailouts: lessons to learn when patience is a virtue. *EuroMed Journal of Business*, 6(2),192–205, https://doi.org/10.1108/14502191111151269

Ossola, G., Giovando, G., & Crovini, C. (2017). Corporate and risk governance: key-drivers for value creation and growth. The case of Italian Credit Cooperative Banks. *Review of Business Research*, 17(2), 7–18.

Ossola, G. (2000). *I bilanci degli enti finanziari*. Milano: Giuffrè.

Ossola, G. (2005). *Gli schemi del bilancio d'esercizio degli enti creditizi*. Milano: Giuffrè.

Rauf, S., & Fu, Q. (2014). *Integrated Model to measure the Impact of E-Banking Services on Commercial banks' ROE: Empirical Study of Pakistan*. Amsterdam, The Netherlands: Atlantis Press.

Sanchez, B. D., Kaufmann, R. & Vrontis, D. (2012). A new organisational memory for cross-cultural knowledge management. *Cross Cultural Management: An International Journal*, 19(3), 336–351.

Santoro, G., Vrontis, D., Thrassou, & Dezi, L. (2017). The Internet of Things: building knowledge management systems for open innovation and knowledge management capacity. *Technological Forecasting and Social Change*, DOI: 10.1016/j.techfore.2017.02.034

Schiniotakis, N. I. (2012). Profitability factors and efficiency of Greek banks. *EuroMed Journal of Business*, 7(2), 185–200, https://doi.org/10.1108/14502191211245606

Tsolas, I. E. (2011). Bank branch-level DEA to assess overall efficiency. *EuroMed Journal of Business*, 6(3), 359–377, https://doi.org/10.1108/14502191111170178

Usai, S. & Vannini, M. (2005). Banking structure and regional economic growth: lessons from Italy. *Annals of Regional Science*, 39, 691–714.

Vasiliadis, L. (2009). Greek banks' internationalisation: a suggested modelling approach. *EuroMed Journal of Business*, 4(1), 88–103.

Vella, F. (2004). La governance delle società cooperative. In C. Borzaga & A. Fici (Eds.), *La riforma delle società cooperative*. Trento.

Zago, A., & Dongili, P., (2014). Financial Crisis, Business Model and the Technical Efficiency of Italian Banche di Credito Cooperativo, Quaderni di ricerca del credito cooperativo, n.4.

7 Applying persuasion science in marketing communications

A comparison of marketing communications professionals in Armenia and Greece

Armine Petrosyan and Nikolaos Dimitriadis

The modern challenge of persuasion

This paper reflects a longitudinal investigation of the complex and rapidly evolving phenomenon of persuasion that has given rise to the development arena of experimental data of new behavioral, neurological models (Lindstrom, 2011). From a macro-perspective, persuasion theorists have investigated the goals, the process of persuasion, and the centrality of attitude. At the micro-level, they have derived a number of persuasion theories to explain behavioral influence. The outcome is a thorough study of traditional persuasive tools and techniques along with the firsthand perspectives of persuasion trends.

Even though academic and practitioner literatures alike suggest that it became increasingly hard "to create unique or even premium content that people are prepared to pay for," unprecedented technological developments have boosted communication professionals' reach of their audiences (Gregory, 2009, p. 14). Hence, the latest attempt by marketing communication professionals is to take advantage of the potential of new media technologies for the purposes of persuasion (Gleitman *et al.*, 2011).

Yeung (2011) confirms that in the last few years the domain of persuasion has been extended. Over the last few decades, researchers have been collecting evidence about the forces and methods that change minds and alter behavior. In laboratory tryouts and field studies that cover situations varying from business negotiations to promotion activities, pioneering scientists have gathered a remarkable body of evidence about the approaches that "encourage or even compel people to change their attitudes and actions" (Yeung, 2011, p. 9). However as Myers *et al.* (2014) state, experiments have frequently focused on the *form* of a message such as style, structure, and delivery, and fewer studies of the *content* of messages in ensuring persuasive influence.

Persuasion, as Funkhouser and Parker (1999) proclaim, whether it be education or propaganda, is "inevitable". Therefore, as Milliman and Fugate (1988, p. 6) claim, the objective is to find ethical ways to persuade "to those on the margin, close to buying, to make the decision to buy".

Although there is an enormous quantity of data and a notable number of theories, "perhaps more data and theory than on any other single topic in the social sciences", there is still an area for study of diverse variables related to persuasion (Petty and Cacioppo, 1986, p. 2). Yeung (2011) asserts that the phenomenon of persuasion is becoming an important field of study for academic researchers and practitioners. It is still a new area of research with several literature gaps, and a need for more rigorous research. These gaps appear to be widening with the introduction of new media technologies for the purposes of persuasion that has led to action-based approaches to the phenomenon, an under-explored context. Hence, the chapter charters the preference within the literature for the use of action-based persuasion rather than other models of it. This issue has provided the initial impetus for this study.

To our knowledge, there has not been an empirical cross-national study on a new issue of a topic of persuasion by exploring the adoption of persuasion methods from different viewpoints and approaches and using a methodological approach that has never been used in Armenia and Greece for the research purposes. Although there are several studies focused on traditional and contemporary persuasion techniques from developed countries, none of them has observed a comparative study between these two countries, alongside introducing neuromarketing in the light of current persuasion perspectives (Eser *et al.*, 2011; Va, 2015). Additionally, this paper synthesizes past research adding new perspectives and extending persuasion-related research to a new level: incorporating measurement of persuasion methods as a critical under-explored objective from the prior research.

If we are to understand more fully the implications of persuasion tools for relational strategies, then a close examination of neuromarketing is also required (Pilelienė, 2012; Senior and Lee, 2008). Therefore, a special consideration is given to neuromarketing issues throughout the review.

On that basis, this chapter focuses on the adoption of contemporary and traditional persuasion methods from the perspective of communication professionals in Armenia and Greece: how do the key stakeholders view persuasion principles and methods?

The main objectives of the study are the following:

> To investigate attitudes of communication professionals concerning persuasion methods
> To highlight which specific persuasion principles they apply and why/how
> To explore techniques by which persuasion methods are measured
> To examine potential differences between different approaches of communication professionals in Armenia and Greece
> To develop suggestions of how persuasion methods can be improved for communication professionals

The prime focus was to obtain preliminary insights rather than test theory. Our findings could be a value to both academics and practitioners and could serve as a reference for future research on persuasion.

Persuasion theories and marketing communications

Current literature, sales books, and training programs tend to be theoretical combinations of motivation and practical guidance but in fact they are restricted in their explanations of the mechanisms of persuasion. Theory of persuasion in marketing is mostly based on opinion or attitudinal rather than behavioral change. From a marketing communication perspective, these attitudinal theories do not provide useful assumptions and implications (Fiore *et al.*, 2015). Yet "practical persuaders" such as advertisement, PR, digital marketing professionals, as well as marketing executives, focus not on changing attitudes but "on getting other people to do what they want them to do" (Funkhouser and Parker, 1999, p. 27).

Such classics of selling found in business communication texts such as Strong's AIDA Model: Attention, Interest, Desire, Action (Strong, 1925), or AIEDA: Awareness, Interest, Evaluation, Decision and Adoption (Stacks and Bowen, 2011), Monroe's motivated sequence (attention, need, satisfaction, visualization, and action), the "four Ps" (Promise, Picture, Prove, and Push) (Shelby, 1986), or Carnegie's "How to Win Friends and Influence People" (Carnegie, 1936) are worth investigating but "...do not offer theories of how persuasion works" (Funkhouser, 1984, p. 17).

Among widely embraced persuasion models are the Elaboration Likelihood Model (ELM) (Cacioppo and Petty, 1984; Petty *et al.*, 1999; Jones, 2004), Heuristic-Systematic Model (HSM) (Chaiken, 1987; Chen and Chaiken, 1999), Information-Processing Model (IMP) (McGuire, 1968; Flay *et al.*, 1980; Scholten, 1996), and Unimodel (Kruglanski and Thompson, 1999; Kruglanski, 2013). One of the theories that gives practical assumptions and explanations of the mechanisms of persuasion is the Action Theory of Persuasion (ATP). A key assumption of ATP is that every action is headed "...by a decision to act" (Funkhouser, 1984, p. 28).

Dos Santos (2015) and Rakić and Rakić (2014) discuss the persuasion model under the umbrella term, integrated marketing communications; they offer five characteristics within different mixes: integration in terms of media, communication methods (traditional promotion), actors (inducted by consumers and consumers), content creation (based on consumer generated and marketing content), and the time of communications for integration (traditional static and dynamic communications). Moreover, Myers *et al.* (2014), while discussing the elements and aspects of persuasion stress that "...we should bear in mind that these models should be understood as 'working' within a specific social context at a particular time" (p. 204).

Cialdini's principles

There are a number of scientifically proven persuasion methods and tactics accessible to communication specialists for designing persuasive messages (Goldstein *et al.*, 2008); however the most widely known and influential is proposed by Robert Cialdini. In Cialdini's (2007) model, the most common types of persuasion principles or shortcuts are the following:

Conformity and consensus: people look to the actions and behaviors of others to determine their own. According to the science of consensus, rather than relying on personal ability to persuade others, communication specialists can point out to a customer what many others are already doing, especially many similar others.

Reciprocity: by virtue of the reciprocity rule, people are obligated to the future "reimbursement" of smiles, favors, gifts, offerings, invitations, and the like or in other words obligation to give when they receive (Horn *et al.* 2013). The key of using the principle of reciprocation is the factor of being the first to give and to ensure that what is given is personalized and unexpected (Goldstein *et al.*, 2008).

Scarcity: the idea of possible loss plays a large role in the decision-making process. According to this rule, people want more of those things there are less of. Marketing communication professionals should point out what's *unique* about the proposition and what they stand to lose if they fail to consider the proposal (Cialdini, 2009). Scarcity influences the content of customers' cognition, the tendency of consumers from lower socioeconomic circumstances "to become materialistic" (Roux and Goldsmith, 2014, p. 215).

Authority: the tendency of following credible and knowledgeable experts (e.g. diplomas, uniform, experience, etc.). This principle is widely used in advertisement campaigns with celebrity endorsement (Hung, 2014; Mishra, 2015; Starcevic, 2013). Tran (2013) asserts that 25% of all ads use celebrities, taking into account the fact that the target market has awareness and strong favorable unique perceptions of the external source.

Liking: people prefer to say, yes, to those whom they like. There are three important factors for this: they like those who are similar to them, who pass compliments, and who cooperate with them towards mutual goals. This can be projected to an online environment as well (Lipsman *et al.*, 2012).

Neuromarketing: Persuasion in the human brain

Neuromarketing approaches are considered to be a new confluence of medical knowledge, technology, and marketing due to the ability to scan the brain as a way of understanding brain stimulations (Almiron-Chamadoira and Dubernat, 2015; Zurawicki, 2010). It is the key to revealing the subconscious thoughts, feelings, and desires that drive the purchasing decisions and of course is the key to sending the right messages to the right part of the brain for the achievement of proper results (Andrejevic, 2012; Butler, 2008). One of the latest studies by Stipp (2015) indicates that adding neuroscience-based methods to a traditional test of commercial creative "can identify advertising creative that leads to more sales..." (p. 121).

Lindstrom (2008) compares neuromarketing with the two circles in a Venn diagram as indicating the two branches of traditional marketing research – quantitative and qualitative –

> ...it's time to make room for the new kid on the block: neuromarketing. And in that overlapping region of these three circles lies the future of marketing: the key to truly and completely understanding the thoughts, feelings, motivations, needs, and desires of consumers...
>
> (Lindstrom, 2008, p. 5)

According to marketers and researchers' growing belief, time-honored traditional practices, theories, and models in advertising had overstated cognitive processes (Varan *et al.*, 2015). Barkin (2013), while discussing prospects and limitations of neuromarketing, states that humans make both intuitive mood-based emotional decisions and more careful, planned, rationally based decisions. The outcome has been progressive interest in consumers' emotional and unconscious reactions to marketing, advertising messages, in other words "... to better understand the role emotion plays in advertising effectiveness" (Stipp, 2015, p. 120). Thus, *neuro* methods offer more detailed and direct information on the principal aspects of consumer response to marketing messages and on consumers' needs and motivations (Adhami, 2013; Page, 2012). If best practices are applied, methods will provide supplementary data points and insights that lead to better decision-making processes (Hart, 2015; Reimann, 2013).

These tools and technologies doubtless raise a range of ethical issues concerning the fact that consumers can be effectively manipulated into buying the product (Flores *et al.*, 2014; Murphy *et al.*, 2008; Stokes, 2015). As Arussy (2009, p. 12) states "...the practice is offensive and contrary to any principle of customer experience. It is advised to focus on the client's heart rather than messing with the brain of the customer". Stokes (2015) points out that the real ethical issues aren't just with treating people as predictable machines (in a sense, all marketing does that anyway) but "...with the extent to which we can fight against...non-argumentative modes of persuasion" (p. 47). Some studies indicate that companies are springing up to offer their clients brain-based information about consumer preferences, intending to bypass focus groups and other marketing research techniques on the premise that "...directly peering into a consumer's brain while viewing products or brands is a much better predictor of consumer behavior" (Murphy *et al.*, 2008, p. 293).

Elden *et al.* (2015) indicate that attitudes and opinions on the usage of neuroscience in marketing and advertising vary mostly based on the department they work in at the agency, calling it "a battle between creatives and strategic planners" (p. 29). However, as Haley *et al.* (2014, p. 111) claim, "... positive, on-going interactions between creatives and planners can lead to acceptance of the value of planning among creative".

It has been noticed that all these viewpoints have value in crafting marketing strategies for certain target populations, improving creative output, providing a better understanding of the consumer. In today's "visual pollution", knowing your audience and understanding their behavior means understanding what stimulates their attention to a campaign (Ciprian-Marcel *et al.*, 2009).

In the light of classic persuasion approaches and of the more contemporary one of neuromarketing, this study strived to explore current opinions and adoption among four types of communications professionals in both Armenia and Greece.

Measurement of persuasion methods

After application of a specific persuasion technique follows the measurement or hypothesis testing process. The latter is considered to be the most important, challenging, and difficult portion of the whole campaign (Smith, 2013). Baskin *et al.* (2010) underline the importance of the evaluation process that plays a vital and prominent role for solving the organizational problem. Conarroe (1971) highlights the importance of measurement process along with the four main steps for the implementation of the communication plan: 1) setting specific goals, not general goals; 2) making a plan of actions aimed directly at the goal or goals; 3) measuring results against the plan at regular intervals; and 4) "based on appraisal and analysis, alter goals, plan and actions" (Conarroe, 1971, pp. 25–27).

Stacks and Bowen (2011), while discussing the strategic approach for designing the measurement process, underline three objectives: informational, motivational, and behavioral. Measurement of informational objectives embraces counts of number of receivers who can accurately recall and remember the key of the message.

The second objective deals with motivation. This consists of outtake measures where we have targeted opinion leaders or selected audiences and assess their agreement with messages and their intended behaviors. Measurement can consist of content analysis of opinion leader columns, blogs, tweets, and other content for tone (positive, negative, neutral), share of voice (competition mentions), and accuracy. It can also look at subsamples or segments of the target audience to gauge message acceptance or rejection, degree of interest, and projected decisions about adoption of the campaign outcome.

Third, the behavioral objective projects to the final outcome of actual expected behaviors; those are "the actions that count toward proving return on the investment, such [as] final adoption, purchasing behavior, recommendation or voting intention" (Stacks and Bowen, 2011, p. 14).

Taking into account that advertising is the purest and most indisputable form of persuasion cost and for many firms also the largest, the measurement approach focuses on "future after-tax cash flows, centers on the profit-productivity of capital and relies on quantitative estimates" (Dean, 1967, p. 81).

While discussing a company's brand credibility measurement, Haig (2015) mentions that brand equity measures such as value or goodwill are too "nebulous to measure" (p. 177). Precisely, the author states that the premise for measurement is based on how we persuade in all communication – interpersonal, company to person, or company to company – and on the communication persuasion model: credible source → message → channel→ receiver (Aureliano-Silva *et al.*, 2015).

Mishra (2015) suggests that advertising effectiveness measures such as advertisement believability and attitude toward the ad were significantly different "while measures such as attitude toward brand and purchase intention were almost similar across the high and low congruent pairs of celebrity endorser and brand" (Mishra, 2015, p. 16).

Kazokiene and Stravinskiene (2011) propose principles for the evaluation of the set objectives based on hierarchical level: criteria for tasks, target audiences, and action plan. As for the impact, standards for the evaluation of diverse results, outputs, outtakes, and outcomes, are offered.

Various studies have examined the reliability, validity, and sensitivity of recall and persuasion measures (Ostlund *et al.*, 1980). The problem with recall and persuasion methods that has been mainly ignored by the academic and business community is "...the fact that both methods measure consumer response after exposure" (Fenwick and Rice, 1991, p. 23). Authors believe that valuable information about the effectiveness of the advertising can be acquired during the viewing experience. This can assist in identifying the specific scenes that might inhibit or enhance the ad's effectiveness. In practice this means a shift to the study of emotions (Aaker *et al.*, 1986; Abe and Izard, 1999). As the authors claim, if emotions change from moment to moment, "we need a moment-to-moment measurement method to capture them effectively" (Fenwick and Rice, 1991, p. 25).

Aaker and Bruzzone (1981) suggest such measurement databases and methodologies as "normal exposure, simple check boxes, mail interviews, and large national samples" and on the contrary "forced exposure, more elaborate scales, and personal interviews" (p. 23).

However, research shows that most persuasion-related studies are quantitative in nature; as Becheur *et al.* (2008) assert, measuring emotions through questionnaires, for instance, may "...lead to an overestimation of the emotional states" (p. 105). In compliance with the above, Derbaix *et al.* (2012) state that this can create difficulty for respondents to express their affective state.

While discussing the two distinct types of central and peripheral route processes Cacioppo and Petty (1984) suggest another measurement tool, the PEAC system, which measures individuals' responses uninterruptedly during the advertisement watching process. According to the study, "continuous measurement was found to exhibit quite high levels of test-retest reliability" (p. 28).

92 *Armine Petrosyan and Nikolaos Dimitriadis*

After careful investigation of the PEAC system, similarities with the contemporary neuromarketing measurement tactics can be noticed (Meckl-Sloan, 2015). As neuromarketing is a science of human decision, in order to understand the behavior process three main metrics are implemented: neurometrics, biometrics, and psychometrics. There are several types of measurement approaches such as: automated facial coding (emotion displayed on their face), eye tracking (where they are looking at in an image), voice analysis (no attention to the words they say, but to the tone of voice), lie-detector (measure the heart-rate, blood pressure, electricity flows between fingers), EEG (electro-encephalography biometrics) (measure the small currents on the top of skulls), implicit association measurement, and MRI (magnetic resonance imaging) scanner (measure the amount of oxygen consumed by the brain in various regions of the brain) (Page, 2012; Patrick Renvoise, 2013). Page (2012) points out that neuromarketing measuring methods improve further understanding of marketing issues, highlighting the fact that "...they add predictive power to our research, and help us explain behavior more effectively" (p. 290).

The expansion of the persuasion research to other populations and the use of measurement instruments are highly recommended.

Methodology

The purpose of this study is exploratory and, therefore, qualitative research methods were considered to be more appropriate (Saunders *et al.*, 2009). Specifically, as Leech and Onwuegbuzie (2010) state, exploration implicates predominantly using "inductive methods to explore...a concept, phenomenon...to develop tentative hunches, inferences..." (p. 62).

The core objective of this study is to investigate the adoption of contemporary and traditional persuasion methods by communication professionals. In particular, this study seeks to shed more light on attitudes, application, and measurement of persuasion methods, principles, and techniques implemented by communication professionals. Since "an emphasis on situational details unfolding over time allows qualitative research to describe processes", it was a proper choice for this study (Gephart, 2004, p. 455). In terms of the latter, due to its interpretive and inductive nature, qualitative research highlights human interactions, meanings, and relationships among variables that are addressed in the field (Denzin and Lincoln, 2009). In addition, qualitative research seeks "to explain research observations by providing well-substantiated conceptual insights that reveal how broad concepts and theories operate in particular cases" (Gephart, 2004, p. 455).

Even though a literature review on the topic of persuasion shows a large body of knowledge in this field, the reason for applying a qualitative research is the notable deficiency in providing a detailed description of this phenomenon from the practical persuaders' perspective, precisely taking into account the specific setting of neuromarketing development as a new approach used for persuasion purposes.

The size of the selected sample was 20 interviewees; that is in compliance with the reference by Onwuegbuzie and Leech (2005) for this kind of research. Parent (total) population encompassed all companies/agencies/individuals in Armenia and Greece that possess communications positions.

The sample of this study used a maximum variation sampling in order to choose the interview participants within all the possible stakeholders of the communication sector (Leech and Onwuegbuzie, 2010). The sample included communication specialists from the following areas: public relations, advertisement, digital marketing, and marketing/consulting. In terms of the latter, all sectors were involved in the target groups of the current research.

As Loh and Dahesihsari (2013) state, the objective of this kind of sampling is to involve specific groups of participants who possess characteristics relevant to the phenomenon being studied. These specialists are considered to have a good varying insight into the phenomenon under investigation (Funkhouser and Parker, 1999). The sample units were chosen taking into account Ritchie *et al.*'s (2003) argumentation that they understand "the central theme and puzzles" of the phenomenon under investigation; this was mainly the experiences and roles that the participants possess (p. 78). In other words, these people were ideal candidates for the discussion of their practices and experiences relevant to the topic.

The selection of respondents was utilized through personal and company networks: interview contacts were mostly referred by respondents that researchers were interviewing, herewith using "snowballing" techniques along with "convenience" sampling (Dilley, 2000).

The study utilized a semi-structured, in-depth personal interview as it allows direct interaction, enables in-depth research, and "...opens new voices, new vistas, new visions" to the investigation of the field (Dilley, 2000, p. 131; Mojtahed *et al.*, 2014). Wengraf (2001) recommends interviews as being a powerful tool for such research areas since they allow the researcher to obtain "in depth matters and rich insights" (p. 3). Correspondingly, Barker *et al.* (2001) claim that this approach aims to acquire an insider's perspective on the studied phenomenon.

The transcription of interviews formed a sizeable quantity of material. Taking into consideration this fact, coding was used to arrange the large amounts of textual data, synthesize it, create meaningful categories "... discovering what is important and what is to be learned...", analyze the data, and present the conclusions (Lawrence and Tar, 2013, p. 29). Due to the defined codes, correlations and patterns had been identified that served as sources for the findings (Huberman and Miles, 2002).

Research results and discussion

Main attitudes of communication professionals concerning persuasion methods

Research findings suggest that the attitudes of communication professionals related to persuasion is to some extent different from the general process described in the literature. Even though they consider persuasion as *"cornerstone for what I do" (1.2a., Advertising PROF, Armenia); "one of the important elements for my job" (1.1c., Social Media PROF, Armenia); "absolutely necessary" (2.2b., Social Media PROF, Greece)*, overall, findings tended to support Funkhouser and Parker's (1999) topical speculation that the ultimate goal of marketing and communication should not concentrate on attitude change *"to make people think, feel, choose whatever you want" (1.3.b., PR PROF, Armenia)*, in some cases *"in a subtle imposing manner" (2.3.a., PR PROF, Greece)*, but rather on precipitate action: *"the mechanism should lead to a specific action: purchase, call, order" (1.4a., Marketing PROF, Armenia)*.

The action-based theory proposes a number of practical constructive implications aimed at influencing the outcomes of decisions made by an actor in his or her action decision sequence. However, phases used by participants from Armenia and Greece indicated that there is a predominant concentration on attitudinal rather than behavioral change approaches:

> ...marketers do not feel deep down that everything they design is to produce action, whatever action, maybe to buy, to visit us, to go, to participate in a competition, to have a test drive... even to talk to other people, which is also an action.
>
> (2.4a., Marketing PROF, Greece)

Even though practitioners agreed that formulating and setting measurable SMART+C (Challenging) objectives for the whole campaign is vital for achieving optimum measurable results, in line with Conarroe (1971) and Stacks and Bowen (2011), the majority of participants emphasized informational, motivational, or attitudinal (e.g. "top of mind", "top of heart") rather than behavioral change oriented objective use. Among stated persuasion variables were content, presentation, source, logical, financial, and audience, which is in agreement with the existing literature.

Lack of persuasion-related skills have been recognized by the majority of participants as one of the important challenges, as Eser *et al.* (2011), Gendusa (2008), Gleitman *et al.* (2011), and many other authors highlight: *"...need of specialists, professional team, practice; and the existing resources are not used productively" (1.4b., Marketing PROF, Armenia)*. This leads to *"the fact that we don't have persuasion schools" (1.2b., Advertising PROF, Armenia); "there is a need of specialized education in the related field" (2.2a., Advertising PROF, Greece)*.

Cacioppo and Petty (1984) emphasize that the central route is more likely to lead to attitude and behavior changes, rather than the peripheral route that may lead merely to superficial and temporary attitude change. However, the majority of participants were more inclined to state that persuasion works better on a subconscious level, rather than a conscious level. The majority of interviewees confirmed that driving customers through their hidden feelings and emotions (fear, hope, happiness, etc.) works better in practice; however some mentioned that it is *"...situational" (2.3.a., PR PROF, Greece)*; *"...spherical and depends on the target, as some argumentative cues can be accepted subjectively" (1.3b., PR PROF, Armenia)*; or *"the process combines both: mostly the unconscious (give them reasons to believe) and then to satisfy the conscious" (2.4a., Marketing PROF, Greece)*.

Research findings provided support for the argumentation that there are two means of classifying situations centered on major persuasion variables: communication channel feedback and the thoroughness of the persuasion objective (Milliman and Fugate, 1988).

Application of specific persuasion principles

While discussing communication processes, Yeung (2011) highlights the importance of using persuasion techniques while constructing the message. Answers revealed that communication practitioners do use persuasion principles; however this is somehow automatic as they are obliged to do so. The application process is complex, with a range of tools that depend on several *factors*, such as: *"...an audience, product, and the level of creativity..." (1.1a., Social Media PROF, Armenia)*.

Practices related to the application of various persuasion techniques are in most cases completed without being thought about in advance; however as Goldstein *et al.* (2008) underline, scientifically proven persuasion methods and tactics are accessible to communication specialists for designing persuasive messages only if they are thought through meticulously beforehand: *"...without thinking in advance of persuasion, we cannot achieve it as it would [be] a matter of luck, unfortunately though this [is] not how the market operates or marketers are trained"*(2.4a., Marketing PROF, Greece).

> they think very introspective, they are very inwards-looking, the only thing that they think about, that is it going to look nice, liked by my CEO, win me an award, am I going to look cool when I meet with other marketing directors.
>
> (2.4a., Marketing PROF, Greece)

Similarly, *"it is a necessity for people working in communications not only to use persuasion but first to understand it deeply" (1.2a., Advertising PROF, Armenia)*.

Among six main persuasion shortcuts selected and presented in the scope of this research, communication specialists highlighted the extensive use of *authority and liking*. The use of the latter refers more to the online environments such as company page likes, votes, comments, etc. Accordingly, the majority of participants stressed the importance of a company's online presence nowadays. As for authority, according to the interviews, it is the most often used persuasion technique by companies in both countries. The interviewees indicated that the authority principles such as use of experts, government, celebrities, etc. could help to assure customers' willingness to cooperate.

As Bednall *et al.*'s (2010) research indicates, some persuasion appeals are considered unethical. However, only the minority of respondents reflected on the use of persuasion appeals as unethical, in addition the majority pointed out the importance of keeping to all ethical standards while implementing the appeals. It seems that communication professionals are taking all ethical issues related to persuasion usages seriously bearing in mind the fact that the professional use of techniques can be a reason for a long-term relationship with the customer.

Even though many authors (Meckl-Sloan, 2015; Stipp 2015; Varan *et al.*, 2015) consider neuroscience-based marketing research a widely accepted tool, nearly all participants considered neuromarketing approaches as something yet to come: *"the application of neuromarketing is a little bit frightening as it goes against the will of a customer" (2.1b., Social Media PROF, Greece).* Moreover, the majority of the participants do not accept neuromarketing as a persuasion tool mostly taking into account the ethical concerns in agreement with an extensive body of literature (Flores *et al.*, 2014; Murphy *et al.*, 2008; Stokes, 2015): *"...it is used for the products that there is no need to have them, in fact" (2.2a., Advertising PROF, Greece).*

Specialists in Armenia and Greece emphasized frequently repeating mistakes when taking the experience of the usage of persuasion methods from other countries; communication professionals try to implement them in their own countries without considering the specification (geographical, cultural, socio-economic, living standards, etc.) of the market: *"...taking example/experience of another country and trying to implement that in Armenia not considering the specification of the market" (1.3b., PR, Armenia).*

Findings revealed that communication professionals perceived persuasion to work better in an online environment (through websites, e-shops, social media) and personal selling, than PR and advertising, This is in agreement with Keller and Fay (2012), who claim the correct use of online platforms combined with face-to-face consumer expressions fosters conversation with the customer; the conversation then converts the prospect that leads to purchase or action.

Techniques by which persuasion methods are measured

The lack of research concerning persuasion methods measurement processes has been recognized as one of the important challenges while dealing with a communication plan that is in line with Aaker and Bruzzone (1981), Fenwick and Rice (1991), and many other authors. Smith (2013) underlines that traditional communication techniques deal with how to do things, but as the field is changing while working on the communication plan practitioners should know what to do and why and of course how to evaluate it.

Taking into consideration the fact that persuasion has a lot to do with the measurement of emotional states, some authors suggest continuous measurement of persuasion methods; however, findings have shown that the measurement mostly took place only after application of a specific objective. This leads to the discussion of the lack of measurable objectives in communication related activities by practitioners in the field. Having in mind that if objectives are not measurable how can they be measured: *"...if you have very specific objectives, you know the function of them, then you measure the action and online is perfect because you know immediately: how many people clicked, voted..."* (2.4a., Marketing PROF, Greece).

Interview participants emphasized the point that the online measurement process is relatively easy compared with others. It allows specialists to measure number of likes, page visits, and information seen, it also allows us to judge the speed of response (especially for websites): *"...is challenging and demanding; in an online environment it is relatively easy to measure"* (2.1a., 2.1c., Social Media PROF, Greece); or *"gradual conversion of comments from negative to positive or neutral, the amount of likes as one of the simple forms"* (1.1c., Social Media PROF, Armenia).

Differences between approaches in Armenia and Greece

As was predicted earlier, communication professionals in Armenia and Greece have many more similarities in their approaches than differences. Gleitman *et al.* (2011) claim that in collectivistic cultures social influence works better in persuasion. It must be noted that both countries are representatives of collectivist culture.

Nonetheless, the findings reveal some differences. Persuasion was mostly portrayed as communication and on the other hand as manipulation (more common answer for Armenian specialists, taking into account the problematic area in which the country is situated). Both representatives emphasized the fact that the use of persuasion is situational; however answers *on a conscious level* prevail for specialists in Greece and *on a subconscious level* in Armenia: marketing communication as a profession has been in a way reinvented after the collapse of the Soviet Union: *"...that is why this is a specialists' formation phase for the Republic of Armenia"* (1.1a., Social Media PROF, Armenia).

Communication specialists in Armenia seem to be more skeptical concerning neuromarketing, which refers to the fact that the country doesn't have professionals and proper techniques for neuromarketing research.

Greek communication specialists (even though not the majority), in contrast, are more or less open to neuromarketing approaches taking into account the fact that the country has several neuromarketing oriented companies in Athens and Thessaloniki, in addition, the country deals with some international companies.

Both representatives considered digital marketing platforms and personal selling to be more productive tools than advertisement and PR. Yet, even though the measurement of persuasion methods is comparatively easy in an online environment, both practitioners pointed out the lack of measurement techniques in their activities.

That led to highlighting of the importance of persuasion-related education (including measurement) for the communication professionals in Armenia and Greece.

Overall, results showed that attitudes, application of specific persuasion principles, and use of measurement techniques by communication specialists in Armenia and Greece mostly coincide and that both countries are in need of advanced persuasion knowledge.

Results also disclosed that nowadays communication professionals are trained *"to present a cool graphic, a nice concept, a clever wordplay and if they do something like this that sounds nice, they feel that they succeeded in developing communication...this is not the case" (2.4a., Marketing PROF, Greece)*; *"...because things have changed dramatically the last few years: consumer behavior, technology and the exposure of people and different messages have also increased" (2.3.a., PR PROF, Greece)*.

Answers led us to the point that marketing/consulting professionals are more interested in action-persuasion than other fields of communication, revealing some insights related to persuasion usage: *"...in the process every word should be thought about beforehand" (1.4a., Marketing PROF, Armenia)* as *"...without thinking in advance of persuasion, we cannot achieve it as it would [be] a matter of luck, unfortunately though this not how the market operates or marketers are trained" (2.4a., Marketing PROF, Greece)*.

Practical implications

The importance of *professional usage of persuasion, reflecting it for action-based activities* and in line with *action-based communication objectives* cannot be overstated. Although considering persuasion techniques as inevitable and vital for use in messages, the majority of communication professionals didn't reflect the usage of persuasion methods for leading the customer to a specific action. The concentration is in most cases for the brand/company to be "top of mind", or "top of heart", "know the brand"; however, creating a nice concept, a clever wordplay is not a guarantee for the success in developing communication. The above-mentioned is also important, yet, it is part of a group of things specialists can do: what, when, who, where, why, how, how to get feedback in order to get to a core, and the core is to get somebody to act.

In order to establish communication between a company and a customer, communication specialists should *step into the shoes of the target audience*, in other words *"be" the target market*. As Gendusa (2008) states, "...you have to get into their head, think like them, be them" (p. 20). Practitioners definitely need to somehow touch their customers very deeply, sometimes very sensitive chords in their hearts or minds, sometimes very trivial things.

Practitioners have to touch the things that the customer cares for or she or he will focus internally a lot: hopes and fears, joys, and when they catch this, the decision is already taken. This means communication professionals need

Persuasion science in marketing 99

to diagnose the pain: understand the customer, primarily not what they want but what pain/fears/hopes they have in their subconscious thoughts. Though, if customers do not agree mentally with the message, they will have internal conflicts: to complete the process practitioners have to give them reasons to believe, to satisfy and fulfill their needs (Ciprian-Marcel *et al.*, 2009).

If practitioners want to move customers towards the specific message, they need to *make the messages more customer-oriented (self-centered), visual, emotional and tangible*; they need to *show contrast, tell a story, differentiate consumers' claims making them look like the only red apple among blue ones* (Rakić and Rakić, 2014).

Liking, especially in an online environment, is the first step, but unfortunately many companies stop there (Lipsman *et al.*, 2012). "I have so many likes" is not the point; due to the online algorithms used by many online platforms, the customer is not even seeing any update on their wall. Persuasion has to be applied in all the steps: professionals have *to persuade the customer to like, to stay, to interact and engage.* This is undoubtedly difficult, challenging, risky, and energy consuming effort.

The practice of credible people/experts and endorsers works in practice but practitioners need to *establish expertise, identify problems solved and search for fit between celebrity and the brand* (Dwivedi *et al.*, 2015). And this is also related to social media activities, since in online platforms endorsers are closer to the target.

From the neuromarketing perspective specialists can gain insights in their activities. Yet, they need *to educate themselves in the use of tools, do research in the field for creating synthesis/integration with the traditional persuasion techniques*, and in compliance with this to be cautious concerning the ethicality of the usage.

Measurement processes can assist practitioners in focusing on their main purpose in the organization; that is to bring specific results, to achieve them: making customers attend, click, try (Stacks and Bowen, 2011). That is why they need *to put a special emphasis on the measurement process while designing the campaign, design measurable objectives and project continuous measurement of persuasion methods before, during, and after application of a specific persuasion technique.*

Another recommendation is the *systematic training and education in the persuasion related field*; this undoubtedly will lead to a change in the marketing mindset and possible rethinking and formation of industry standards.

Conclusions

The importance of using persuasion methods in marketing communications to induce action cannot be overstated. A persuasion model cannot provide a cookbook to prescribe what to do in every particular situation. Rather, an in-depth study of a practical persuasion framework will offer communication specialists an insightful use of persuasion principles.

Although this study found that professionals considered persuasion techniques inevitable and vital, most didn't use persuasion for leading customers to a specific action. As mentioned earlier, the aim in most cases is for the brand to be top-of-mind or top-of-heart. This means that professionals' attitudes do not match their actions. In order for persuasion to be applied for behavioral purposes education, training, and more research is needed. The ethical issue of persuasion, especially for neuromarketing, needs to be addressed effectively in order for adoption in the field to accelerate.

In order to break through the clutter, the use of such tactics as integrated marketing communications (IMC), repetition through storytelling, and the influence process with a high involvement, when the consumer is motivated enough to become part of the campaign, is recommended by various academicians. The beneficial consequences of this are positive with progressive word of mouth and customer retention (Evanschitzky and Walsh, 2005). In accordance with this, Keller and Fay (2012) claim that the correct use of such persuasive platforms as online social media combined with face-to-face consumer expressions enhance the correlation between word-of-mouth and paid advertising. They highlight the need for a new advertising model, one in which a key goal of the ad is "…to foster conversation; the conversation then persuades the prospect, which leads to purchase" (Keller and Fay, 2012, p. 459).

In addition to the above it is worth highlighting that some persuasion methods have been used a lot and people have developed a kind of immunity towards these actions. This should mean a lot for communication professionals; they should always be looking for the clever, creative, fitting, and fresh ways of using persuasion methods; not just automatically, as research reveals in some cases (Christofi *et al.*, 2015).

Without thinking in advance of persuasion, specialists cannot achieve it as it would be a matter of luck. In regard to the effects of source credibility and message frame, future studies should involve larger samples in terms of size and geography and quantitative measures should be used to strengthen the current findings and acquire a better view of the phenomenon under investigation. Also future studies should include consumers' perspectives to present a more complete picture of persuasion, principles, methods, and other related issues discussed in the research. In addition, this study raises many opportunities for future research in specific variables. For instance, what is the incremental effectiveness of each of the various persuasion techniques presented in this research and to what extent are these persuasion techniques important and how are they measured separately.

The future of persuasion in marketing communications will be very exciting and revealing indeed.

References

Aaker, D. & Bruzzone, D. (1981). Viewer Perceptions of Prime-Time Television Advertising. *Journal of Advertising Research*, 21 (5), 15–23.

Persuasion science in marketing 101

Aaker, D., Stayman, D. & Hagerty, M. (1986). Warmth in Advertising: Measurement, Impact, and Sequence Effects. *Journal of Consumer Research*, 12 (4), 365–381.

Abe, J. & Izard, C. (1999). The Developmental Functions of Emotions: An Analysis in Terms of Differential Emotions Theory. *Cognition and Emotion*, 13 (5), 523–549.

Adhami, M. (2013). Using Neuromarketing to Discover How We Really Feel About Apps. *International Journal of Mobile Marketing*, 8 (1), 95–103.

Almiron-Chamadoira, P. & Dubernat, A. (2015). Neuroeconomics and consumer neuroscience, the last ten years, the next decade agenda. *Neuropsychoeconomics Conference Proceedings*, p. 24.

Andrejevic, M. (2012). Brain Whisperers: Cutting through the Clutter with Neuromarketing. *Somatechnics*, 198–215.

Arussy, L. (2009). Neuromarketing Isn't Marketing. *CRM Magazine*, 13 (1), 12.

Aureliano-Silva, L., Lopes, E., De Lamônica Freire, O. & da Silva, D. (2015). The Brand's Effect on the Evaluation of Advertising Endorsed by Celebrities: an Experimental Study. *Brazilian Business Review (English Edition)*, 12 (4), 57–78.

Barker, A., Nancarrow, C. & Spackman, N. (2001). Informed eclecticism: a research paradigm for the twenty-first century. *International Journal of Market Research*, 43 (1), 3–27.

Barkin, E. (2013). The Prospects and Limitations of Neuromarketing. *CRM Magazine*, 17 (7), 46–50.

Baskin, O., Hahn, J., Seaman, S. & Reines, D. (2010). Perceived effectiveness and implementation of public relations measurement and evaluation tools among European providers and consumers of PR services. *Public Relations Review*, 36 (2), 105–111.

Becheur, I., Dib, H., Merunka, D. & Valette-Florence, P. (2008). Emotions of Fear, Guilt or Shame in Anti-Alcohol Messages: Measuring Direct Effects on Persuasion and the Moderating Role of Sensation Seeking. *Advances in Consumer Research-European Conference Proceedings*, 8, 99–106.

Bednall, D., Adam, S. & Plocinski, K. (2010). Ethics in practice. *International Journal of Market Research*, 52 (2), 155–168.

Butler, M. R. (2008). Neuromarketing and the perception of knowledge. *Journal of Consumer Behaviour*, 7 (4/5), 415–419.

Cacioppo, J. T. & Petty, R. E. (1984). The Elaboration Likelihood Model of Persuasion. *Advances in Consumer Research*, 11, 673–675.

Carnegie, D. (1936). *How to Win Friends and Influence People*. New York: Simon and Schuster.

Chaiken, S. (1987). The heuristic model of persuasion. *Social influence: the Ontario symposium*, 5, 3–39.

Chen, S. & Chaiken, S. (1999). The heuristic-systematic model in its broader context. *Dual-process theories in social psychology*, 73–96.

Christofi, M., Vrontis, D., Kitchen, P. and Papasolomou, I. (2015). Innovation and Cause-related Marketing Success: a Conceptual Framework and Propositions. *Journal of Services Marketing*, 29 (5), pp. 354–366

Cialdini, R. (2007). *Influence, the Psychology of Persuasion*. United Kingdom: HarperCollins.

Cialdini, R. (2009). *Influence: Science and Practice*. Boston: Allyn and Bacon.

Ciprian-Marcel, P., Lăcrămioara, R., Ioana, M. & Maria, Z. (2009). Neuromarketing-Getting Inside the Customer's Mind. *Annals of the University of Oradea, Economic Science Series*, 18 (4), 804–807.

Conarroe, R. (1971). How to plan and organize a public relations program. *Public Relations Quarterly*, 16 (3), 5.

Dean, J. (1967). Measuring the Productivity of Investment in Persuasion. *Journal of Industrial Economics*, 15 (2), 81.

Denzin, N. K. & Lincoln, Y. S. (2009). *Qualitative research*. Yogyakarta: PustakaPelajar.

Derbaix, C., Poncin, I., Droulers, O. & Roullet, B. (2012). Measuring Affective Reactions Induced by Social Campaigns: Complementarity and Convergence of Iconic and Verbal Measures. *Recherche et applications en marketing (English Edition) (AFM C/O ESCP-EAP)*, 27 (2), 71–90.

Dilley, P. (2000). Conducting Successful Interviews: Tips for Intrepid Research. *Theory into Practice*, 39 (3), 131.

Dos Santos, M. A. (2015). Integrated marketing communication through neuromarketing. *Neuropsychoeconomics Conference Proceedings*, p. 44.

Dwivedi, A., Johnson, L. & McDonald, R. (2015). Celebrity endorsement, self-brand connection and consumer-based brand equity. *Journal of Product and Brand Management*, 24 (5), 449–461.

Elden, M., Bakir, U. & Geçit, E. (2015). Neuromarketing from the perspective of advertising professionals: a battle between creatives and strategic planners. *Neuropsychoeconomics Conference Proceedings*, 29.

Eser, Z., Isin, F. & Tolon, M. (2011). Perceptions of marketing academics, neurologists, and marketing professionals about neuromarketing. *Journal of Marketing Management*, 27 (7/8), 854–868.

Evanschitzky, H. & Walsh, G. (2005). Investigating the Moderators of the Customer Satisfaction-Loyalty Link: Evidence From Retailing. *AMA Winter Educators Conference Proceedings*, 16, 220–221.

Fenwick, I. & Rice, M. (1991). Reliability of Continuous Measurement Copy-Testing Methods. *Journal of Advertising Research*, 31 (1), 23–29.

Fiore, M., Contò, F., Vrontis, D. & Silvestri, R. (2015). Innovative Marketing Behaviour Determinants in Wine SMEs: the Case of an Italian Wine Region. *International Journal of Globalisation and Small Business*, 7 (2), 107–124.

Flay, B., DiTecco, D. & Schlegel, R. (1980). Mass media in health promotion: An analysis using an extended information-processing model. *Health Education and Behavior*, 7 (2), 127–147.

Flores, J., Baruca, A. & Saldivar, R. (2014). Is Neuromarketing Ethical? Consumers Say Yes. Consumers Say No. *Journal of Legal, Ethical and Regulatory Issues*, 17 (2), 77–91.

Funkhouser, G. R. (1984). A Practical Theory of Persuasion Based on Behavioral Science Approaches. *Journal of Personal Selling and Sales Management*, 4 (2), 17–25.

Funkhouser, G. & Parker, R. (1999). An Action-Based Theory of Persuasion in Marketing. *Journal of Marketing Theory & Practice*, 7 (3), 27.

Gendusa, J. (2008). Marketing that Pulls. *Marketing Health Services*, 28 (1), 18–21.

Gephart, R. P. (2004). Qualitative Research and the Academy of Management Journal. *Academy of Management Journal*, 47 (4), 454–462.

Gleitman, H., Gross, J. & Reisberg, D. (2011). *Psychology*. New York: W.W. Norton and Company.

Goldstein, N., Cialdini, R. & Martin, S. (2008). *YES! 50 Scientifically Proven Ways to Be Persuasive*. New York: Simon and Schuster.

Gregory, H. (2009). Why old planning models must go. Media Week, 14.

Haig, B. (2015). Brand credibility measurement: A new measure for brand equity/brand value: Part 1. *Journal of Brand Strategy*, 4 (2), 177–189.

Hart, L. (2015). Neuromarketing Offers Tips to Impact Decision Making. *Kitchen and Bath Design News*, 33 (4), 18.

Haley, E., Taylor, R. & Morrison, M. (2014). How Advertising Creatives Define Excellent Planning. *Journal of Current Issues and Research In Advertising (Routledge)*, 35 (2), 167–189.

Horn, C, Fries, A. & Gedenk, K. (2013). My Vote for My Mailman: Appeals to Reciprocity in Communication Campaigns. *Schmalenbach Business Review (SBR)*, 65 (3), 248–269.

Huberman, M. & Miles, M. B. (2002). *The qualitative researcher's companion*. Sage.

Hung, K. (2014). Why Celebrity Sells: A Dual Entertainment Path Model of Brand Endorsement. *Journal of Advertising*, 43 (2), 155–166.

Jones, L. S. (2004). Promoting exercise behaviour: An integration of persuasion theories and the theory of planned behavior. *British Journal of Health Psychology*, 9 (4), 505–521.

Kazokiene, L., Stravinskiene, J. (2011). Criteria for the Evaluation of Public Relations Effectiveness. *Engineering Economics*, 22 (1), 91–105.

Keller, E. & Fay, B. (2012). Word-of-Mouth Advocacy: A New Key to Advertising Effectiveness. *Journal of Advertising Research*, 52 (4), 459–464.

Kruglanski, A. & Thompson, E. (1999). Persuasion by a Single Route: A View From the Unimodel. *Psychological Inquiry*, 10 (2), 83–109.

Kruglanski, A. (2013). *Lay epistemics and human knowledge: Cognitive and motivational bases*. Springer Science and Business Media.

Leech, N. and Onwuegbuzie, A. (2010). Guidelines for Conducting and Reporting Mixed Research in the Field of Counseling and Beyond. *Journal of Counseling and Development*, 88 (1), 61–69.

Lindstrom, M. (2008). *Buyology: Truth and Lies About Why We Buy*. New York: Random House.

Lindstrom, M. (2011). *Brandwashed: Tricks Companies Use to Manipulate Our Minds and Persuade Us to Buy*. New York: Random House.

Lipsman, A., Mud, G., Rich, M. & Bruich, S. (2012).The Power of "Like": How Brands Reach (and Influence) Fans Through Social-Media Marketing. *Journal of Advertising Research*, 52 (1),. 40–52.

Lawrence, J. & Tar, U. (2013). The use of Grounded Theory Technique as a Practical Tool for Qualitative Data Collection and Analysis. *Electronic Journal of Business Research Methods*, 11 (1), 29–40.

Loh, J. & Dahesihsari, R. (2013). Resilience and Economic Empowerment: A Qualitative Investigation of Entrepreneurial Indonesian Women. *Journal of Enterprising Culture*, 21 (1), 107–121.

McGuire, W. (1968). Personality and attitude change: An information-processing theory. *Psychological foundations of attitudes*, 171–196.

Meckl-Sloan, C. (2015). Neuroeconomics and Neuromarketing. *International Journal of Business Management and Economic Research*, 6 (2), 133–136.

Mishra, A. S. (2015). Brand-Celebrity Match and its Impact on Advertising Effectiveness. *DLSU Business and Economics Review*, 25 (1), 16–27.

Milliman, R. & Fugate, D. (1988). Using Trust-Transference as a Persuasion Technique: An Empirical Field Investigation. *Journal of Personal Selling and Sales Management*, 8 (2), 1–7.

Mojtahed, R., Nunes, M., Martins, J. and Peng, A. (2014). Equipping the Constructivist Researcher: The Combined use of Semi-Structured Interviews and Decision-Making maps. *Electronic Journal of Business Research Methods*, 12 (2), 87–95.

Murphy, E., Illes, J. & Reiner, P. (2008). Neuroethics of neuromarketing. *Journal of Consumer Behaviour*, 7 (4/5), 293–302.

Myers, D., Abell, J. & Sani, F. (2014). *Social Psychology*. McGraw Hill Higher Education.

Onwuegbuzie, A. & Leech, N. (2005). On Becoming a Pragmatic Researcher: The Importance of Combining Quantitative and Qualitative Research Methodologies. *International Journal of Social Research Methodology*, 8 (5), 375–387.

Ostlund, L, Clancy, K. & Sapra, R. (1980). Inertia in Copy Research. *Journal of Advertising Research*, 20 (1), 17–23.

Page, G. (2012). Scientific realism: what 'neuromarketing' can and can't tell us about consumers. *International Journal of Market Research*, 54 (2), 287–290.

Patrick Renvoise at TEDxBend (2013). Is There a Buy Button Inside the Brain. [online]. Available at: www.youtube.com/watch?v=_rKceOe-Jr0

Petty, R. & Cacioppo, J. (1986). *The Elaboration Likelihood Model of Persuasion*, pp. 1–24, New York: Springer.

Petty, R., Wheeler, S. & Bizer, G. (1999). Is There One Persuasion Process or More? Lumping Versus Splitting in Attitude Change Theories. *Psychological Inquiry*, 10 (2), 156.

Pieliene, L. (2012). Marketing Luxury: Neuro Insight. *Management Theory and Studies for Rural Business and Infrastructure Development*, 34 (5), 148–153.

Rakić, B. & Rakić, M. (2014). Integrated Marketing Communications Paradigm in Digital Environment: The Five Pillars of Integration. *Megatrend Review*, 11 (1), 187–203.

Reimann, M. (2013). Transformative Consumer Neuroscience. *Advances in Consumer Research*, 41, 43–48.

Ritchie, J., Lewis, J. & Elam, G. (2003). Designing and selecting samples. *Qualitative research practice: A guide for social science students and researchers*, 2, 111–145.

Roux, C. & Goldsmith, K. (2014). Scarcity, Poverty, and their Implications for Consumers' Cognitions, Judgment and Behavior. *Advances in Consumer Research*, 42, 215–219.

Saunders, M., Lewis, P. & Thornhill, A. (2009). *Research Methods for Business Students*. 5th Edition, Harlow: FT Prentice Hall.

Senior, C. & Lee, N. (2008). A manifesto for neuromarketing science. *Journal of Consumer Behaviour*, 7 (4/5), 263–271.

Shelby, A. N. (1986). The Theoretical Bases of Persuasion: A Critical Introduction. *Journal of Business Communication*, 23 (1), 5–29.

Scholten, M. (1996). Lost and found: the information-processing model of advertising effectiveness. *Journal of Business Research*, 37 (2), 97–104.

Smith, R. (2013). *Strategic planning for public relations*. New York: Routledge.

Stacks, D. & Bowen, S. (2011). The strategic approach: Writing measurable objectives. *Public Relations Tactics*, 18 (5), 14.

Stipp, H. (2015). The Evolution of Neuromarketing Research: From Novelty to Mainstream. *Journal of Advertising Research*, 55 (2), 120–122.

Strong, E. K. (1925). *The Psychology of Selling*. New York: McGraw-Hill.

Stokes, P. (2015). Brain Power. *Acuity*, 2 (7), 44–47.

Starcevic, S. (2013). The Influence of Celebrity Endorsement on Advertising Effectiveness and Brand Image (English). *Zbornik Radova Ekonomskog Fakulteta U Istocnom Sarajevu*, 7, 147–161.

Tran, G. A. (2013). The Role of Celebrity Endorsers. *Society for Marketing Advances Proceedings*, 25, 156–159.

Va, K. P. (2015). Reinventing the Art of Marketing in the Light of Digitalization and Neuroimaging. *Amity Global Business Review*, 10, 75–80.

Varan, D., Lang, A., Barwise, P., Weber, R. & Bellman, S. (2015). How Reliable are Neuromarketers' Measures of Advertising Effectiveness? *Journal of Advertising Research*, 55 (2), 176–191.

Wengraf, T. (2001). *Qualitative research interviewing: Biographic narrative and semi-structured methods*, Sage.

Yeung, R. (2011). *I is for Influence: The new science of persuasion*, London: Macmillan.

Zurawicki, L. (2010). *Neuromarketing: Exploring the Brain of the Consumer*. Springer.

8 Innovative tertiary strategies on improving satisfaction level of students

Demetris Vrontis, Sam El Nemar and Amani Mallat

Introduction

A university is defined as a place where a group of people with different principles, thoughts and academic background is assembled together under a common institutional logo or name (Michael, 1997). Students are seen as critical customers and key stakeholders since they are the main customers of any university (Hill, 1995). The university or higher education institution is a service industry with the main goal to help students fulfill their expectations and needs (Vrontis et al., 2007; Elliott & Shin, 2002). Therefore, an organization should work on its relationship (Franco and Haase, 2017; Festa et al., 2017; Bresciani et al., 2012; Christofi et al., 2015) with its most valuable resources, students, (Helfert et al., 2002) and develop a long-term customer relationship (Grönroos, 1989). Nowadays, due to competitive environments in higher education, universities find themselves facing a problem that might threaten their existence. In the literature, business-orientated education institutes are found to be moving toward services-oriented marketing where the main 'P' is people. Moreover, student satisfaction is found to be the main reason for their persistence where it is defined as the students' evaluation of their experiences with the services provided. Measuring the level of student satisfaction through service quality dimensions has been conducted by numerous researchers to understand how customers react to services or products offered.

Usually, service quality is commonly viewed from an organizational perspective. To succeed, such vision should be translated in favor of what students' want, as their perception is vital for institution market success.

The fact that satisfaction has an effect on both individual and organizational performance makes it interesting to study the factors that satisfy customers in both academic and non-academic settings.

Addressing all the factors that most students rely on to judge service quality has not been totally recognized. For this reason, it becomes necessary to investigate if the measurements have taken all the factors significant for students into consideration and whether these factors are based on a particular perspective. Since the service quality judgment is subjective, building a given construct for assessment will generate a better vision of student satisfaction.

Customer satisfaction construct is frequently used by organizations to find out how students perceive the offered services or products and how satisfied they are. This leads to a better understanding of services that students prefer and allows organizations to maximize their service quality and to engage the maximum of their resources in enhancing the relationship with their customers (Anderson et al., 1994). This is the purpose of this study, to identify the factors that positively impact student satisfaction in higher education and to measure satisfaction by checking students' opinions about some factors. To achieve this purpose, a comprehensive student survey was implemented at the Lebanese International University for the following reasons:

RO1) To identify which factors satisfy university students during their university year
RO2) To measure, among the identified factors, which aspects students discuss most frequently or see as the most impactful.
RO3) To construct a conceptual framework on university student satisfaction.

Literature review

Student satisfaction

Abu Hasan (2008) expressed that "satisfaction is a state felt by a person who has experienced a performance or an outcome that fulfills his or her expectation". While student satisfaction is described as the subjective students' evaluation of different experiences and outcomes related to education, it is not something fixed. That is, it changes continually based on repeated experiences during the period of university education that is reflected through students' behavior (El Nemar and Vrontis, 2016; Elliott and Shin, 2002; Gide and Shams, 2011; Andronikidis, 2009; Rossi et al., 2014; Chebbi et al., 2016).

Measuring the level of student satisfaction differs across methods. The basic method defined by Kotler and Clarke (2012) is *periodic surveys* that directly assess student satisfaction, their evaluation of the institution and their possible recommendations. Student satisfaction is not dependent on only one factor, which is education. There are many other factors that influence and impact student satisfaction. An accurate measure is very difficult to obtain because it is subjective among researchers.

Customer satisfaction refers to the level of satisfaction expressed by customers for the quality of offered services (Athiyaman, 1997; Brown and Schwartz, 1989; Shams, 2011). Thus, due to the rise in the service-marketing sector, service quality is significantly associated with customer satisfaction (Tajeddini, 2011). Service quality is "the discrepancy between consumers' perceptions of services offered by a particular firm and their expectations about firms offering such services" (Parasuraman et al., 1985). Thus, it is the difference between customers' expectations and their real experience (Aldridge and Rowley, 1998; Shams, 2016a; 2016b).

Many theoretical models have been designed to explain this discrepancy, as seen in "*service quality model*" by Grönroos (1984), the "*GAP model*" by Parasuraman et al. (1985), the "*model of perceived service quality and satisfaction*" by Spreng and Mackoy (1996), and the "*service encounter model*" by Bitner (1990).

Colleges and higher education institutions are interested in better understanding customer satisfaction and their reaction to offered services or products. Once understood, these organizations become able to engage the best of their resources, "time, money, employees, production process, and so on", more effectively in order to enhance their relationship with customers (Anderson et al., 1994; Shams and Lombardi, 2016; Trequattrini et al., 2016).

The relationship between student satisfaction and college experience has also been studied. The first factor studied is if this relationship is different between genders. It was found that social/relational factors are important for women's satisfaction but not for men's. However, career factors were important for men's satisfaction and not for women's and this was supported by major certainty findings. On the other hand, "*confidence in being a student*" and "*having attractive courses*" are of great importance for both genders and are highly affected by campus faculty members who have the ability to influence students' confidence and to change their courses to make them more relevant and exciting (Bean and Vesper, 1994). Also, the first and second year students' contact with the faculty is critical for college experience.

The reviews on student satisfaction and how students perceive the educational experience are extremely unpredictable. Therefore, universities should adopt the customer approach in order to satisfy students and win the competition battle of all universities. To build competitive advantage and consumer preferences, universities have to focus on the importance of quality and satisfaction (Elliott and Shin, 2002). Seymour (1972) suggested that higher education's main goal should be to gain a bulk of highly satisfied customers regardless of whether they are students, parents of students, alumni, or industry employers. Thus, word of mouth or personal recommendations (James, 2002; Shams, 2015a; 2015b; Shams and Kaufmann, 2016) should be greatly considered as they come mainly from friends, family members, teachers and advisors (Bolton and Drew, 1991) and have the strongest impact (Day, 1971; Richins, 1983; Murray, 1991; Kaufmann and Shams, 2015). In higher education, students who had a very good experience will share it, which leads to better expectations of prospective students (Bolton and Drew, 1991). Therefore, word of mouth must be considered a powerful tool because it has a direct impact on customers' decisions and behaviors (Lovelock et al., 2001).

There are many perspectives of student satisfaction since it is a very complex construct that requires university best practices (El Nemar and Vrontis, 2014; Elliott and Shin, 2002). In addition, student integration theory of persistence or retention can be the result of the relationship between students and institutions (Tinto, 1987). Students are retained through two commitments: obtaining a college degree and achieving this degree at a particular institution (institutional commitment). Combining these two commitments has an impact on retention at a specific institution. Thus, the institution will meet the student expectations by combining students' motivation, academic ability and the institution's ability (Kara and De Shields, 2004).

As mentioned earlier, literature on student satisfaction and student perception of the academic experience is very complex. Alongside this, many authors have implied the presence of comparable factors (Harvey, 2001; Hill, 1995). In their studies, they suggested the following factors: "library services, accommodation services, course content, teaching quality, catering service, academic workload and so on". Moreover, in 2001, UCC Student Services Evaluation Report studied student satisfaction using the following categories: "general climate, admissions/records, financial aid and awards, counseling, assessment center, academic advising, athletics, health clinic, computer labs, library, bookstore".

As satisfaction has an effect on both individual and organizational performance, it becomes interesting to study the factors of satisfaction in both academic and non-academic settings (Cranny et al., 1992; Decenzo et al., 2010).

Service quality measurement in higher education

Many studies have been conducted on service quality measurement in higher education institutions. In 1995, Hill studied the relationship between expectations and perceptions of university services. He showed that students have a maintained level of expectation at the time of university experience that has been built prior to enrollment. Since this level of expectation may decrease over time, he suggested measuring students' expectations before they enter the university. A study done by Brenders et al. (1999) also showed that the best time to measure expectations is before students enroll in the university program because, at that time, their expectations are based on high school. Thus, measuring the students' perceptions was at the center of all research.

The dimensions of quality that should be measured in higher education are different among researchers. Eight quality dimensions have been proposed by Owlia and Aspinwall (1996) which are: 1) Tangibility (adequate equipment and facilities), 2) Competence (teaching expertise), 3) Attitude (understanding students' needs), 4) Personal attention (willingness to help), 5) Content (curriculum, flexibility of knowledge), 6) Delivery (effective presentation, feedback from students), 7) Reliability (trustworthiness), and 8) Handling complaints (solving problems).

This framework only considered the link between students and teachers, it did not consider the campus and the communication processes. However, many higher education institutions have proposed this framework to address student satisfaction (Mishra, 2007).

110   *Demetris Vrontis et al.*

In 1996, Wright used the SERVQUAL model through factor analysis to analyze the factors linked to student satisfaction at a university. He distributed a questionnaire of 31 items to 149 third year business students and came up with the following degree of impact: the diversity of courses and student body ranked first among the factors, the ease of use of facilities came second, the interaction between students and teachers came in third place, the fourth place went to the student quality followed by the educational process, the faculty quality, the technological capabilities of the university and finally the professors' teaching experience. All the factors are concerned with the relation between teachers and students and do not include any administrative or communication issues.

However, based on a study on 182 British students done by Cook in 1997, several factors were relevant to relate to good quality. They are: "1) Academic staff factors, 2) Study factors (library and private study facilities, computer access and an atmosphere conducive to study), 3) General welfare factors, 4) Practice factors, and 5) Extra-curricular activity factors".

Thus, the interaction between students and academic staff is perceived as the most important regardless of the way administrative staff communicates with students and teachers. Moreover, a study on 718 undergraduate students in the Netherlands was done by Berger and Milem in 1999 to find out the factors that influence students' persistence. It appeared that students with social family backgrounds integrate more in the university system. Another study conducted on 145 Australian students to explore students' perceptions regarding universities focused on the academic experience. It appeared that the lack of administrative components and communication has a negative impact on students' perception of university service quality (Brenders et al., 1999).

An alternative study was performed at two universities in Singapore on a sample of 958 students. This study was built based on the SERVQUAL model. It was found that students expected a higher level of services, especially communication services, and the presence of channels to transmit their opinions to management (Tan and Kek, 2004).

A study conducted on business students in Brazil focused on factors related to students' satisfaction and loyalty revealed that other factors such as the economic and financial level along with employment and marital status influence the level of satisfaction (Walter, 2006).

A study in Egypt on 508 students from four different universities was conducted to measure service quality. It used the SERVQUAL tool combined with Importance-Performance (IP) analysis. It was shown that the five SERVQUAL dimensions couldn't be met but three other dimensions were acquired: first, all activities related to registration, fee payment and enrolment; second, the students' orientation from the university staff; and finally, the role of the physical service environment (Mostafa, 2006).

Over the years, the study of how to measure students' perceptions continued. In 2009, another study was done on 38 Brazilian production engineering program students to measure junior students' expectations and on 28 seniors for perception measurement. The SERVQUAL instrument was implemented but couldn't be validated. The move was applied to the dimensions obtained by Mostafa (2006) (de Oliveira and Ferreira, 2009). As clearly seen the SERVQUAL instrument measures the service quality (Carlos Pinho et al., 2007).

Further studies have also measured service quality in higher education, such as Brown and Mazzarol (2009) and Jurkowitsch (2006).

Based on studies already discussed focusing on measuring similar quality factors, it was difficult to draw a framework for service quality in higher education. These studies done on service quality dimensions showed wide differences in the identification of these dimensions. Thus, identifying a clear structure of dimensions of service quality in advanced education is not easy. The 5Qs model was proposed by Zineldin (2007) to characterize the quality dimensions into five groups which were then analyzed.

Conceptual framework

Based on the literature, the most important factors associated with student satisfaction were selected from models that were constructed to assess student satisfaction. Using these models, this study designed a conceptual model modified to adapt to the purpose of this study. Researchers mentioned four major groups of factors as independent variables, which are assumed to influence student satisfaction. These are institutional factors, out-of-school factors, student expectations and demographic factors. Lebanese students' satisfaction is the dependent variable. Institutional factors comprise the educational component "quality of teaching, communication with teachers during and outside the course, curriculum, textbooks and other teaching materials" and the administrative components (the principles and practices of the university administrators). Out-of-school activities include all activities and facilities provided on the campus. Demographic factors are age, gender, course attendance, cumulative average and so on. Finally, factors of expectations discuss what the student expects from the higher education institution. Based on this conceptual framework, the hypotheses of this study are illustrated in Figure 8.1.

All four factors – institutional factors (educational and administrative), out of school factors, demographics and expectations – will be tested with student satisfaction.

> H1: Institutional factors have a positive relationship with overall student satisfaction.
> H2: Out of school factors have a positive relationship with overall student satisfaction.
> H3: Demographics have a positive relationship with overall student satisfaction.

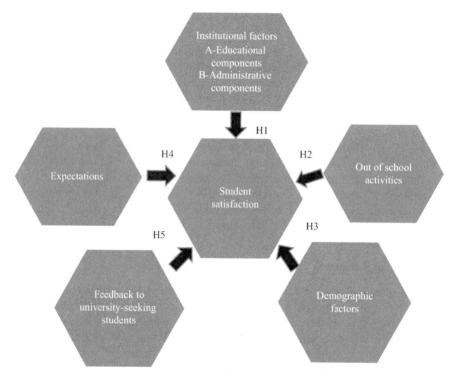

Figure 8.1 Student satisfaction conceptual framework

H4: Expectations have a positive relationship with overall student satisfaction.

H5: Current satisfied university students provide positive feedback to university-seeking students.

Research methodology

This study adopted the student satisfaction questionnaire as the research instrument to achieve the objectives of the study. The questionnaire was subdivided into two sections: demographic factors and student satisfaction factors (67 questions). The demographic category of each respondent included age, gender and year of study. Another category of questions was concerned about factors related to student satisfaction, the relationship between service quality and student satisfaction, and the outcome generated from their level of satisfaction.

This research utilized non-probability sampling type known as convenient sampling, because the researcher wanted to access students' satisfaction levels towards their university.

Therefore, data was collected from the sample during the 2016 academic year from business students at Lebanese International University (LIU). One hundred and thirty questionnaires were distributed and 100 acceptable completed forms from full-time business students were obtained. In order to collect valid responses, a self-completion questionnaire to students of the university was adopted. In the questionnaire, different aspects of student satisfaction were addressed and a Likert scale of five options for respondents to select from was provided. All the students' data collected through the questionnaire was analyzed using SPSS. Demographic variables in the questionnaire were coded alphanumerically (1 for male and 2 for female) and a Likert scale was used for all independent and dependent variables (from 5 to 1 where: 5 = I completely agree; 4 = I generally agree; 3 = I slightly agree; 2 = I do not agree; 1 = No experience of the topic). Cronbach's alpha was used to test the reliability and Chi-square correlation to test the relationship of the conceptual framework as the researcher needed to confirm if parts of the model were correlated with the process.

Analysis and results

The results obtained through the questionnaire were introduced to the statistical program SPSS for statistical analysis. The descriptive analysis shows that 55% of LIU students are female and 45% are male. The majority of students (61%) are between 20 and 24 years old, 31% of students are between 17 and 19 years old and 6% are above 24.

Consequently, the researcher applied the Cronbach's alpha to test the reliability of the scales used. The results of the reliability coefficients are shown in Table 8.1 representing our confidence that the following test is accurate and reliable.

Table 8.1 Reliability of institutional factors, out of school activities and expectations

Factors of satisfaction	Reliability
Factors affecting studying arrangements	0.949
Studying	0.949
Factors affecting student assessment	0.950
Factors affecting teaching and learning	0.950
Factors affecting training	0.950
Factors affecting premises	0.948
Factors affecting library	0.949
Factors affecting cleaning services	0.950
Factors affecting café services	0.950
Factors affecting expectations	0.948

Cronbach's Alpha ($\alpha = 0.5$ is considered as acceptable, $\alpha = 0.7$ as good, $\alpha = 0.8$ and above as excellent).

114 *Demetris Vrontis et al.*

Table 8.2 Correlation of variables with student satisfaction

Variables	Student satisfaction
Institutional factors (H1)	0.127
Out of school activities (H2)	0.124
Demographics (H3)	0.081
Students' expectations (H4)	0.131

Hypothesis testing

For hypothesis testing, a correlation coefficient is used to assess if student satisfaction and studied factors are correlated. A bivariate correlation was used.

H1: Institutional factors are positively related to overall student satisfaction.
H2: Out of school factors are positively related to overall student satisfaction.
H3: Demographics are positively related to overall student satisfaction.
H4: Expectations are positively related to overall student satisfaction.

Table 8.2 shows a significant positive relationship between student satisfaction and institutional factors ($r = 0.127$, $p < .05$), student satisfaction and out of school activities ($r = 0.124$, $p < .05$), student satisfaction and demographics ($r = 0.081$) and student satisfaction and expectations ($r = 0.131$). It was hypothesized that institutional factors, out of school activities, demographic factors and expectations are positively associated with overall student satisfaction. These results indicate that positive institutional factors, positive out of school activities, demographics and expectations are associated with higher satisfaction.

H5: Current satisfied university students provide positive feedback to university-seeking students.

Table 8.3 describes the correlation coefficient assessment of student satisfaction and university recommendations; this bivariate correlation test shows if student satisfaction and university recommendations are correlated. Results revealed a significant positive relationship between student satisfaction and students' recommendations ($r = 0.137$, $p < 0.05$). It was hypothesized that current satisfied university students provide positive feedback to university-seeking students. These results indicate that the students' type of recommendation is associated with higher satisfaction. So H5 is accepted. This means, the higher the level of current student satisfaction, the more likely it will positively affect the recommendation of the institution to potential students.

Strategies to improve student satisfaction   115

Table 8.3 Correlation of student satisfaction and students' recommendations

		Student satisfaction	*What type of recommendations will you make about the university?*
Student satisfaction	Pearson correlation	1	.137
	Sig. (2-tailed)		.02
	N	100	100
What type of recommendations will you make about the university?	Pearson correlation	.137	1
	Sig. (2-tailed)	.02	
	N	100	100

Table 8.4 Chi-square tests: student satisfaction and institutional factors

(a)

	Value	*Df*	*Asymp. sig. (2-sided)*
Pearson Chi-square	54.189[a]	41	.041
Likelihood ratio	58.393	41	.038
Linear-by-linear association	33.914	1	.000
No of valid cases	100		

a. 83 cells (98.8%) have expected count less than 5. The minimum expected count is .21.

(b)

		Value	*Asymp. std. error[a]*	*Approx. T[b]*	*Approx. sig.*
Interval by interval	Pearson's R	.585	.085	7.146	.000[c]
Ordinal by ordinal	Spearman correlation	.526	.066	6.119	.000[c]
No of valid cases		100			

Conceptual framework testing

In order to examine if our conceptual model is valid, a Chi-square testing was done to test the relationships.

Table 8.4 describes the Chi-square test for student satisfaction and institutional factors. Results revealed the Pearson Chi-square value is 54.189 where p is 0.041<0.05, this means that there is strong evidence of a relationship between institutional factors and student satisfaction. The Pearson's R value

116 Demetris Vrontis et al.

Table 8.5 Chi-square tests: student satisfaction and school activities

(a)

	Value	df	Asymp. sig. (2-sided)
Pearson Chi-square	58.978[a]	35	.007
Likelihood ratio	62.507	35	.003
Linear by linear association	33.819	1	.000
No of valid cases	100		

a. 70 cells (97.2%) have expected count less than 5. The minimum expected count is .21.

(b)

		Value	Asymp. std. error[a]	Approx. T[b]	Approx. sig.
Interval by interval	Pearson's R	.584	.080	7.131	.000[c]
Ordinal by ordinal	Spearman correlation	.536	.066	6.279	.000[c]
No of valid cases		100			

a Not assuming the null hypothesis
b Using the asymptotic standard error assuming the null hypothesis

is 0.585 which reinforces the good and strong correlation between student satisfaction and institutional factors. The more the educational components and administrative components at the university are up to the students' expectations, the more students are satisfied.

Table 8.5 shows that there is also strong evidence of a relationship between students' satisfaction and out of school activities (Chi-square = 58.978; p = 0.007 <0.05). Also, the Pearson's R is 0.584 which confirms the good and strong correlation. Thus, the more service facilities provided by the university, the more students are satisfied.

Table 8.6 describes the Chi-square test for student satisfaction and their expectations. Results revealed the Pearson Chi-square value is 22.777 and p = 0.01 < 0.05, this means there is evidence of a relationship between students' satisfaction and expectations. Moreover, the Pearson's R is 0.418 meaning that the relation exists but it is moderate to strong compared with other factors that showed better correlation (institutional factors and out of school activities).

Table 8.7 describes the Chi-square test for student satisfaction and demographics. Results revealed there is a strong evidence of relationship between student satisfaction and demographics (Chi-square = 38.115 and

Table 8.6 Chi-square tests: student satisfaction and expectations

(a)

	Value	df	Asymp. sig. (2-sided)
Pearson Chi-square	22.777[a]	16	.01
Likelihood ratio	26.687	16	.045
Linear-by-linear association	17.312	1	.000
No of valid cases	100		

a. 31 cells (91.2%) have expected count less than 5. The minimum expected count is .21.

(b)

		Value	Asymp. std. error	Approx. T	Approx. sig.
Interval by interval	Pearson's R	.418	.087	4.557	.000[c]
Ordinal by ordinal	Spearman correlation	.391	.084	4.209	.000[c]
No of valid cases		100			

Table 8.7 Chi-square tests: student satisfaction and demographics

(a)	Value	df	Asymp. sig. (2-sided)
Pearson Chi-square	38.115[a]	15	.001
Likelihood ratio	41.129	15	.000
Linear-by-linear association	25.396	1	.000
No of valid cases	100		

a. 27 cells (84.4%) have expected count less than 5. The minimum expected count is .21.

(b)

		Value	Asymp. std. error	Approx. T	Approx. sig.
Interval by interval	Pearson's R	.506	.089	5.815	.000[c]
Ordinal by ordinal	Spearman correlation	.468	.085	5.249	.000[c]
No of valid cases		100			

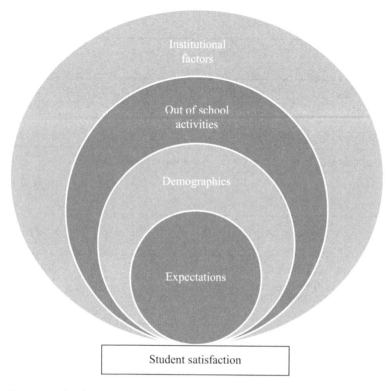

Figure 8.2 Student satisfaction model – factors of satisfaction from weakest to strongest

p = 0.001 < 0.05). Also, the Pearson's R is 0.506 which confirms the good and strong relation, as strong as the institutional and out of school activities factors.

As a result, it has been shown that all the factors tested are important for student satisfaction but their importance can be drawn as shown in Figure 8.2 from weakest to strongest.

Conclusion

The aim of this research was to identify the factors affecting the satisfaction level of university students and those holding a significant impact and, more importantly, the factors that can be included in the construct of a conceptual framework. Using the literature, this study tested the identified factors to produce a conceptual framework based on Harvey's (2001) model, who found that institutional factors, out of school activities, demographic factors and students' expectations are the most impactful factors.

In this study, the factors that enhance student satisfaction and ensure their persistence have been examined:

1. It was strongly proved that the quality of teaching is an important factor for student satisfaction. Students showed high satisfaction with the quality of teaching, curriculum and teaching materials.
2. The principles and practices of the university administrators were shown to be another important factor of satisfaction for students.
3. The good relationship of students with the faculty (director, non-teaching staff, instructors, student affairs office) as part of the advising process was of high importance and relates to their connectedness to the faculty. This comes in accordance with studies that have revealed the importance of the academic programs and showed that students' relationship with faculty staff will enhance the students' feelings of belonging and welcome and reflect their satisfaction level (Tinto, 1987). Elliott and Healy (2001) showed that the more students feel connected to the faculty, the more they will feel satisfied. Faculty serves as the most important factor for students since it helps them to adjust to college life and achieve more intellectually and personally. It also enhances their educational aspirations (Lamport, 1993).
4. One of key factors contributing to student satisfaction was revealed through students' opinions about the university facilities (out of school activities including the library, premises, café and cleaning services). They were highly satisfied with the activities and facilities provided by the university. These results are supported by Peters (1988) who states that campus life has an importance not less than institutional factors for students' satisfaction (almost similar beta coefficient).
5. For hypothesis H3, the relationship between students' satisfaction and demographic factors (more specifically "educational level") has been tested. The results revealed that high satisfaction is associated with positive demographic factors.
6. Another contributing factor to satisfaction is the extent to which students felt "their expectations fit". They reinforce their commitment through agreeing on recommending the university again.

In H5, how student satisfaction and their types of recommendations for the faculty are correlated has been studied. The results showed that student satisfaction and recommendations are positively related: high satisfaction is associated with positive recommendations. This is in accordance with the fact that word of mouth (personal recommendation) has a great effect on the university's reputation or brand image. Students base their decisions on others' recommendations and especially family, friends, teachers or advisors who have the biggest impact. What students perceive will have an influence on their decision-making process. Thus, personal recommendation is the most powerful source of information for students.

120 *Demetris Vrontis et al.*

At the end of our study on student satisfaction with a Lebanese university in relation to the different services it offers, the researcher has been able to achieve the various objectives set for this study: measuring the level of satisfaction, dissatisfaction, the ranking of these criteria and finally the proposal for priority areas for improvement.

Indeed, the highly competitive environment of higher education requires a continuous improvement of the quality of the services offered in order to satisfy a clientele whose requirements are increasing.

It should also be stressed that achieving the objective of increasing student satisfaction would benefit LIU at all levels. Not only would it consolidate the position of excellence advocated by the school, but it would also improve its competitiveness. It is therefore up to this prestigious institution to make the necessary efforts in this direction.

Through this study, many dimensions of student satisfaction have been identified. Educational guidance, quality of classroom arrangements, the thoroughness of the curriculum, students' feelings about their classroom, connections with staff and the quality of campus life all enhance the relation of students with the institutions through building a feeling of belonging. The life outside the classroom (campus life or out of school activities) is as important as institutional factors to student satisfaction.

As there are studies focusing on the reasons that lead to student departure, many others including this study look for factors that enhance student retention. Student centeredness can be created through positive students' perceptions of the institutional and out of school factors. Through this built feeling, students will feel accepted and welcomed in the institution, which leads them to feel more likely to be attached to the school and more satisfied with their overall experience.

The high level of satisfaction shown by the students here will ensure their persistence until degree completion. A positive relationship with faculty staff will ensure stronger commitment to the institution. Also, the more effective and powerful the academic advising, the more students perceive the institution positively. Moreover, students who expect that the program of study will fit their career goals will have positive feelings about the institution and show stronger attachment.

Universities use students' surveys to help them identify challenges and find ways to improve them as well as target their goals toward more strategic planning programs. In fact, universities that consider recalling student satisfaction factors are the most successful, allowing them to enjoy a greater level of institutional success.

This study was able to reveal the factors that bring satisfaction to Lebanese university students. Furthermore, by building a conceptual model, this research was able to identify the factors that have the most likelihood of satisfaction. Further tests of such model should be adopted at other Lebanese universities as well in order to be able to generalize the findings and explore satisfying factors so as to compete in this increasingly competitive environment. Further studies will not only approve the model but also generate a

Strategies to improve student satisfaction 121

valuable measurement for institutions in higher education. Through this valid model, universities become able to optimize their offerings in favor of students and, therefore, to their retention. Investigating a larger sample can help to explore the differences and similarities among students. Universities should increase their marketing programs to attract talented students and to better market themselves by showing their strengths to parents and students. They should also put significant investment into salaries and funds to ensure a more diversified and qualified faculty. Finally, and most importantly, to be able to generalize the conceptual model, it should be supported with qualitative research on a larger population.

Limitations

This study focused only on business students at LIU due to time constraints. Further research should access multiple universities with different majors.

References

Abu Hasan, F.H. (2008). Service quality and student satisfaction: A case study at private education institutions. *International Business, 1*(3), 163–175.

Anderson, E.W., Fornell, C. and Lehmann, D.R. (1994). Customer satisfaction, market share, and profitability: Findings from Sweden. *The Journal of Marketing, 58* (3), 53–66.

Andronikidis, A. (2009). Linking dimensions of perceived service quality to actual purchase behaviour. *EuroMed Journal of Business, 4*(1), 4–20.

Athiyaman, A. (1997). Linking student satisfaction and service quality perceptions: the case of university education. *European Journal of Marketing, 31*(7), 528–540.

Berger, J. and Milem, J. (1999). The role of student involvement and perceptions of integration in a causal model of student persistence. *Research in Higher Education, 40*, 641–664.

Bolton, R. and Drew, J. (1991). A multistage model of customers' assessment of service quality and value. *Journal of Consumer Research*, March, *17*, 375–384.

Brenders, D.A., Hope, P. and Ninnan, A. (1999). A systemic, student-centered study of university service. *Research in Higher Education, 40*(6), 665–685.

Bresciani, S., Thrassou, A. and Vrontis, D. (2012). Human Resource Management – Practices, Performance and Strategy in the Italian Hotel Industry. *World Review of Entrepreneurship, Management and Sustainable Development, 8* (4), 405–423.

Brown, S.W. and Swartz, T.A. (1989). A gap analysis of professional service quality. *The Journal of Marketing, 53* (2), 92–98.

Brown, R.M. and Mazzarol, T.W. (2009). The importance of institutional image to student satisfaction and loyalty within higher education. *Higher Education, 58*(1), 81–95.

Carlos Pinho, J., Macedo, I.M. and Monteiro, A.P., (2007). The impact of online SERVQUAL dimensions on certified accountant satisfaction: The case of taxation services. *EuroMed Journal of Business, 2*(2), 154–172.

Chebbi, H., Yahiaoui, D., Vrontis, D. and Thrassou, A. (2016). The Impact of Ambidextrous Leadership on the Internationalization of Emerging Market Firms (EMF): The Case of India. *Thunderbird International Business Review*, 421–436.

122 *Demetris Vrontis et al.*

Christofi, M., Vrontis, D., Kitchen, P. and Papasolomou, I. (2015). Innovation and Cause-related Marketing Success: a Conceptual Framework and Propositions. *Journal of Services Marketing*, 29 (5), 354–366.

Cook, M.J. (1997). A student's perspective of service quality in education. *Total Quality Management*, 8(2–3), 120–125.

Cranny, C.J., Smith, P.C. and Stone, E. (1992). Job satisfaction: How people feel about their jobs. *Administrative Science Quarterly*, 39(1), 186–89.

Day, G., (1971). Attitude change, media and word of mouth. *Journal of Advertising Research*, 11(6), 31–40.

DeCenzo, D.A., Robbins, S.P. and Verhulst, S.L. (2010). *Fundamentals of human resource management*. Hoboken, NJ: John Wiley.

El Nemar, S. and Vrontis, D. (2014, September). What factors do student choice models identify as aspects of influence over school leavers when selecting a university in Lebanon. In *7th Annual EuroMed Conference of the EuroMed Academy of Business, 18–19 September 2014, Kristiansand, Norway.*

El Nemar, S. and Vrontis, D. (2016). A higher education student-choice analysis: the case of Lebanon. *World Review of Entrepreneurship, Management and Sustainable Development*, 12(2–3), 337–351.

Elliott, K.M. and Shin, D. (2002). Student satisfaction: An alternative approach to assessing this important concept. *Journal of Higher Education Policy and Management*, 24(2), 197–209.

Elliott, K.M. and Healy, M.A. (2001). Key factors influencing student satisfaction related to recruitment and retention. *Journal of Marketing for higher Education*, 10(4).1–11.

Franco and Haase. (2017). Success factors in university sport partnerships: a case study. *EuroMed Journal of Business*, 12 (1), 87–102.

Festa, G., Ciasullo, V.C., Vrontis, D. and Thrassou, A. (2017). Cooperating for Competing – a Small Italian Wineries' Internationalisation Strategy Case Study. *Global Business and Economics Review*, 19 (5), 648–670.

Gide, E. and Shams, S.M.R. (2011). The use of e-CRM database to promote a value-breeding bond network: The case of Hawthorn football club of Australian Rules. *Procedia Computer Science*, 3, 1083–1088.

Grönroos, C. (1984). A service quality model and its marketing implications. *European Journal of Marketing*, 18(4), 36–44.

Harvey, L. (2001). Student feedback: a report to the higher education funding council for England. Birmingham: Centre for Research and Quality, the University of Central England.

Helfert, G., Ritter, T. and Walter, A. (2002). Redefining market orientation from a relationship perspective: Theoretical considerations and empirical results. *European Journal of Marketing*, 36(9/10), 1119–1139.

Hill, F.M. (1995). Managing service quality in higher education: the role of the student as primary consumer. *Quality Assurance in Education*, 3(3), 10–21.

Jurkowitsch, S., Vignali, C. and Kaufmann, H.R. (2006). A student satisfaction model for Austrian higher education providers considering aspects of marketing communications. *Innovative Marketing*, 2(3), 9–23.

Kara, A. and DeShields, O.W. (2004). Business student satisfaction, intentions and retention in higher education: An empirical investigation. *Marketing Educator Quarterly*, 3(1), 1–25.

Kaufmann, H.R. and Shams, S.M.R. (Eds.). (2015). *Entrepreneurial challenges in the 21st century: Creating stakeholder value co-creation.* Hampshire, UK: Palgrave Macmillan.

Kotler, P. and Clarke, R.N. (2012). *Marketing for health care organizations.* New Jersey: Prentice-Hall.

Lamport, M.A. (1993). Student-faculty interaction and the effect on college student outcomes: A review of the literature. *Adolescence, 28*(112), 971.

Lovelock, C.H., Patterson, P.G. and Walker, R.H. (2001). *Services Marketing: An AsiaPacific Perspective.* 2nd ed. Sydney: Prentice Hall.

Michael, S.O. (1997). American higher education system: consumerism versus professorialism. *International Journal of Educational Management, 11*(3), 117–130.

Mishra, S. (2007). *Quality assurance in higher education: An introduction.* Vancouver: National Assessment and Accreditation Council, India and commonwealth of Learning.

Mostafa, M.M. (2006). A comparison of SERVQUAL and IP analysis: Measuring and improving service quality in Egyptian private universities. *Journal of Marketing for Higher Education, 16*(2), 83–104.

Murray, K. (1991). A test of services marketing theory: consumer information acquisition activities. *Journal of Marketing,* 55 (1), 10–25.

De Oliveira, O.J. and Ferreira, E.C. (2009). Adaptation and application of the SERVQUAL scale in higher education. In Proceedings of POMS 20th Annual Conference Orlando, Florida USA.

Owlia, M.S. and Aspinwall, E.M. (1996). A framework for the dimensions of quality in higher education. *Quality Assurance in Education, 4*(2), 12–20.

Parasuraman, A., Zeithaml, V.A. and Berry, L.L. (1985). A conceptual model of service quality and its implications for future research. *Journal of Marketing,* 49 (4), 41–50.

Peters, T.J. (1988). Individual attention: The key to keeping students in school. *ACU-1 Bulletin,* pp.4–8.

Richins, M.L. (1983). Negative Word of Mouth by Dissatisfied Consumers: A Pilot Study. *Journal of Marketing, 47,* 68–78.

Rossi, M., Vrontis, D. and Thrassou, A., (2014). Agro Business in a Changing Competitive Environment – Campania firms' strategic, marketing and financial choices. *World Review of Entrepreneurship, Management and Sustainable Development,* 10 (2), 321–333.

Shams, S.M.R. (2011). A relationship marketing model to enable sustainable growth of the Bangladesh Cricket Board: A stakeholder causal scope analysis (doctoral thesis). Rockhampton: Central Queensland University.

Shams, S.M.R. (2015a). Branding destination image: A stakeholder causal scope analysis for internationalisation of destinations. *Tourism Planning & Development, 13* (2), 140–153.

Shams, S.M.R. (2015b). Stakeholders' perceptions and reputational antecedents: A review of stakeholder relationships, reputation and brand positioning. *Journal of Advances in Management Research, 12* (3), 314–329.

Shams, S.M.R. (2016a). Capacity building for sustained competitive advantage: A conceptual framework. *Marketing Intelligence & Planning, 34* (5), 671–691.

Shams, S.M.R. (2016b). Sustainability issues in transnational education service: A conceptual framework and empirical insights. *Journal of Global Marketing, 29* (3), 139–155.

124 *Demetris Vrontis et al.*

Shams, S.M.R. and Kaufmann, H.R. (2016). Entrepreneurial co-creation: A research vision to be materialized. *Management Decision, 54* (6), 1250–1268.

Shams, S.M.R. and Lombardi, R. (2016). Socio-economic value co-creation and sports tourism: Evidence from Tasmania. *World Review of Entrepreneurship, Management & Sustainable Development, 12* (2–3), 218–238.

Spreng, R.A. and Mackoy, R.D. (1996). An empirical examination of a model of perceived service quality and satisfaction. *Journal of Retailing, 72*(2), 201–214.

Tajeddini, K. (2011). Customer orientation, learning orientation, and new service development: an empirical investigation of the Swiss hotel industry. *Journal of Hospitality & Tourism Research, 35*(4), 437–468.

Tan, K.C. and Kek, S.W. (2004). Service quality in higher education using an enhanced SERVQUAL approach. *Quality in Higher Education, 10*(1), 17–24.

Tinto, V. (1987). *Leaving college: Rethinking the causes and cures of student attrition.* Chicago: University of Chicago Press.

Trequattrini, R., Shams, R., Lardo, A. and Lombardi, R. (2016). Risk of an epidemic impact when adopting the Internet of Things: The role of sector-based resistance. *Business Process Management Journal, 22* (2), 403–419.

Vrontis, D., Thrassou, A. and Melanthiou, Y. (2007). A contemporary higher education student-choice model for developed countries. *Journal of Business Research, 60*(9), 979–989.

Walter, S.A. (2006). *Antecedentes da satisfação e da lealdade de alunos de uma instituição de ensino superior. 2006. 167 f* (Doctoral dissertation, Dissertação (Mestrado em Administração)–Programa de Pós-Graduação em Administração, Centro de Ciências Sociais Aplicadas, Universidade Regional de Blumenau, Blumenau).

Wright, R.E. (1996). Quality factors in higher education: The students' viewpoint. *College Student Journal, 30,* 269–271.

Zineldin, M. (2007). The quality of higher education and student satisfaction self-assessment and review process a trm philosophy and 5Qs model. In Second International Conference Education, Economics, and Law: Traditions and Innovations. Växjö University, Sweden. Available at: http://tempus.ulim.md/proj_dis.php

9 Relationship marketing and entrepreneurial innovation

A B2B context of stakeholder relationship management

Hasina Idris and S. M. Riad Shams

Introduction

Relationship marketing (RM) as a stakeholder relationship value-centred approach of the contemporary marketing practices ensures the mutually beneficial stakeholder relationships and interactions, while the stakeholders work interdependently toward reciprocally advantageous multifarious goals. Incorporating the traditional 4Ps, RM extends a long-term commitment and relationship bond among the associated stakeholders/business partners to nurture the mutually beneficial stakeholder relationship value, with the aim of innovating further product/service value for customers and share that innovated/enhanced value among the stakeholders. From this context, this study focuses on analysing the entrepreneurial initiatives of the England and Wales Cricket Board (ECB) and their inter-organisational (business partners') mutually beneficial relationship value, cause and consequence of their relationships and interactions and the impact of RM on their business-to-business (B2B) interactions, while they work interdependently in order to align and/or realign their wider B2B strategies and marketing processes through a planned and organised product/service innovation process for their target markets, with the aim of optimising their B2B relationship and its further potentials of value innovation and economic growth.

Eleven RM perspectives emerge as value-innovating RM perspectives from the ECB's entrepreneurial initiatives. The ECB has been utilising these RM perspectives to innovate product/service value for customers through the underlying mutually beneficial relationship value of their partners. Such a B2B service innovation approach of ECB appears to be feasible across markets and industries.

Evaluative viewpoint

Relationship marketing (RM) and mutually beneficial relationship value

RM focuses on rational perspectives of business management, while centralising the cause and consequence of stakeholders' mutual relationships

126 *Hasina Idris and S. M. Riad Shams*

and interactions (Shams, 2012a; Evangelista et al., 2015; Shams, 2017a). RM engages the key stakeholders to work interdependently to align and/or realign processes in order to pursue their mutually beneficial multifarious goals and subsequent relational value. Primarily, there is a continual and mutually beneficial attempt to pursue the associated stakeholders' multifarious goals towards a cooperative and prolific relationship/partnership, and an understanding of long-term commitment (Tomer, 1998).

This long-term commitment originates a bond among the business partners, which gradually becomes more valuable and forms a chain of relationships (Gordon, 1998) among the involved stakeholders. Underlying this valuable chain of relationships, the associated stakeholders establish, maintain and enhance their mutually beneficial relationship value through their joint power in order to collectively sustain their competitive advantage. The inter-organisational mutually beneficial relationship value enables the involved organisations (external stakeholders) to align and/or realign their business processes in a way that helps them to rely on each other in order to work interdependently based on their initial understanding and joint power towards a win-win outcome. In fact, underlying this mutually beneficial relationship value of the concerned stakeholders, RM helps them to mutually create value for customers through innovated product/service value, and share that innovated value among themselves in a venture (Gordon, 1998). More specifically, RM systemises the

> Mutually beneficial relationship value and multifarious goals of associated stakeholders, while the stakeholders work interdependently in order to (identify) establish, maintain and enhance (regulate and sustain) value for customers by meeting and exceeding customers' anticipation (needs) in a way that (the targeted) customers expect and accept, and share that value with the involved stakeholders towards a win-win outcome.
>
> (Shams, 2012a, p. 244).

Consequently, creating mutually beneficial superior relational value for all associated stakeholders, including customers is a crucial factor of the contemporary business practices in order to sustainably retain and enhance relational bonds (Shams, 2012b; Shams, 2017b; Trequattrini et al., 2016). However, it requires a logical long-term outlook to let the associated stakeholders know what they can expect from an organisation and be sure that the organisation will deliver the promised/contracted value to the stakeholders. When such a mutual understanding will be established among the associated stakeholders, it would be convenient to sustain that relational bond (Sanchez et al., 2012). RM works from this viewpoint incorporating the traditional 4Ps of marketing management philosophy and including logical flow of long-term outlook from a stakeholder relationship management perspective (Gummesson, 2002), while the associated stakeholders work interdependently toward mutually beneficial

Stakeholder relationships in a B2B context   127

multifarious goals in order to innovate value for customers and share that innovated value among the key stakeholders to enhance their mutually beneficial relational value.

As a result, relationships and value networks structure the vertebrae of businesses in B2B marketing (Håkansson, 1982; Håkansson and Lundgren, 1995; Håkansson et al., 2009, as cited in Zolkiewski, Story and Burton, 2012), particularly when innovating (identify, establish, maintain, enhance, regulate and sustain) mutually beneficial relational value. Value is defined as, "what customers (and other stakeholders) receive in comparison to what they give" (Ioannou, 2012, p. 170). More expressively,

> Value is perceived as an anticipated outcome of any sort of planned and organized activity. The activity could be derived from monetary, psychic, or physical resources. The more the outcome meets initial anticipation, the more the possibility of win-win outcomes or value optimization for all involved stakeholders.
>
> (Shams, 2012a, p. 244; 2012b, p. 263)

Mutually beneficial relationship value to entrepreneurial innovation in a B2B setting

From this perspective, aiming for an anticipated outcome (for example, the result of a prospective value innovation for customers) of any sort of planned and organised product/service development/re-development activity of the business partners/associated stakeholders, RM integrates their inter-reliant relational bond and their mutually beneficial relational value, towards an innovative effort of the stakeholders to attain and enhance the anticipated outcome with a win-win viewpoint for all associated stakeholders, in order to sustain their competitive advantage. Innovation is considered as a "process of value creation, through the implementation and setting of one or several ideas" (Chebbi et al., 2013, p. 267), where the mutually beneficial relationship value of the associated stakeholders plays a crucial role in organising the setting and implementation of ideas from an inter-organisational perspective, in order to mutually innovate further value for the target markets, and share that innovated value among the involved stakeholders. Accordingly, Ritter and Gemünden (2003) described that organisations that have resolute relationships with the associated stakeholders (internal and external) are able to generate more possibility to gain greater product/service and process innovation success. For the purpose of this study, innovation is recognised as:

> (…) a firm's tendency to engage in and support new ideas, novelty, experimentation and creative processes that may result in new products, services or technological processes. Innovativeness represents a basic willingness to depart from existing practices and venture beyond the current state

of the art (in order to sustain the competitive advantage underlying the innovation).

(Lumpkin and Dess, 1996, p. 142, as cited in Vrontis et al., 2012, pp. 422–423).

Again, Chebbi et al. (2013, p. 274) described that "innovation requires the mobilisation of customers, as well as partners" (associated stakeholders), in order to extend an organisation's capacity to engage in and support new ideas, novelty, experimentation and creative processes to innovate new products or services for customers. As a consequence, the mutually beneficial inter-organisational relationship value among the associated stakeholders/business partners, underlying the cause and consequence of their relationships and interactions, stimulates the involved stakeholders to work interdependently and clarifies what they can expect from each other, while the business partners mutually identify, establish, maintain and enhance creative ideas to innovate and promote new products or services for their target markets (Rossi et al., 2014; Christofi et al., 2015a, 2015b, 2017; Conta et al., 2015; Festa et al., 2017). Consequently, innovation originates knowledge through the use and execution of those creative ideas of new products and/or services (Van de Ven et al., 1989, as cited in Vrontis et al., 2012), and that innovated knowledge further adds to the stakeholders' initial mutually beneficial relationship value to augment their competitive advantage. Furthermore Vrontis et al. (2012, p. 423) cited Bresciani et al. (2011),

Innovation is in fact, an important strategic resource that companies use to achieve competitive advantage. Innovation is inevitably also an element that researchers use to define and evaluate businesses' wider strategies and specific marketing processes. It is ultimately a crucial point in the effort to understand the capabilities of companies, their procedural capacities and potential in terms of surviving and competing in the global economy.

(Vrontis et al., 2012, p. 423)

Indeed, successful innovation drives growth and wealth creation (Barringer and Ireland, 2008, as cited in Vrontis et al., 2012; Shams et al., 2017; Santoro et al., 2017) by integrating an organisation's market (internal and external stakeholders) orientation and capabilities to influence the target market in a way where the mutually innovated product/service meets or exceeds the market needs (Banterle et al., 2010; Shams, 2016a). As a result, an organisation's capabilities to optimise the potentials of the cause and consequence of their stakeholders' (inter-organisational) relationships and interactions appear to be a central force of successful product/service innovation from the B2B context. Further, "network competence (favourable cause and consequence of stakeholders' relationships and interactions and their subsequent mutually beneficial relationship value) has a strong positive influence on the extent of interorganizational (B2B) collaborations

Stakeholder relationships in a B2B context 129

and on a firm's product and process innovation success" (Ritter and Gemünden, 2003, p. 745). Indeed, the participatory co-creation/co-innovation approach of the involved stakeholders "enables to understand and respond and reduces the inherent risks of innovation" (Maklan et al., 2008, p. 221). Moreover, the inter-organisational interactions between the business partners in the B2B markets enhance the bonds among the associated stakeholders that make it difficult to terminate the stakeholders' relationships (Wilson, 1995).

On the other hand, an enterprising entrepreneurial culture is the pre-cursor of business success and a crucial determinant for overall economic performance (Hundley and Hansen, 2012; Kaufmann and Shams, 2015). As a consequence, recognising how the entrepreneurial culture nurtures an entre-preneurial mindset that encourages a firm and their allied stakeholders to engage in and mutually support new ideas, novelty, experimentation, creative proposition and other key elements of the overall innovation process within a value network that helps to mutually innovate value and ultimately facilitates business success and ensures favourable economic performance is an impera-tive consideration for entrepreneurial innovation in the B2B setting.

> Entrepreneurial mindset refers to a specific state of mind which orientates human conduct towards entrepreneurial activities and outcomes. Individuals with entrepreneurial mindsets are often drawn to opportun-ities, innovation and new value creation. Characteristics include the ability to take calculated risks and accept the realities of change and uncertainty.
> (*The Financial Times*, 2014, np)

Consequently, entrepreneurial innovation in the B2B setting could be acknowledged as the initiatives of an entrepreneurial mindset or an entre-preneurial organisation to manipulate the resources of the associated stakeholders of a value network in a way that creates/co-creates value through product and/or service innovation, in order to supplement an existing utility of an entity or to create new utility that meets and/or exceeds the target market's anticipation. However, the rewarding value innovation and delivery process to the ultimate consumers does not rely only on an organisation's or its entrepreneur's inspired effort. Stakeholders, the most important associates of a value-delivery network, and their significant contributions are certainly required for a win-win outcome for all parties involved in the innovation pro-cess. Therefore, a well-organised, mutually beneficial relational value man-agement process of the associated stakeholders is a significant concern of an entrepreneurial organisation to integrate the co-innovation route into the value innovation incubator, where the key stakeholders work interdependently toward their mutually beneficial multifarious goals, in order to co-innovate value and share that co-innovated value with the allied stakeholders (Shams and Kaufmann, 2016). Indeed, stakeholder relationship value management appears as an antecedent of entrepreneurial innovation in the B2B setting.

From these perspectives, the focus of this study is to analyse the case of the England and Wales Cricket Board (ECB), as an entrepreneurial organisation and their inter-organisational (business partners') mutually beneficial relationship value, cause and consequence of their relationships and interactions and the impact of relationship marketing on their B2B interactions, while they work interdependently in order to align and/or realign their wider B2B strategies and marketing processes through a planned and organised product and/or service innovation for their target markets, with the aim of optimising their B2B relationship and its further potentials of innovation and growth. Value is recognised as a vital element of strategic and procedural innovation (Vrontis et al., 2012), where the mobilisation of the business partners (also from a B2B context) and their significant contribution to the value network is crucial for successful innovation (Chebbi et al., 2013).

Relevant research gap, aim and method of the study

Maklan et al. (2008) cited from Roberts et al. (2005) that focusing on the progressive participatory approach to stakeholder relationships and interactions, contemporary business management is more and more endorsing stakeholders' engagement towards their mutual contribution to value innovation/creation in order to survive and prosper. The earlier analysis of this chapter reveals that underlying the RM approach of the contemporary marketing and the cause and consequence of stakeholders' relationships and interactions, their mutually beneficial relationship value extends a vital utility to collaboratively innovate products/services that reflect through the market needs and facilitate organisational growth, while minimising the risk of innovation. However, Lagrosen (2005) described that the recognised courses of action of stakeholder engagement and involvement are still rather limited. Therefore, innovative organisations are from their experience and anticipation, promoting their relationships and interactions to both internal and external stakeholders, because these stakeholders have a superior influence to identify, establish, maintain, evaluate and enhance product/service innovation (Maklan et al., 2008) for their target markets. Likewise Weerawardena (2003) prescribed that

> The new research agenda must explore the role of distinctive marketing capabilities as they relate to innovative and entrepreneurial firm behaviour. However, the literature on the role of marketing capabilities (that extend innovation) in competitive strategy has been limited. Similarly there have been inadequacies in the conceptualization and operationalization of innovation and sustained competitive advantage constructs (or variables).
> (Weerawardena, 2003, p. 15)

More specifically in the B2B context, various cross-functional business and management procedures that impel stakeholders' contemporary relationships and interactions, challenge the existing understanding of stakeholders' decision making processes (Maklan et al., 2008). From these perspectives, the aim of this study is to contribute to our current understanding of stakeholders' relationships and interactions of an entrepreneurial organisation (in this case, the ECB), and the implications of RM against various inter-organisational business management procedures through such relationships and interactions. The purpose here is to leverage various relational (RM) perspectives that engage the associated stakeholders to work interdependently in a B2B setting, in an attempt to mutually create value for customers through innovated product/service offerings, where such an innovation extends entrepreneurial initiatives, organisational marketing capabilities and growth and meet and/or exceed the needs of the associated stakeholders, including the customers.

In order to attain this aim, the study adopts a qualitative case study method, utilising a single case, the ECB's entrepreneurial initiatives and their relationships and interactions with their key stakeholders/ business partners. Case studies comprise a comprehensive method and are one of the most common ways to do qualitative research (Stake, 2000), especially when the focus is on contemporary phenomena within some real-life context (Yin, 2003, 2009). In essence, case studies have a clear place in research and most importantly provide a way to explain the causal links in real-life interventions that are too complex for the survey or experimental strategies (Gomm et al., 2001; Yin, 2003, 2009). Consequently, based on the contemporary phenomenon within the real-life B2B context and the causal links between the interventions of the cause and consequence of the stakeholders' relationships and interactions of the ECB, another purpose of studying the ECB value network is because ECB has been experiencing steady growth in recent years, where their stakeholder-focused entrepreneurial initiatives help them to prolifically utilise the cause and consequence of their stakeholders' relationships and interactions, in order to facilitate the following issues for them:

- Engaging the ECB's stakeholders to work interdependently to align and/ or realign business processes to pursue their multifarious goals.
- Stimulating the mutually beneficial relationship value of the ECB stakeholders through their interdependence to mobilise the cause and consequence of their relationships and interactions in order to co-innovate products/services for their customers from a B2B context.
- The innovated product/service facilitates the transformation from the existing practice of ECB to a new state-of-the-art, value-centred and stakeholder engaging business practice that favourably contributes to their product/service innovation from a B2B context, as well as ensuring their steady growth, where the innovated product/service meets the needs of the associated stakeholders.

The study utilises scholarly literature and media contents review in depth. Creswell (1998) described that case studies are analysed by making a "...

132   Hasina Idris and S. M. Riad Shams

detailed description of the case and its settings" (p. 78). Stavros (2005) suggests that the issues, concepts and variables from a case would be useful to pursue the aim of the study, where the "...insight, intuition and impression" (Dey, 1995, p. 78) of the collected data are important components of analysis. Accordingly, a pattern is adapted for analysing the cause and consequence of ECB's entrepreneurial initiatives and their stakeholders' relationships and interactions, where the prospective variables/constructs (various RM perspectives) identified from the case have been analysed through insight, intuition and impression for comprehending the impact of the identified variables/constructs on the aim of the study. For example, how various RM perspectives extend the ECB's entrepreneurial initiatives and nurture their inter-organisational (among the key stakeholders) business management procedures through the cause and consequence of their stakeholder relationships and interactions, and engage the key stakeholders and business partners to work interdependently from a B2B context in order to innovate products/services for their target markets from a win-win perspective.

The case of the England and Wales Cricket Board (ECB)

Building partnership as a stakeholder relationship value-driven initiative

The Chief Executive Officer of the ECB clarified the goals of the Building Partnership (2009), which is a five year strategic plan framework as: ECB needs to acclimatise as a customer/stakeholder-focused organisation by promoting relationship and service values, while reducing bureaucracy (Collier, 2009). The Building Partnership gives a clear, focused and assessable target for ECB and its business partners to meet that goal. ECB have set out the following areas where they need improvements in order to adapt to the transforming business requirements (Building Partnership, 2009):

- improve accountability;
- streamline management;
- slash paperwork and bureaucracy;
- performance management;
- efficiency;
- commercial awareness.

ECB wanted to promote trust with stakeholders by efficient communication, service and reduced bureaucracy in order to establish long-term stakeholder commitment and subsequent relationship bond (Gide and Shams, 2011a). Therefore, ECB endeavours to let their stakeholders know what they can expect from ECB and be sure that ECB will deliver. At the beginning of 2008, ECB established a communication system by which 80% of their communication can be done online to reduce paperwork and bureaucracy (Building Partnership, 2009). To achieve the Building Partnership goals, ECB has adapted a more customer and other stakeholder value-driven culture by implementing relationship and service values instead of bureaucratic legal values.

ECB's initiative towards organisational change through the Building Partnership (2009), including stakeholder management, helps ECB to adapt to contemporary business challenges, focusing on promoting mutually beneficial stakeholder relationship value with their key stakeholders. ECB prioritises the type of stakeholders and the relevance of individual stakeholder's significance to their financial and other operational goals, with the aim of a value-innovating win-win outcome for all associated stakeholders (Building Partnership, 2009). Such an adaptation and relationship and service value-centred RM initiative allows ECB to put into practice the competitive product or service innovation opportunities for their target markets in association with their key stakeholders. ECB's initiative to create a customer/stakeholder-driven organisation, reducing bureaucracy, and defining roles and responsibilities clearly across their business as a whole (Building Partnership, 2009), offers the opportunity to innovate new and more dynamic services for ECB's stakeholders, including their customers.

Moreover, ECB's initiatives (Building Partnership, 2009) of improving the way the game is led, through effectual leadership and governance, building a vibrant domestic game, enthusing participation and following, especially among young people, developing successful England teams, ECB's continuous innovative effort on developing partnerships across various industries as per the needs of the ECB and the potential partners and ECB's Focus Club and Clubmark approach of partnership with the cricket clubs across England and Wales are nothing, but the modification of ECB's existing services with new and different characteristics that innovates additional benefits/value for the target markets of ECB and their commercial and operational partners. As a result, such an initiative to modify the existing service with more value-oriented stakeholder relationship and interaction helps these key stakeholders to realise their latent mutually beneficial relationship value that may be originated and utilised through the cause and consequence of business relationships and interactions with ECB, focusing to create value for their target market and sharing that value among themselves (Shams, 2011, 2012a).

ECB categorises their sponsors and partners into seven different business requirements and opportunities, which helps them analyse how to best serve the partners, as well as bring out the most value from the partners, aiming to foster certain business requirements and subsequent relational value (Commercial Partners, 2010). Moreover, such a further segmentation of a segmented market or niche marketing (the different categories and sub-categories of sponsorship and partnership requirements and opportunities) helps ECB to realise the different needs of their businesses and creatively niche those needs by identifying and offering innovative mutually beneficial relational value to the sponsors and business partners towards a further value innovation process for their (ECB and its partners) target markets.

Broadcasting partners

Sky Sports (2010) have exclusive live broadcast rights to all international cricket played under the auspices of the ECB. They also have exclusive live broadcast rights to all domestic competitions. Sky Sports sponsors ECB's Coach Education Programme too. Channel Five (2010), BBC Radio (2010) and talkSPORT (2010) radio are ECB's other co-broadcast partners. ECB is able to innovate further services to develop their coaches as another key stakeholder through the joint power and effort of their broadcasting partners. Moreover, ECB sub-segments the broadcasting partnership segment of the total partnership market into television and radio broadcasting sub-segments, wherein the partners realise the significance of mutually beneficial relational value by associating with ECB's businesses (Shams, 2011).

Team sponsors

Brit Insurance (2010) is the official team sponsor of ECB. Brit Insurance's logo appears on the England teams' shirts. Brit Insurance (2010) demonstrates the significance of mutually beneficial relational value with the ECB as, "our association with cricket is an excellent way to increase the profile of Brit Insurance with those that purchase and advise on business insurance" (np). More discussion on ECB's insurance partnership is presented in the 'other partners' section (pp. 000–000). ECB also sub-segments their team sponsorships with other partnership opportunities.

Competition sponsors

Leading energy supplier Npower (2010) has been sponsoring all domestic international test cricket since 2001 and their agreement ran up to 2013. Npower will continue to enjoy significant commercial access to the England team, as well as an extensive package of rights including ticketing at test matches and image rights. The deal will also provide Npower with the opportunity to build a greater brand presence at test match venues through advertising, branding and sampling. Npower (2010) will also continue its successful grassroots initiative to spread cricket around the UK, Npower Urban Cricket, which it runs in partnership with the ECB. These initiatives provide a permanent and safe space for children to learn the basics of cricket, aiming to increase participation and leave a long-term, sustainable legacy for the sport. Kevin Miles, Chief Executive of Npower Retail described the scheme:

> We're delighted to announce our continued sponsorship: to be at the heart of the game for eleven years is something we can be extremely proud of. Our Urban Cricket initiative continues to go from strength to strength. Renewing our contract ensures future investment in this scheme, which is vital for the development of cricket from playground to test arena.

From a brand perspective, not only has our cricket sponsorship provided us with great visibility, it has also provided a strong marketing platform for our other products and services like our gas boiler installation service, Npower home team. We're already looking forward to the next two seasons.

(Shams, 2012b, p. 253; Npower 2010, np)

ECB chief executive David Collier added, "its (Npower) Urban Cricket initiative has helped give thousands of children across the country a chance to play cricket for the first time" (Npower 2010, np). LV= (2010), the insurance and investment group, has been sponsoring English county cricket since 2002; they renewed the contract with ECB and announced that they will continue their sponsorship. ECB Chief Executive, David Collier described the renewal of the sponsorship contract:

This renewal underlines the benefits that sponsorship can bring to commercial partners. This announcement is fantastic news for domestic cricket, and LV's continued support will play a key role in the future success of our national summer sport.

(LV=, 2010, np)

LV=chief executive Mike Rogers added:

Our sponsorship of the LV County Championship has proved very successful in getting our message across to cricket fans far and wide. We look forward to strengthening our partnership with the ECB.

(LV=, 2010, np)

Friends Provident (2010), the life and pensions company, is proud to be a long-term domestic competition sponsor of ECB. Following three successful years as the title sponsor of the domestic fifty-over competition, the sponsorship of the ECB's new enhanced Twenty20 competition provides a natural evolution for Friends Provident and its involvement in domestic cricket. Friends Provident also supports Chance to Shine (a cricket development programme of ECB), the Cricket Foundation's campaign to regenerate competitive cricket in state schools, and the Professional Cricketer's Association.

NatWest (2010), part of the Royal Bank of Scotland Group, has been a major sponsor of English cricket for more than twenty-five years. Over the last two decades more than £35 million has been invested into the game both at international and grassroots levels. This includes the highly successful NatWest Interactive Road show and NatWest Speed Stars competition, the Interactive Cricket Programme taking cricket into secondary schools, the Volunteers in Cricket initiative, as well as the innovative "Sun Safety–Don't get caught out" campaign to raise awareness of skin cancer in the UK.

136   *Hasina Idris and S. M. Riad Shams*

Clydesdale Bank and Yorkshire Bank (2010) sponsor the Twenty20 Cup, which is hosted by ECB. The partnership continues to support cricket at all levels of the game. Gareth Johnson, Promotions Executive for Clydesdale Bank and Yorkshire Bank, explains:

> Our support for Twenty20 continues to generate great feedback from our customers and our employees – the pace and energy of this form of the game is something that we can all identify with.
>
> (Clydesdale Bank and Yorkshire Bank, 2010, np)

Other partners

Buxton (2010) Natural Mineral Water is the official water supplier to the England cricket team. As part of the agreement Buxton provides the England cricket team with bottled mineral water to be used during all home international matches and training sessions. ECB commercial director John Perera described the partnership:

> We feel there is an excellent brand fit between Buxton and the England Cricket Team and are confident this partnership will further demonstrate that cricket can have a positive impact in a business (B2B) environment.
>
> (Buxton, 2010, np)

Paolo Sangiorgi, Nestlé Waters UK Managing Director, commented:

> Buxton and the ECB share several important mutual characteristics, a rich heritage and a strong sense of Britishness – and this is why we believe our new sponsorship deal will work so well. Buxton has always used strong sports associations to increase its awareness and promote healthy and active lifestyles, and we are confident that the new partnership will benefit everyone.
>
> (Buxton, 2010, np)

Hewitt Associates (2010), a global human resources services company with offices in thirty-five countries, is proud to be an official Human Resource Management Partner of the ECB.

> Maximising human resources is what Hewitt is all about. Cricket, while a team sport thrives on the importance of specialist skills and individual strengths as key elements of success – just as ECB does at Hewitt.
>
> (Hewitt Associates, 2010, np)

Through this partnership, Hewitt can reach out to employees, clients, associates and a wide range of ECB's stakeholders and audiences. As one of the commercial partners of the ECB, the Hewitt name will be a fixture at some of the world's most famous grounds. Marshall Wooldridge Ltd, a general and financial services insurance company is the insurance partner of ECB (ECB Extra Cover Insurance, nd). In the partnership with Marshall Wooldridge Ltd, ECB provides discounted Extra Cover (2010) to its affiliated Focus Clubs and Clubmark clubs as an official insurance scheme. The ECB strongly recommends all affiliated clubs to consider the Extra Cover scheme to protect their assets and overcome liabilities. Extra Cover is the ideal way for cricket clubs to insure against a wide range of risks, all in one simple policy. It provides a flexible and customised range of cover designed solely for cricket clubs around the UK, who are one of the target markets of Marshall Wooldridge, as well as the key stakeholders of the ECB in order to spread cricket more widely.

Suppliers

Maximuscle, the UK leader in sports nutrition, was the official partner of ECB for sports nutritional products up to the end of 2010 (Cricket World, 2010). Maximuscle and the ECB worked at new methods to improve performance with Maximuscle providing proven products like Viper and Recovermax, offering expert advice from their team of nutritionists and creating new sports nutrition solutions to the rigorous demands of international cricket. According to James O'Shea, Marketing Director for Maximuscle (Cricket World, 2010, np): "this is an exciting opportunity for Maximuscle to showcase the virtues of sports nutrition to anyone looking to improve their performance".

Grassroots and recreational partners

ASDA (2010), the leading European conglomerate corporate house is ECB's grassroots level's development partner. More discussion is presented on this in the following sub-section. On the other hand, Npower (2010) and NatWest (2010) extended their partnership with the ECB into ECB's grassroots level development and recreational activities along with their competition sponsorship. Again, as a broadcast partner of ECB, Sky Sports (2010) extended their support to ECB into ECB's recreational activities.

ECB Focus Club, ECB Clubmark and partnership with schools

ECB develops school and junior cricket and other local cricket through ECB affiliated Focus Clubs around the UK.

> Affiliation to the ECB allows clubs and, where appropriate, leagues to access a range of tangible benefits. Affiliation is via the County Board within whose area the club or League is based. We provide those benefits

centrally by the ECB – individual County Boards will provide additional benefits and may charge additional affiliation fees for these benefits.

(Play Cricket Making A Difference, 2006, p. 10)

Centrally and regionally through the regional County Boards, ECB provides guidance, resources, development planning and initiatives, technical and expertise support for business and game development to these affiliated Focus Clubs in association with their sponsors and commercial partners (Shams, 2011; Play Cricket Making A Difference 2006). Furthermore, in return for this huge amount of support, ECB's regional County Boards charge an affiliation fee to the clubs. ECB provides this support to the clubs through their prolific relationship with their sponsors and partners, which helps to develop cricket country-wide, as well as helps sponsors and commercial partners to meet their business targets. Simultaneously, ECB and their regional county bodies earn additional revenue from the club affiliation fees. This shows that only through the cause and consequence of stakeholder relationships development and maintenance initiatives and subsequent interactions, ECB has been increasing their revenue and innovating the routes for growth through their innovated services to the affiliated clubs.

There are in excess of 1,400 Focus Clubs which have been strategically identified across England and Wales. On average each Focus Club will work in partnership with four schools and one community group. This equates to over 5,600 schools and 1,400 community groups. On the other hand, the ECB Clubmark is a motivational programme for the Focus Clubs, which boosts the competition among the Focus Clubs to achieve and support from ECB and set an example for other Focus Clubs. These Focus Clubs are currently registered and actively working towards the ECB Clubmark. More than 850 Focus Clubs have achieved the prestigious ECB Clubmark accreditation by putting in place and maintaining the required minimum operating standards for community club cricket (Play Cricket Making A Difference, 2006). Under the Clubmark (2010) scheme, with the partnership of the UK Government department Sport England, ECB and cricket clubs can play a key role in building partnerships with the key stakeholders by supporting the delivery and implementation of various businesses, promotional and operational activities. A Focus Club has to meet the criteria of seven steps to obtain and maintain the prestigious ECB Clubmark status (ECB Clubmark Process, 2010).

ECB always encourages the affiliated Focus Clubs and Clubmark clubs to have their own sponsors and commercial partners from local and national businesses to get sufficient funds to run the clubs. For this, ECB helps the clubs through their expert sponsorship marketing guidelines, as well as helping the clubs to get grant aid through their Sources of Grant Aid and Funding for Cricket Clubs (2009) publication.

ECB is concerned to develop and nurture cricket talent from grassroots level for which they established and maintain partnerships with schools through country-wide local ECB Focus Clubs and Clubmark Clubs. ECB introduced cricket activities for primary and secondary school boys and girls (Cricket in Partnership with Education, 2010) in partnership with their grassroots partner ASDA (2009; 2010) and the local ECB affiliated clubs. ASDA works in partnership with the ECB to develop and implement two major campaigns designed to use ASDA Kwik Cricket as a vehicle to educate children about the benefits of healthy living and also raise the profile of the sport within communities. A core element of these campaigns will involve the ECB, in conjunction with the eighteen first-class County bodies, and ASDA establishing a series of recreational junior cricket festivals across the country. This will also include new girls' tournaments aimed at increasing levels of participation. These festivals will be attended by high-profile professional cricketers who, in addition to passing on coaching tips, will also talk to kids about the benefits of healthy eating (ASDA, 2010). ASDA Kwik Cricket is played in 8,000 primary schools and over 4,500 of the 6,000 ECB affiliated clubs. It is designed to provide children, between the ages of 7 and 11, with an introduction to cricket and can be played through various flexible and adaptable ways (ASDA, 2010). Deborah Whitehead, Local Marketing & ASDA in the Community General Manager, said:

> ASDA Kwik Cricket is proving to be very popular with the number of primary schools participating increasing each year. It's perfectly aligned to our strategy to focus on Kids within local communities. In 2008 we added to the program by educating children around the benefits of healthy eating and doing more to support cricket within the local communities.
>
> (ASDA, 2010, np)

ECB's entrepreneurial capabilities explain to their business partners what they can expect from ECB and ECB's logical assurance to their partners ensures that ECB will provide the promised value. Such entrepreneurial capabilities of ECB extend their marketing proficiency. Underlying their partners' and other associated stakeholders' mutually beneficial relationship value, these enhanced entrepreneurial capabilities and marketing proficiencies help them to mutually innovate services for their target markets (all associated stakeholders, including customers) in a planned and organised way that has ensured the economic growth of ECB in recent years. Figure 9.1 shows ECB's growth.

Findings

The favourable remarks of the ECB's partners and sponsors clearly demonstrate the significance of the mutually beneficial relational value of these stakeholders and ECB through their joint initiatives of innovating services for their different target markets. The partners are able to meaningfully innovate and promote their offerings to their target markets while ECB are also able to nurture and innovate further value for their target markets through the

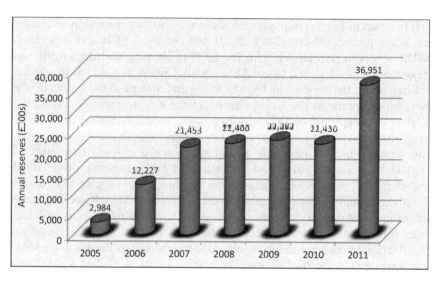

Figure 9.1 Growth in annual reserves of the England and Wales Cricket Board
Source: Annual Report (2012, 2008)

mutually beneficial relational value of their stakeholders. RM-centred value innovation keeps an inquisitive eye on changes that help timely adaptation of the innovation process with any transforming circumstances (Gummesson, 2002) by taking advantage of further opportunity and/or minimising weakness and threat. Accordingly, in order to achieve the Building Partnership goals by prolifically utilising the mutually beneficial stakeholder relationship value with the aim of innovating further value for all of the involved stakeholders' target markets, ECB has adapted a more stakeholder focused culture by implementing relationship and service values instead of bureaucratic legal values. Similarly, Gummesson (2002) further added that RM promotes relationships and service values in a value network rather than bureaucratic legal values. Such a relationships and service value smoothes the progress of joint value innovation processes by promptly responding to the anticipation of the involved stakeholders/business partners and avoiding any bureaucratic complications.

Furthermore, RM entrusts and ensures that all staff members of an organisation (and other external stakeholders, such as business partners) deliver superior service quality to their customers (Kurtz, 2009; Shams, 2016a, 2016b). Likewise, Stavros (2005) summarises that "in RM, it is the responsibility of all employees to promote the quality because RM is not just concerned with relationships administered by a marketing department within an organisation, but with all departments of an organisation" (as cited in Shams, 2012a, p. 224), as well as the associated business partners. Therefore,

Stakeholder relationships in a B2B context 141

quality is the concern of all, as a RM perspective signifies its prominence in value innovation processes for customers, while the dedication and innovative value contribution of all involved stakeholders are encouraged during the service innovation, delivery and evaluation process.

Consequently, the previous analysis in this chapter shows that ECB fund its regional bodies, Focus Clubs and Clubmarks Clubs based on their annual performance, which indicates that ECB promotes quality as the concern of all in their intra-organisation (B2B) practice. ECB introduced the Clubmark status for the Focus Clubs, which can only gain the Clubmark status after fulfilling ECB's standards. Therefore, quality as a concern for all is involved from this perspective too. Moreover, the overall stance towards organisational change from a traditional practice to the more customer/stakeholder driven practice of ECB indicates that high stakeholder service, stakeholder commitment and stakeholder contact are entrenched in ECB's transformed B2B practice, and become the key to ECB's success through their reformed customer/stakeholder driven organisational practice. Likewise, another RM perspective is acknowledged from ECB's organisational change, as high stakeholder service, stakeholder commitment and stakeholder contact. These are the crucial factors of RM (Stavros, 2005; Shams and Belyaeva, 2017) in order to nurture mutually beneficial relational value through superior stakeholder commitment, service (Kurtz, 2009) and contacts. Moreover, RM is based on customers' and other stakeholders/business partners' preferences in terms of innovating alternative products and services value for customers. RM helps to realise customer and other stakeholders' contemporary and latent needs, wants, demands, anticipation and preferences through high stakeholder commitment, contact, interaction and service (Shams, 2011).

The next recognised RM perspective of this study is further segmentation of a segmented market, or niche marketing. "The division of the total market into smaller, relatively homogeneous group is called segmentation" (Kurtz, 2009, p. 28).

> RM helps marketers to identify, meet, satisfy and delight the latent needs of the market by further segmenting of a segmented market. The further segmentation of a segmented market helps to closely realize and serve (design/innovate offering) every single and even smaller needs, wants and demands of the market through niche marketing.
>
> (Shams, 2012a, p. 221)

According to Kotler et al. (2009, p. 228) a "niche is a more narrowly defined segment of a market or customer group seeking a distinctive mix of benefits. Marketers usually identify niches by dividing a segment into sub-segments". As a consequence, the sub-segments of a segmented market of the total target market(s) make convenient to closely scrutinise the alternative needs, wants and demands of the total target market, where the mutually beneficial stakeholder/business partners' relationship value collaboratively engages the stakeholders to advantageously design product or service offerings to meet and delight that needs, wants and demands. As per their business requirements, ECB categorises and sub-categorises their sponsors and partners into seven different segments and underlying sub-segments of the sponsorship and partnership opportunities. Such a further segmentation of a segmented market, or niche marketing (the different categories and sub-categories of sponsorship and partnership requirements), helps ECB to realise the different needs of their businesses and creatively niche those needs by identifying and proffering innovative offerings to the sponsors and commercial partners towards a win-win outcome (Shams and Lombardi, 2016).

Joint power of the associated stakeholders is recognised as a relevant RM perspective that also significantly contributes to the value innovation process. Based on the mutually related trust, commitment and relational bond, RM develops a joint power among the associated stakeholders (Kurtz, 2009), which helps an organisation to utilise the stakeholder/business partners' mutually beneficial relationship value that originates from their relational bond to innovate further value for customers. Likewise, ECB has been developing cricket throughout the UK through the resources and opportunities gained by the joint power of their sponsors and business partners. Simultaneously, in general, sharing of dependency, risk and uncertainty is always involved among the business partners, based on the partnership contract. RM also shares the dependency, risk and uncertainty among the key stakeholders (Gummesson, 2002).

RM inspires B2B interaction based on stakeholder cooperation and trust (Kurtz, 2009). In return, stakeholders are able to share the mutually beneficial relational value at a profit, as well as share any unforeseen risk and uncertainty during the value innovation and delivery process that minimises the risk of innovation. Another RM perspective, "orientation on benefits" or "knowledgeable customers and/or other stakeholders", is involved in ECB's RM practice too. ECB tries to enlighten potential sponsors or business partners about the potential benefits of sponsoring or partnering with ECB, as ECB ensures to let their stakeholders know what ECB can offer them and be sure ECB will deliver that (Building Partnership, 2009). An encouraging approach is likely as part of the stakeholders' relationships and interactions. The relational interaction should be consequential through customers' and/ or other stakeholders' adequate knowledge about the organisation or about the offering (Gummesson, 2002). Client knowledge is positively allied to the quality of relational interaction (Rajaobelina and Bergeron, 2009). Consequently, RM emphasises stakeholders' orientation on benefits about the business with an organisation that helps stakeholders to properly allocate resources in the B2B innovation process. On the other hand, a Value-Breeding Bond (VBB) network is acknowledged as:

> A significant value proliferating network of RM, centred on a steady and continuously re-processable approach "to identify, establish, maintain and enhance value" (Grönroos, 2004, p. 101) within and some

time beyond the value network or group of stakeholders, so that value can be generated repeatedly through the re-productiveness of existing value, while each stakeholder plays some value added role, by way of stakeholders working interdependently towards mutually beneficial, multifarious goals.

(Shams, 2012a, p. 228, 2011, p. 43; Gide and Shams, 2011c, p. 1086)

Similar to the other value-innovating RM perspectives, VBB also shares the mutually beneficial relational value among the key stakeholders/business partners to innovate further value for customers (Shams, 2015a). For example, in the partnership with the sponsors and business partners, ECB provides grassroots cricketing facilities to the ECB affiliated clubs. Based on those facilities, the affiliated clubs continue the cricketing activities among school kids country-wide. Through such ventures, all involved stakeholders are benefiting and breeding further value towards their future interest. Commercial partners and sponsors are gaining promotional advantage by partnering and/or sponsoring ECB, which enhances their potential sales. Again, affiliated clubs are gaining cricketing facilities from ECB and County Boards because of ECB's partnership with their business partners and sponsors, which encourages affiliated clubs' growth too.

Simultaneously, schools throughout the country are gaining the opportunity to involve their students in sports activities, which helps young students to gain sustainable physical fitness from childhood, as well as helps the school to promote their extra-curricular activities. On the other hand, ECB and their regional bodies are gaining club affiliation fees from such ventures too. As a result, the VBB is found in ECB's B2B value innovation process. All of the involved stakeholders are gaining their individual interests through the venture, which breeds further value among the ECB's VBB network. Again, the previous analysis of this chapter shows that ECB and their insurance partner customise various insurance services for ECB's Focus Clubs. RM is based on customers' and other stakeholders/business partners' preferences in terms of innovating alternative products and service value for customers. RM helps to realise customer and other stakeholders' contemporary and latent needs, wants, demands, anticipation and preferences through high stakeholder contact, commitment and interaction.

> RM service providers gain a better knowledge of the client's requirements and needs. This knowledge can then be combined with social rapport built over a number of service encounters to tailor and customize the service to client's specifications.
>
> (Little and Marandi, 2003, as cited in Shams, 2012a, p. 223)

Similarly, Kurtz (2009) illustrated that the level of customisation is advanced in RM, compared with transactional marketing. As a result, customisation is found in ECB's B2B innovation process as another value-innovating RM

144　*Hasina Idris and S. M. Riad Shams*

perspective, which keeps a keen eye on customers' and other stakeholders' requirements, while attempting to innovate value. Furthermore, these value-innovating RM perspectives are also recognised from various intra-disciplinary perspectives that collectively stimulate the associated stakeholders' mutually beneficial relationship value (Shams, 2013, 2012a, 2012b; Gide and Shams, 2012a, 2011b, 2011c; Shams, 2015b).

Discussion and conclusion

The commitment and bond among the ECB's stakeholders, based on ECB's initiative to let their stakeholders know what they can expect from ECB and be sure that ECB will deliver, extend the cause and consequence of relationships and interactions of the stakeholders, alongside their interdependency towards their multifarious goals. The multifarious goals of ECB and their stakeholders could be envisioned from the findings of this chapter. Table 9.1 outlines these multifarious goals.

Based on ECB and their stakeholders' understandings (commitment and bond) of their interdependency and mobilisation to achieve these diverse goals, they identify, establish, maintain and enhance their mutually beneficial relationship value, where this mutual value and initial commitment and bond are inter-reliant too. At this stage, ECB and their stakeholders integrate the needs of their target markets, centred on the implications of the applicable RM perspective(s) through a planned and organised process of alignment/realignment with new ideas, novelty, experimentation and creative input to innovate new services in order to meet those market needs. For example, in association with their grassroots partner (ASDA), ECB engage their country-wide affiliated clubs and schools to nurture young cricket talent nationwide. Following such an idea and relevant planned and organised activities, ECB and their county bodies earn affiliation fees from the affiliated clubs, entrench

Table 9.1 Multifarious goals of ECB and their stakeholders

ECB's goals	*Goals of ECB's stakeholders (business partners)*
Spread cricket across England and Wales	Optimise their brand awareness
Engage more young people in cricket	Maximise their business opportunities
Develop and enhance sustainable infrastructure	Enhance competitive advantage
Build successful national team	Spread their company messages and receive feedback from their target markets
Drive profitable businesses to secure sufficient funds	Promote their products and services
Contribute to various social and communal issues, such as awareness of skin cancer, benefits of healthy eating and so forth	Meet their business targets and so forth

the cricketing facilities at the grassroots level, associated schools are able to enhance their extra-curricular activities, the affiliated clubs can diversify their activities to various age groups, the young people can realise the importance of a sporting and healthy life style from the early stages of their lives and ASDA can promote their offerings to their target markets.

The joint power of all of the associated stakeholders as a fundamental RM perspective of this process and idea stimulates the mutually beneficial relationship value of the involved stakeholders from at least two other RM perspectives. The Focus Clubs have to ensure the quality of their dedication, facilities and support against this venture that ultimately helps them to achieve additional annual funding from ECB by gaining the Clubmark status. Therefore, quality as the concern of all is involved here, alongside the orientation of benefits RM perspective. Prior to sponsoring this idea, ASDA should have had a feasible understanding of what they could expect from ECB through such ventures, i.e. how they could reach their target markets (kids and parents) with their offerings for young people. The win-win outcome was recognised in the remark of the General Manager, Local Marketing & ASDA in the Community (see p. 000). Accordingly, Figure 9.2 portrays this process of B2B product/service innovation, where the evaluation procedure should be linked to the actual outcome of the process.

In terms of managerial and scholarly perspectives, the stakeholder relationship-focused entrepreneurial initiatives for B2B product/service innovation could be applicable and further nurtured from any industry and

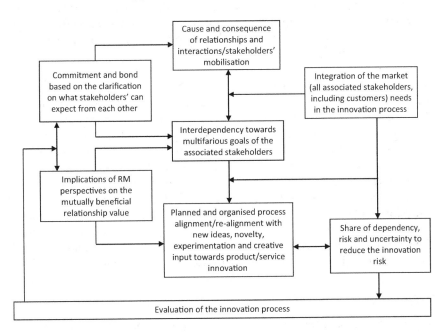

Figure 9.2 Mutually beneficial relationship value-centred B2B innovation process

market setting; however the relationship portfolio should pursue only the given situation of the targeted setting (Gummesson, 2002). Donaldson and O'Toole (2007) showed that the relational approach of marketing has an influence on the innovative product/service development process through the degree of stakeholders' interaction in a network, where RM helps to proffer new and existing ways to innovate products/services, including from the prospective value identification phase to the design phase, product testing phase, product marketing phase and even product life-cycle management phase. Ultimately this identifies alternative routes to enhance the associated stakeholders' mutually beneficial relationship value in order to collectively contribute to the innovation process. Therefore, further theoretical and empirical research in the following areas would be beneficial to augment the findings of this study:

- Correlate even further the concepts of mutually beneficial relationship value, commitment, bond, cause and consequence of relationships and interactions, chain of relationships, creativity, experimentation, innovation, competitive advantage and economic growth.
- Further studies in different markets and industries could strengthen the validity of these RM perspectives, and a broader range of other emerging perspectives could be acknowledged and utilized.
- Further studies on product/service life-cycle management and different stages (value identification phase to the design phase, product testing phase, product marketing phase and so forth) of product/service development and innovation could be studied in order to recognise the impact of the analysed concepts of this chapter on the specific stage of the life of a product/service.

On the other hand, in a world with limited resources, value innovation is perceived as the key to socio-economic development. Entrepreneurial initiative is recognised as an antecedent of this value innovation (Shams, 2016c). Entrepreneurs need to be engaged, from management and marketing to finance and investing and so forth, where entrepreneurs and their stakeholders face challenges, mutually benefit from opportunities and innovate value. Underlying this entrepreneurial perspective, the findings of this chapter could attract inter-disciplinary interests to understand issues from various cross-disciplinary contexts against the cause and consequence of stakeholders' relationships and interactions, in order to mutually innovate value to sustainably respond to socio-economic challenges. Besides the academic interest, further research will also satisfy the need for explicit guidance for practice.

References

ASDA. (2009). ASDA from A to Z, ASDA-saving you money every day. Retrieved from www.asda.co.uk/corp/home.html (accessed 02 February 2010).

ASDA. (2010). England & Wales Cricket Board, ECB partners. Retrieved from www.ecb.co.uk/ecb/partners/asda,949,BP.html (accessed 02 February 2010).

Annual Report. (2012). England & Wales Cricket Board annual report 2012, Annual report including financial statement. Retrieved from http://static.ecb.co.uk/files/1282-ecb-2012-annual-report-digital-12445.pdf (accessed 26 October 2013).

Annual Report. (2008). England & Wales Cricket Board annual report 2008, ECB annual report. Retrieved from http://static.ecb.co.uk/files/ecb-annual-report-2008–10494.pdf (accessed 26 October 2013).

Banterle, A., Cavliere, A., Stranierj, S. and Carraresi, L. (2010). The relationship between innovation and marketing in SMEs in the EU food sector. Paper presented in the International European Forum on System Dynamics and Innovation in Food Networks, 2010 International European Forum, February 8–12, 2010, Innsbruck-Igls, Austria.

BBC Radio. (2010). England & Wales Cricket Board, Commercial partners. Retrieved from www.ecb.co.uk/ecb/partners/bbc-sport,52,BP.html (accessed 02 February 2010).

Brit Insurance. (2010). England & Wales Cricket Board, Commercial partners. Retrieved from www.ecb.co.uk/ecb/partners/brit-insurance,2102,BP.html (accessed 02 February 2010).

Building Partnership. (2009). Cricket's Strategic Plan 2005-2009-From Playground to Test Arena. London: England and Wales Cricket Board.

Buxton. (2010). England & Wales Cricket Board, Commercial partners. Retrieved from www.ecb.co.uk/ecb/partners/buxton-water,1284,BP.html (accessed 03 February 2010).

Channel Five. (2010). England & Wales Cricket Board, Commercial partners. Retrieved from www.ecb.co.uk/ecb/partners/five,952,BP.html (accessed 02 February 2010).

Chebbi, H., Yahiaoui, D., Thrassou, A. and Vrontis, D. (2013). The exploration activity's added value into the innovation process. *Global Business and Economics Review*, *15*, (2/3), 265–277.

Christofi, M., Vrontis, D., Kitchen, P. and Papasolomou, I. (2015a). Innovation and Cause-related Marketing Success: a Conceptual Framework and Propositions. *Journal of Services Marketing*, 29 (5), 354–366.

Christofi, C., Leonidou, E. and Vrontis, D. (2015b). Cause–related Marketing, Product Innovation and Extraordinary Sustainable Leadership: the Root towards Sustainability. *Global Business and Economics Review*, *17* (1), 93–111.

Christofi, M., Leonidou, E. and Vrontis, D. (2017). Marketing Research on Mergers and Acquisitions: a Systematic Review and Future Directions. *International Marketing Review* (published online ahead of print, DOI: 10.1108/IMR-03-2015-0100).

Clubmark. (2010). England & Wales Cricket Board, Clubmark club. Retrieved from www.ecb.co.uk/development/clubs-and-leagues/clubmark/ (accessed 02 February 2010).

Clydesdale Bank and Yorkshire Bank. (2010). England & Wales Cricket Board, Commercial partners. Retrieved from www.ecb.co.uk/ecb/partners/national-australia-bank,569,BP.html (accessed 02 February 2010).

Collier, D. (2009). Building partnership. *Building Partnership-Cricket's Strategic Plan 2005-2009-From Playground to Test Arena*, 1, 1–24.

Commercial Partners. (2010). England & Wales Cricket Board, Commercial partners, Retrieved from www.ecb.co.uk/ecb/partners/ (accessed 02 February 2010).

Conta, F., Fiore, M.,Vrontis, D. and Silvestri, R. (2015). Innovative Marketing Behaviour Determinants in Wine SMEs: the Case of an Italian Wine Region. *International Journal of Globalisation and Small Business, 7* (2), 107–124.

Creswell, J. W. (1998). *Qualitative Inquiry and Research Design: Choosing Among Five Traditions.* Thousand Oaks, California: Sage.

Cricket in Partnership with Education. (2010). Cricket in Partnership with Education. London: England and Wales Cricket Board.

Cricket World. (2010). Maximuscle is official England nutrition supplier, Commercial partner. Retrieved from www.cricketworld.com/health/article/?aid=18436 (accessed 03 February 2010).

Dey, I. (1995). *Reducing Fragmentation in Qualitative Research in Computer Aided Qualitative Data Analysis: Theory, Methods and Practice.* London: Sage.

Donaldson, B., and O'Toole, T. (2007). *Strategic Market Relationships: From Strategy to Implementation,* 2nd edn. Brisbane: John Wiley & Sons Ltd.

ECB Clubmark Process. (2010). England & Wales Cricket Board, Clubmark club. Retrieved from www.ecb.co.uk/development/clubs-and-leagues/clubmark/clubmark-process/#photos=gallery_null (accessed 02 February 2010).

ECB Extra Cover Insurance. (nd). England & Wales Cricket Board, Commercial partners, Retrieved from http://static.ecb.co.uk/files/are-you-adequately-insured-10323.pdf (accessed 02 February 2010).

Evangelista, S., Lombardi, R., Russo, G. and Shams, S. M. R. (2015). Exploring structural capital from business administration perspective: A general framework on the existing literature. *Sinergie Italian Journal of Management, 33* (1), 145–160.

Festa, G., Ciasullo, V. C., Vrontis, D. and Thrassou, A. (2017). Cooperating for Competing – a Small Italian Wineries' Internationalisation Strategy Case Study. *Global Business and Economics Review,* 19 (5), 648–670.

Friends Provident. (2010). England & Wales Cricket Board, Commercial partners. Retrieved from www.ecb.co.uk/ecb/partners/friends-provident,1057,BP.html (accessed 03 February 2010).

Gide, E., and Shams, S. M. R. (2011a). The role of web-based promotion on the development of a relationship marketing model to enable sustainable growth. *Procedia Computer Science, 3,* 1060–1073.

Gide, E. and Shams, S. M. R. (2011b). The impact of relationship marketing on reinforcing corporate brand, identity and reputation: analysis of five sport cases. Paper presented in the Academy of Marketing Science 7th Global Brand Conference on Brand, Identity and Reputation: Exploring, Creating New Realities and Fresh Perspectives on Multi-Sensory Experiences, April 05-07, 2011, University of Oxford, UK.

Gide, E., and Shams, S. M. R. (2011c). The use of E-CRM database to promote a Value-Breeding Bond Network: the case of Hawthorn Football Club of Australian Rules. *Procedia Computer Science, 3,* 1083–1088.

Gomm, R., Hammersley, M. and Foster, P. (2001). *Case Study and Generalization in Case Study Method.* London: Sage.

Gordon, I. (1998). *Relationship Marketing: New Strategies, Techniques and Technologies to Win the Customer You Want and Keep Them Forever.* Ontario: John Wiley & Sons Canada Ltd.

Gummesson, E. (2002). *Total Relationship Marketing.* London: Butterworth-Heinemann.

Hewitt Associates. (2010). England & Wales Cricket Board, Commercial partners. Retrieved from www.ecb.co.uk/ecb/partners/hewitt-associates,1143,BP.html (accessed 02 February 2010).

Hundley, G. and Hansen, S. D. (2012). Economic performance and the enterprise culture', *Journal of Enterprising Culture*, 20 (3), 245–264.

Ioannou, M. (2012). Customer relationship management (CRM): a one-size-fits-all philosophy?', in Kaufmann, H., and Panni, M. F. A. K. (Eds.), *Customer Centric Marketing Strategies: Tools for Building Organizational Performance*, pp. 150–170. Hershey, PA: Business Science Reference.

Kaufmann, H. R. and Shams, S. M. R. (Eds.). (2015). *Entrepreneurial challenges in the 21st century: Creating stakeholder value co-creation*. Hampshire, UK: Palgrave Macmillan.

Kotler, P., Keller, K.L., Ang, S.H., Leong, S.M. and Tan, C.T. (2009). *Marketing Management: An Asian Perspective (5th ed.)*. Singapore: Prentice Hall.

Kurtz, D. L. (2009). *Contemporary Marketing*, 2009 edn. Singapore: South-Western Cengage Learning.

Lagrosen, S. (2005). Customer involvement in new product development: a relationship marketing perspective. *European Journal of Innovation Management*, 8 (13), 424–436.

LV=. (2010). England & Wales Cricket Board, Commercial partners. Retrieved from www.ecb.co.uk/ecb/partners/lv,44,BP.html (accessed 02 February 2010).

Maklan, S., Knox, S. and Ryals, L. (2008). New trends in innovation and customer relationship management: a challenge for market researchers. *International Journal of Market Research*, 50 (2), 221–240.

NatWest. (2010). England & Wales Cricket Board, Commercial partners. Retrieved from www.ecb.co.uk/ecb/partners/natwest,46,BP.html (accessed 03 February 2010).

Npower. (2010). England & Wales Cricket Board, Commercial partners. Retrieved from www.ecb.co.uk/ecb/partners/npower,47,BP.html (accessed 02 February 2010).

Play Cricket Making a Difference. (2006). *Play Cricket Making a Difference.* London: Tobasgo Creative.

Rajaobelina, L. and Bergeron, J. (2009). Antecedents and consequences of buyer-seller relationship quality in the financial service industry. *International Journal of Bank Marketing, 27* (5), 359–380.

Ritter, T. and Gemünden, H. G. (2003). Network competence: its impact on innovation success and its antecedents. *Journal of Business Research*, 56 (9), 745–755.

Rossi, M., Vrontis, D. and Thrassou, A., (2014). Agro Business in a Changing Competitive Environment – Campania firms' strategic, marketing and financial choices. *World Review of Entrepreneurship, Management and Sustainable Development, 10* (2), 321–333.

Sanchez, B. D., Kaufmann, R. and Vrontis D. (2012). A new organisational memory for cross-cultural knowledge management. *Cross Cultural Management: An International Journal, 19*, (3), 336–351.

Santoro, G., Vrontis, D., Thrassou, and Dezi, L. (2017). The Internet of Things: Building knowledge management systems for open innovation and knowledge management capacity. *Technological Forecasting and Social Change*, (published online ahead of print, DOI: 10.1016/j.techfore.2017.02.034).

Shams, S. M. R. (2017a). Transnational education and total quality management: A stakeholder-centred model. *Journal of Management Development, 36* (3), 376–389.

Shams, S. M. R. (2017b). International education management: Implications of relational perspectives and ethnographic insights to nurture international students' academic experience. *Journal for Multicultural Education, 11* (3), 206–223.

150   *Hasina Idris and S. M. Riad Shams*

Shams, S. M. R. and Belyaeva, Z. (2017). Quality assurance driving factors as antecedents of knowledge management: A stakeholder-focussed perspective in higher education. *Journal of the Knowledge Economy*, published ahead of print (doi. org/10.1007/s13132-017-0472-2).

Shams, S. M. R., Vrontis, D. and Czinkota, M. (2017). Innovation management and entrepreneurial development: The antecedent role of stakeholder engagement. Journal of Business Research. Retrieved from www.journals.elsevier.com/journal-of-business-research/call-for-papers/innovation-management-and-entrepreneurial-development-the-an (accessed on 25 September, 2017).

Shams, S. M. R. (2016a). Capacity building for sustained competitive advantage: A conceptual framework. *Marketing Intelligence & Planning, 34* (5), 671–691.

Shams, S. M. R. (2016b). Sustainability issues in transnational education service: A conceptual framework and empirical insights. *Journal of Global Marketing, 29* (3), 139–155.

Shams, S. M. R. and Kaufmann, H. R. (2016). Entrepreneurial co-creation: A research vision to be materialised. *Management Decision, 54* (6), 1250–1268.

Shams, S. M. R. and Lombardi, R. (2016). Socio-economic value co-creation and sports tourism: Evidence from Tasmania. *World Review of Entrepreneurship, Management and Sustainable Development, 12* (2/3), 218–238.

Shams, S. M. R. (2015a). Stakeholders' perceptions and reputational antecedents: A review of stakeholder relationship, reputation and brand positioning. *Journal of Advances in Management Research, 12* (3), 314–329.

Shams, S. M. R. (2016c). Branding destination image: A stakeholder causal scope analysis for internationalisation of destinations. *Tourism Planning & Development (formerly Tourism and Hospitality Planning & Development), 13* (2), 140–153.

Shams, S. M. R. (2013). Competitive advantage in market space: implications of relationship marketing. In Gohari, E. and Eid, R. (Eds.), *E-Marketing in Developed and Developing Countries: Emerging Practices* (19–38), Hershey, PA: Business Science Reference.

Shams, S. M. R. (2012a). Implications of relationship marketing indicators to enable organisational growth: a stakeholder causal scope analysis. In Kaufmann, H., and Panni, M. F. A. K. (Eds.), *Customer Centric Marketing Strategies: Tools for Building Organizational Performance* (214–244). Hershey: PA: Business Science Reference.

Shams, S. M. R. (2012b). Stakeholder causal scope centric market positioning: implications of relationship marketing indicators. In Kaufmann, H., and Panni, M. F. (Eds.),*Customer-Centric Marketing Strategies: Tools for Building Organizational Performance* (245–263). Hershey, PA: Business Science Reference.

Shams, S. M. R. (2011). *A relationship marketing model to enable sustainable growth of the Bangladesh Cricket Board: A stakeholder causal scope analysis* (doctoral dissertation). Central Queensland University, Australia.

Sky Sports. (2010). England & Wales Cricket Board, Commercial partners. Retrieved from www.ecb.co.uk/ecb/partners/sky-sports,51,BP.html#photos=gallery_null (accessed 02 February 2010).

Sources of Grant Aid and Funding For Cricket Clubs. (2009). *Sources of Grant Aid and Funding For Cricket Clubs*. London: Tobasgo Creative.

Stake, R. E. (2000). *Case Studies*. California: Sage.

Stavros, C. (2005). *Relationship marketing in Australian professional sport: an organizational perspective* (doctoral dissertation), Griffith University, Australia.

talkSPORT. (2010). England & Wales Cricket Board, Commercial partners. Retrieved from www.ecb.co.uk/ecb/partners/talksport-radio,56,BP.html (accessed 02 February 2010).

The Financial Times. (2014). Definition of international mindset, Financial Times Lexicon. Retrieved from http://lexicon.ft.com/Term?term=entrepreneurial-mindset (accessed 02 April, 2014).

Tomer, J. F. (1998). Beyond transaction markets toward relationship: marketing in the human firm: a socio-economic model. *The Journal of Socio- Economics*, 27 (2), 207–228.

Trequattrini, R., Shams, S. M. R., Alessandra Lardo, A. and Lombardi, R. (2016). Risk of an epidemic impact when adopting the Internet of Things: The role of sector-based resistance. *Business Process Management Journal*, 22 (2), 403–419.

Vrontis, D., Tharassou, A., Chebbi, H. and Yahiaoui, D. (2012). Transcending innovativeness towards strategic reflexivity. *Qualitative Market Research: An International Journal*, Vol. 15 (4), 420–437.

Weerawardena, J. (2003). The role of marketing capacity in innovation-based competitive strategy. *Journal of Strategic Marketing*, 11 (1), 15–35.

Wilson, D. T. (1995). An integrated model of buyer-seller relationships. *Journal of the Academy of Marketing Science*, 23 (4), 335–345.

Yin, R. K. (2003). *Application of Case Study Research*. California: Sage, Thousand Oaks.

Yin, R. K. (2009). *Case Study Research: Design and Methods*, 4th edn. California: Sage.

Zolkiewski, J., Story, V. and Burton, J. (2012). Role of relationships and networks in radical innovation. Special issue call for papers from Journal of Business & Industrial Marketing. Retrieved from www.emeraldinsight.com/products/journals/call_for_papers.htm?id=3738&PHPSESSID=enehif8ib1ho5nccm31r4p6u86 (accessed 22 September 2012).

10 Disclosure of electric mobility in annual reports of automotive companies

Risks, strategies, and environment

Giuseppe Ianniello, Michela Piccarozzi and Fabrizio Rossi

Introduction

This chapter intends to use the narrative section of annual reports to investigate the role of electric mobility from the perspective of automobile companies. Because the electric mobility market is new and rapidly evolving, it may be of interest to investigate the vision communicated in the narrative section of annual reports of car manufacturers. As noted by the European Automobile Manufacturers Association in a press release on 5 February 2015 (www.acea.be), in 2014, approximately 75,000 new electric vehicles (EV) were registered in the European Union, a growth rate of 37% in comparison to the previous year. The largest increment is observed in the UK (+ 300%), followed by Germany (+ 70%), and France (+ 30%). In the EFTA (European Free Trade Association) countries, Norway is at the top, with approximately 20,000 new registrations, which is more than double the EVs registered in 2013 (+ 141%). Table 10.1 shows the total registration of EVs in 2014, with differences in comparison with the previous year. This explorative analysis focuses on the following aspects of the EV market: risks, strategies, and environmental impact. In addition, an analysis of the relation between economic performance and the disclosure of electric mobility in annual reports is conducted. For the empirical analysis, we used a sample of major automobile manufacturers active in the European market.

This chapter draws upon legitimacy theory to develop one testable hypothesis. The research method is based on the thematic content analysis (Krippendorff, 2013; Weber, 1988) applied to the narrative section of annual reports (Beattie et al., 2004). This section of annual reports increased in importance in recent years to satisfy the information needs of several stakeholders (IASB, 2010; IIRC, 2013; Teodori and Veneziani, 2013, Scaltrito 2016). The chapter continues with a literature review, followed by the electric mobility aspects investigated and the research method. Thereafter, the results of the empirical analysis are presented, followed by the conclusions.

Table 10.1 Registration of electric vehicles (electrically charged vehicles*) in Europe

Country	2014	2013	Variation %
Austria	3,641	3,227	12.8
Belgium	2,032	819	148.1
Bulgaria	2	1	100.0
Czech Republic	583	475	22.7
Denmark	1,612	650	148.0
Estonia	402	150	168.0
Finland	440	218	101.8
France	12,488	9,622	29.8
Germany	13,118	7,706	70.2
Greece	64	4	1,500.0
Hungary	43	16	168.8
Ireland	256	50	412.0
Italy	1,473	1,174	25.5
Latvia	391	13	2,907.7
The Netherlands	12,920	22,495	- 42.6
Poland	3,968	1,900	108.8
Portugal	289	221	30.8
Romania	7	4	75.0
Slovakia	169	136	24.3
Spain	1,405	883	59.1
Sweden	4,667	1,547	201.7
UK	15,361	3,833	300.8
European Union	*75,331*	*55,144*	36.6
EU 15	*69,766*	*52,449*	33.0
EU New Member	*5,565*	*2,695*	106.5
Norway	19,767	8,210	140.8
Switzerland	2,693	1,717	56.8
EFTA	22,460	9,927	126.3
Total Europe (EsU + EFTA)	97,791	65,071	50.3
West Europe (EU 15 + EFTA)	92,226	62,376	47.9

Source: www.acea.be

* Electrically charged vehicles = pure electric vehicles + extended-range electric vehicles + plug-in hybrid electric vehicles

Literature review

The relevance of research on the narrative section of annual reports has been shown in its historical evolution by Beattie (2014). From the literature review related to the content analysis of the narrative section of annual reports, it appears that a specific analysis on the electric mobility in automobile companies is missing. However, a common theoretical framework for this type of research can be found in the vision of the annual report as a communication tool, particularly in a context of the growing usage of information technology. The narrative section of annual financial statements has widened its role of annual accounts from the area of financial communication to a business reporting tool covering several aspects of the business activity, which allows a form of integrated communication (e.g., Busco et al., 2013). As observed in the literature on earnings quality (e.g., Dechow et al., 2010), the disclosure process in narrative form can also raise the issue of manipulation, which is considered to be behavior targeted towards hiding results or negative aspects of the business performance (e.g., Adelberg, 1979), or the quality of the linguistic characteristics that influence the understandability of the text (e.g., Jones and Smith, 2014). In theory, the narrative section of annual reports is an opportunity for the management to discuss and analyze financial performance and other aspects of the business activity, such as social and environmental issues. As stated in IASB (2010, §9):

> management commentary should provide users of financial statements with integrated information that provides a context for the related financial statements. Such information explains management's view not only about what has happened, including both positive and negative circumstances, but also why it has happened and what the implications are for the entity's future".

Using this communication tool, the management sends signals to several stakeholders, revealing key messages they want to divulge. Analyzing the theme of electric mobility, we are able to show what is disclosed; in addition, the less discussed topics may indicate a company approach to the issue under investigation.

Electric mobility: Risks, strategies, and environment

The orientation towards a green economy and sustainability have stimulated company behavior in the direction of social responsibility, environmental protection, and alternative sources of energy (Caulfield, 2013; Stokes et al., 2013). This general statement can be applied to the transport sector (Oberhofer and Fürst, 2012), and in this context, the issue of electric mobility can be analyzed. In particular, we attempt to capture the following aspects as communicated in the annual reports: risks, strategies, and the environmental impact. In general, those aspects are noted in the framework suggested by the IASB (2010) with the purpose to improve corporate communication. IASB (2010) emphasizes the disclosure of risk factors and business strategy: "That type of commentary will help users of the financial reports understand, for example: (a) the entity's risk exposures, its strategies for managing risks and the effectiveness of those strategies" (IASB, 2010, §14).

The notion of business risk is strictly linked to the concept of value creation; maximizing value creation can be viewed as optimizing growth and performance targets with the relative risks (PWC, 2006). From auditing, the standard definition of business risk is "risk resulting from significant conditions, events, circumstances, actions or inactions that could adversely affect an entity's ability to achieve its objectives and execute its strategies, or from the setting of inappropriate objectives and strategies" (ISA No. 315, 2009, § 4.b). Disclosure of business risks is a key component of financial reporting and strategic planning, in particular, for growing companies willing to communicate with the financial market. Strategic risks applied to electric mobility can be considered in general terms; this is not linked to a short-term performance target but is in relation to the strategic vision and the medium to long-term objectives in the framework of corporate mission and values (Coda, 1992). In this aspect, the strategic risk is different from compliance, reporting, and operational risks (PWC, 2006). In addition, strategic risks may be internal, which is linked to behaviors, decisions, and circumstances stemming from corporate management, or external, which means stemming from factors not controlled by the management, such as government policy and other institutional changes.

Among the types of strategic risk related to electric mobility, we can note the following:

- technological risks, linked to product development and the recharging infrastructure;
- market risk, linked to the market share of EVs;
- financial risk, linked to the return rate on investment in electric mobility.

We attempted to use this framework in gathering information on the risk aspects during the annual reports' content analysis process. In terms of corporate strategy (e.g., Coda, 1992; Porter, 1985), electric mobility requires complex analysis and a forecast of uncertain scenarios in terms of political and institutional policy and consumer behavior regarding the electric mobility issue. In this respect, content analysis of annual reports can reveal the approaches used by automobile companies. Regarding environmental information, the literature has discussed the relation between financial information and the environmental impact of the business activity (e.g., Al-Tuwaijri et al. 2004; Catturi, 1993; Endrikat et al., 2014; Matacena, 1984). The focus on social and environmental aspects has been recognized with international standards, such as the GRI (Global Reporting Initiative), which refers to the general notion of corporate social responsibility (e.g., Carroll, 1999; Caulfield, 2013; Rusconi and Dorigatti, 2004; Terzani, 1984). In the European Commission Recommendation (2001/453/EC),

> the term environment refers to the natural physical surroundings and includes air, water, land, flora, fauna and non-renewable resources such as fossil fuels and minerals (…) environmental issues should be disclosed to the extent that they are material to the financial performance or the financial position of the reporting entity. Depending upon the item, disclosures should be included in the annual and consolidated annual report or in the notes to the annual and consolidated accounts.

156 *Giuseppe Ianniello et al.*

In this context, we attempt to capture the environmental aspect of information linked to electric mobility. Overall, our arguments can be framed in the context of legitimacy theory. According to this theory, an organization is unable to develop and survive if its aims and methods are not in line with the expectations of society (economic, social, and political factors). Brown and Deegan (1998), Lindblom (1994), and Patten (1995) are examples of social and environmental disclosure studies in the accounting literature that used a legitimacy framework. In particular, Lindblom (1994) describes various reporting strategies that corporations can adopt in their process of legitimation. In the case under investigation, we can hypothesize that automobile companies may try to manipulate the perception of electric mobility focusing on strategies and environmental benefits for society, obfuscating issues of concern such as risks and EVs drivers obstacles. For this reason, we formulate the following hypothesis:

> (H1) disclosure of electric mobility in annual report of automotive companies emphasize strategies and environmental aspects in comparison to risks.

Research method and sample selection

The research method refers to the content analysis (e.g., Krippendorff, 2013) applied in social science. Our research was conducted by searching for certain key words in the text under observation. We selected our sample on the basis of the European car market in April 2014 as reported in a commercial magazine (*Quattroruote*, No. 705/2014), constructed using the database of the European Association of Car Manufacturers (ACEA). This choice is motivated by the fact that 2013 annual reports are generally published during that period of time. We considered one year (2013) showing intercompany differences. We used eleven annual reports for 2013 with a closing date of 31 December; however, in seven cases, the closing date was 31 March 2013. For each company, we downloaded the annual report from the corporate website. Because the business entities included in our sample are multinational companies with headquarters in different countries, we used the English version of the website, and the document download is always labelled as the annual report.

Using the approach of Beattie et al. (2004), we considered the unit text of a sentence containing a single piece of information as the object of observation. As shown by Jones and Shoemaker (1994), the classification of a text in particular groups can be implemented with reference to specific themes or single words. In the first level of analysis, we attempted to measure the presence or absence of discourses related to electric mobility. As suggested by Beattie (2000), we sought to show certain aspects of the information provided. First, we classified the information into the framework of general topics (risk, strategy, and environment). Second, for each piece of information, we attempted to show other features: time orientation (historical/forward-looking), financial/non-financial, qualitative/quantitative. This research is focused on the theme of electric mobility (Emobility, sustainable mobility); therefore, the reasoned choice of key words is oriented towards that issue. In particular, to identify such key words, we made reference, in general, to IASB (2010) and specifically, to operative publications showing advantages and disadvantages stemming from the EV market (e.g., IEA, 2013; PWC, 2014).

The list of key words is as follows:

- Electric vehicle/EV/EVs/electric car/electric cars: these key words relate to vehicles (automobiles) operated with a battery. We excluded the specific search of the term 'hybrid', which refers to vehicles operated with a traditional internal combustion engine and a battery.
- CO_2: this term relates to the issue of CO_2 emissions and the related environmental pollution caused by the circulation of internal combustion engine vehicles, whereas those emissions are zero in the case of EVs.
- E-mobility/electromobility/electromotive mobility/sustainable mobility: these key words relate to the theme of electric and sustainable mobility in terms of environmental impact.
- Charging infrastructure/recharging/charge point/charging: these terms refer to the issue of the existence or absence of recharging infrastructure for EVs, the manner in which they work, the charging time; these issues may be an obstacle for drivers or potential drivers of EVs.

The hypothesis implicit in this approach is that the frequency of key words is an indicator of interest towards electric mobility and related issues. The presence or absence of discourses regarding specific themes linked to electric mobility has been the main object of observation. In fact, because the range of information provided in the annual report may be very wide, it is reasonable to focus on specific information. In this perspective, the most relevant examples are known in the research field devoted to environmental and social information (e.g., Hooks and Van Staden, 2011).

In our analysis, we considered the frequency number in absolute value terms and in relation to the total number of document pages. In addition, we considered the frequency in relation to the total number of words contained in the annual report. This approach was adopted by Bowman and Haire (1976) and Trotman and Bradley (1981); they attempted to measure the social information disclosed in annual reports as a percentage of the total length of the document investigated. We used annual reports in a pdf file format downloaded from each company website. Each pdf file was converted into Word format (or a text file) for subsequent analysis. In particular, the conversion to Word format (or a text file) allowed the counting of words of interest in comparison to the total words contained in the document. Thus, we may

158 *Giuseppe Ianniello et al.*

obtain an indicator of the importance of electric mobility in the aspects analyzed.

In detail, the methodology is as follows. For each key word, we counted the frequency number. For each occurrence, the entire sentence (single information) was collected and analyzed for its meaning. Thus, for each single information, we implemented two levels of classification. The first level refers to the aspects of risk, strategy, and environmental impact. The second level refers to certain information features: time orientation (historical/forward looking), financial/non-financial, qualitative/quantitative. In accordance with this approach, we are able to gather a series of elements that may be present or absent in the narrative section of the annual report. The research method's objective is to show what is disclosed and what is not discussed regarding electric mobility. Thus, we can show the different approaches followed in the automobile industry.

To compare the emphasis on electric mobility, as revealed in the annual report, with economic performance, we gathered certain financial information for each company: return on equity (ROE) before tax, return on sales (ROS), and return on investment (ROI). This information is collected from the Osiris database and manually from the annual report. Using the Spearman's rank correlation index, we tested the relation between economic performance and the emphasis on electric mobility.

Empirical results

The descriptive analysis of the evidence we obtained is reported in Table 10.2. Overall, we analyzed eighteen annual reports. The average number of pages in the annual reports is 147. The total number of pages is 2,639, with an average number of words of 69,282. The first level of analysis shows the frequency of key words and its relative relevance in the annual report. The total key words frequency is 624. With the exception of Suzuki, Table 10.2 shows that the theme of electric mobility is discussed in the annual report with intercompany differences. The key words with the highest frequency are CO_2 (48%), which clearly refers to environmental issues, followed by EVs (29%). The issue of the recharging infrastructure (9%), which may be an obstacle for the circulation of EVs, is nearly neglected. In particular, using the percentage of key words relative to the total number of pages as an indicator of interest, it is possible to identify automobile companies that emphasize the electric mobility theme at different levels.

The companies are listed in Table 10.2 according to the above noted indicator from high to low. It is worth noting that the top companies, Nissan and Renault, have a strategic and investment alliance. Using a different indicator, the percentage of key words relative to the total number of words in the document, the order presented in Table 10.2 is substantially confirmed. As an additional test, we considered the average number of words (445) per page as a standard page, recalculating the indicator of key words relative to the total number of standard pages. In addition, in this case, we observe similar results; in particular, the top five and the bottom five companies are the same as shown in Table 10.2. It would be of interest to compare this scoring with the percentage of EVs production over the total production of cars, but this data is not provided. However, it is worth noting that Nissan claims in its annual report to be the world leader in the EV market (Nissan's Annual Report, 2013, p. 13) and Mitsubishi aims to achieve a 20% or higher total production ratio of EVs (Mitsubishi's Annual Report, 2013, p. 28). The case of Suzuki is of interest because it shows that the pattern towards electro mobility is not totally accepted in the automobile industry.

From the analysis of each key word in the context of the narrative reporting, we identified 189 sentences (Table 10.3). We define a sentence (single information) as text appearing between punctuation signs, having a meaning, and containing at least one key word. We excluded from the notion of a sentence the cases in which the key words are presented in graphics, glossary, and other notes. It is possible to note that the theme of CO_2 is highly discussed by VW group (40% of words = 119/297; 12% of sentences = 6/49), Mercedes (24% of words = 70/297; 12% of sentences), and BMW group (8% of words = 25/297; 12% of sentences = 6/49); together these German companies reach a total of 74% of the words CO_2 (214/297) and 36% (18/49) of the sentences on that issue. In addition, considering the relevance of EVs in terms of sentences, it is confirmed that companies in the top positions are Mitsubishi, Renault, VW, and Nissan.

The analysis continues with the classification of the information in the aspects of risk, strategy, and environmental impact. In this segment of the analysis, we focus on the meaning of the sentences in the context of the narrative reporting. Additionally, we observe certain information features: time orientation (historical, forward-looking), financial/ non-financial, qualitative/quantitative. Regarding this aspect, it is worth noting that each sentence has been analyzed in connection with the immediately preceding and following sentences. Moreover, in certain cases, we counted one sentence, although formally there were two or more, when their meaning was strictly linked. In some cases, a sentence was classified in more than one general topic or features according to its meaning and information content. Table 10.4 shows that most information regards corporate strategy and opportunity stemming from electric mobility (64%), followed by the environmental impact (32%), and finally the discussion of risks (4%) linked to the EV market. Considering the null hypothesis of identical proportion of the information in the three categories, the disclosure of risks is significantly ($z = -7.78$, p=0.00) lower in comparison with the information about strategies and environment. Therefore, we can state that H1 is corroborated. We can sustain that annual reports tend to depict the positive aspect of electric mobility, whereas the story of potential risks (recharging infrastructure, range anxiety, consumers' behavior, market growth, alternative technologies, and new regulations) is discussed less.

Table 10.2 Description of annual report 2013 and frequency of key words

Company name	No. pages (a)	Key words						Indicators		
		No. words (b)	EV	CO_2	Electric mobility	Charging infrastructure		Total key words (c)	% (c)/(a)	% (c)/ (b)
Nissan	46	14,502	17	8	2	6		33	72	0.228
Renault group	71	20,301	39	6	0	2		47	66	0.232
Mitsubishi	66	29,849	29	10	0	3		42	64	0,141
VW Group	424	195,488	15	119	35	22		191	45	0.098
Kia	68	37,415	21	3	4	1		29	43	0.078
Jaguar Land Rover	85	57,956	7	21	0	0		28	33	0.048
Mercedes	284	147,243	7	70	5	7		89	31	0.060
BMW Group	208	153,635	4	25	22	6		57	27	0.037
Toyota	124	78,002	15	6	1	4		26	21	0.033
Hyundai	77	27,653	8	6	0	2		16	21	0.058
PSA Group	148	58,334	3	15	0	0		18	12	0.031
Honda	68	23,575	1	3	3	1		8	12	0.034
Volvo	198	102,428	6	1	12	1		20	10	0.020
Mazda	60	3,938	1	2	0	0		3	5	0.076
Fiat Group	366	141,159	5	2	7	0		14	4	0.010
Ford	152	71,877	2	0	0	0		2	1	0.003
GM Group	130	59,377	1	0	0	0		1	1	0.002
Suzuki	64	24,336	0	0	0	0		0	0	0.000
Total	2,639	1,247,068	*181 (29%)*	*297 (48%)*	*91 (15%)*	*55 (9%)*		624 (100%)		
Mean	147	69,282								

EV = EV, EVs, electric vehicle/s, electric car/s; Electric mobility = e-mobility, electromobility, electromotive mobility, sustainable mobility; Charging infrastructure = recharging, charge point, charging

Table 10.3 Sentences for each key word

Company name	EV			CO_2			Electric mobility			Charging infrastructure		
	No. sentences	No. words	n/a	No. sentences	No. words	n/a	No. sentences	No. words	n/a	No. sentences	No. words	n/a
VW Group	9	15	1	6	119	69	13	35	5	7	22	8
PSA Group	2	3	0	4	15	0	0	0	0	0	0	0
Renault	11	39	1	4	6	0	0	0	0	2	2	0
Ford	2	2	0	0	0	0	0	0	0	0	0	0
GM Group	1	1	0	0	0	0	0	0	0	0	0	0
BMW Group	3	4	0	6	25	4	7	22	0	2	6	0
Fiat Group	4	5	0	2	2	0	4	7	2	0	0	0
Mercedes	5	7	0	6	70	9	4	5	0	4	7	1
Nissan	7	17	0	3	8	0	2	2	0	1	6	0
Toyota	1	15	0	2	6	0	1	1	0	2	2	0
Hyundai	1	8	6	1	6	2	0	0	0	2	2	0
Kia	4	21	0	2	3	1	2	4	0	1	1	0
Volvo	5	6	0	1	1	0	5	12	0	1	1	0
Jaguar Land Rover	3	7	0	3	21	0	0	0	0	0	0	0
Mazda	1	1	0	2	2	0	0	0	0	0	0	0
Honda	1	1	0	2	3	0	3	3	0	0	1	0
Suzuki	0	0	0	0	0	0	0	0	0	0	0	0
Mitsubishi	14	29	3	5	10	3	0	0	0	3	3	0
	74	181	11	49	297	88	41	91	7	25	55	9
Total words	624											
Total sentences	189											
Total n/a	115											

n/a = information not classified; EV = EV, EVs, electric vehicle/s, electric car/s; Electric mobility = e-mobility, electromobility, electromotive mobility, sustainable mobility; Charging infrastructure = recharging, charge point, charging

Table 10.4 Information features

Key words	General topics				Features								
	Risk	Strategy	Environment	Total	Qualitative	Quantitative	Total	Financial	Non-Financial	Total	Historic	Forward-looking	Total
EV	2	65	19	86	64	15	79	0	73	73	59	19	78
CO$_2$	3	24	39	66	27	26	53	0	50	50	40	14	54
Electric mobility	0	36	15	51	39	5	44	0	42	42	32	12	44
Charging infrastructure	4	20	1	25	20	8	28	0	24	24	18	6	24
Total	9	145	74	228	150	54	204	0	189	189	149	51	201
%	4%	64%	32%	100%	74%	26%	100%	0%	100%	100%	75%	25%	100%

EV = EV, EVs, electric vehicle/s, electric car/s; Electric mobility = e-mobility, electromobility, electromotive mobility, sustainable mobility; Charging infrastructure = recharging, charge point, charging

From the content analysis of annual reports, it is possible to show some of the topics discussed. With reference to the risk, sentences discuss certain fundamental issues for electric mobility: the theme of batteries, in particular, their cost and the weak recharging infrastructure. With reference to the strategy, the topics discussed in the sentences are broad, and the most noted are: objectives in terms of production; interest in sustainable strategies for company growth; and the critical factor of success, such as the manner by which to recharge EVs. Regarding the environmental impact, the discussion of automobile companies is focused on and linked to corporate social responsibility. The topics most analyzed are: reduction of gas emissions; alternative sources of energy; stimulating the culture of the green economy; and the role of government policy and regulation to stimulate sustainable mobility. Examining the information features, Table 10.4 shows that there is no financial information, whereas there is technical information, such as the level of CO_2 reduction and the range in km per single charge. The time orientation is largely (75%) toward historical information. The forward-looking information (25%) refers to business strategies and opportunities. In addition, there is more qualitative information (74%) than quantitative information. Therefore, there is more of a tendency to describe rather than to provide quantitative information regarding the aspects of electric mobility we searched for.

Overall, this evidence shows that there is difficulty in providing quantitative information and future information regarding electric mobility. As additional evidence, we report that the information regarding electric mobility is presented at the beginning of the annual report, in the President's letter and in the Management Discussion and Analysis (or Management commentary in the language of International Financial Reporting Standards). Often, this information is included in the section that relates to environmental impact and R&D activities, such as, "Sustainability", "Clean mobility", "Eco friendly car", and "Environmental initiatives".

The final part of the analysis is devoted to the relation of economic performance to the emphasis accorded to electric mobility in the annual report (Table 10.5 – Panel A). Using the Spearman's rank correlation index, Table 10.5 (Panel – B) shows no significant link between financial performance and the disclosure of information on electric mobility. The substantial equivalence between the two indicators (the percentage over the total number of pages and the percentage over the total number of words) that we used to measure the interest toward electric mobility is confirmed. Moreover, using total sales as a proxy for company size, we can observe that the theme of electric mobility is not linked to such firm characteristics.

Conclusion

The content analysis of annual reports reveals that, with the sole exception of Suzuki, automobile companies discuss the theme of electric mobility in the

164   *Giuseppe Ianniello et al.*

Table 10.5 Panel A Economic performance and indicators of the content analysis of annual reports

Company name	Sales (thousand €)	ROI (%)	ROE before tax (%)	ROS (%)	% of pages	% of words
VW Group	203,170,000	3.55	13.80	5.66	45.05	0.098
Toyota	173,080,000	3.72	10.99	6.36	20.97	0.033
Mercedes	119,465,000	6.65	23.38	9.38	31.34	0.060
GM Group	112,701,764	3.08	17.50	3.30	0.77	0.002
Ford	106,531,073	2.71	26.96	3.73	1.32	0.003
Fiat Group	86,884,000	7.98	15.19	4.03	3.83	0.010
Honda	82,575,000	3.96	7.80	5.52	11.76	0.034
Nissan	76,691,900	4.09	9.95	5.44	71.74	0.228
BMW Group	76,500,000	5.62	22.20	10.71	27.40	0.037
Hyundai	59,984,546	6.23	22.52	9.52	20.78	0.058
PSA Group	54,109,000	−2.30	−29.12	−2.54	12.16	0.031
Renault	41,677,000	−0.23	4.86	−0.42	66.20	0.232
Kia	32,702,045	8.78	23.84	6.67	42.65	0.078
Volvo	30,773,235	2.08	6.10	2.63	10.10	0.020
Suzuki	21,337,500	4.61	11.67	4.44	0.00	0.000
Land Rover & Jaguar	18,704,100	13.38	47.30	10.88	32.94	0.048
Mazda	18,250,000	2.73	7.10	2.45	5.00	0.076
Mitsubishi	15,021,400	4.63	17.27	3.71	63.64	0.141

Table 10.5 Panel B Correlation (Spearman's rank) between economic performance and indicators of the content analysis of annual reports

	Sales	ROI	ROE before tax	ROS	% of pages	% of words
Sales	1.0000					
ROI	−0.0733	1.0000				
	(0.7726)					
ROE before tax	0.1331	0.7007	1.0000			
	(0.5985)	(0.0012)				
ROS	0.2343	0.7915	0.6883	1.0000		
	(0.3495)	(0.0001)	(0.0016)			
% of pages	−0.0196	0.0010	−0.2941	0.0010	1.0000	
	(0.9384)	(0.9968)	(0.2361)	(0.9968)		
% of words	−0.1600	−0.0134	−0.2755	−0.0588	0.8989	1.0000
	(0.5261)	(0.9579)	(0.2684)	(0.8167)	(0.0000)	

% of pages = total number of key words/total number of pages in the annual report; % of words = total number of key words/total number of words in the annual report

aspects we investigated. In particular, it appears that a group of companies (Nissan, Renault, Mitsubishi, Volkswagen, and Kia) is highly interested in electric mobility, whereas another group of business entities (Mazda, Fiat, Ford, General Motors, and Suzuki) presents a lower level of emphasis on this theme in their annual reports.

The information discussed in the narrative section of the annual reports is primarily devoted to business strategies (64%) and environmental impact (32%), whereas the discourse regarding the risk of the EV market (cost of the batteries, recharging point) is nearly neglected (4%). We interpret this evidence in the framework of legitimacy theory, corroborating our hypothesis that automobile companies may seek to manipulate the perception of electric mobility focusing on strategies and environmental benefits for society, obfuscating issues of concern such as risks and EVs drivers obstacles.

Our evidence is in line with studies confirming the validity of the legitimacy framework in interpreting environmental reporting strategies used by management in corporate annual reports (e.g., Campbell, 2003). In addition, the information features are primarily qualitative (74%) and non-financial (100%), and have a historical time orientation (75%). This evidence is explicable because forward-looking and quantitative information may be private information for each company and, to maintain a competitive advantage, the management may not want to disclose this. Regarding the relation between economic performance and the emphasis on electric mobility in the annual reports, it appears that there is no significant association. Moreover, company size is not linked to the level of interest in electric mobility, as revealed by the content analysis.

Among the limits of this paper, there is subjectivity in the classification process of the information; however, this is in accordance with our research purpose. In addition, the small number of companies analyzed is a consequence of the automobile industry and European car market that we considered when selecting our sample. Future research implications may be a longitudinal analysis, a comparison with EVs produced by each company, and an analysis of related industries, such as manufacturers of batteries and utilities.

References

Adelberg, A. H. (1979). Narrative disclosures contained in financial reports: means of communication or manipulation? *Accounting and Business Research*, 9(35), 179–190.

Al-Tuwaijri, S. A., Christensen, T. E., & Hughes, K. E. (2004). The relations among environmental disclosure, environmental performance, and economic performance: a simultaneous equations approach. *Accounting, organizations and society*, 29(5), 447–471.

Beattie, V. (2000). The future of corporate reporting: a review article. *Irish Accounting Review*, 7(1), 1–36.

Beattie, V., McInnes, B., & Fearnley, S. (2004, September). A methodology for analysing and evaluating narratives in annual reports: a comprehensive descriptive profile and metrics for disclosure quality attributes. *Accounting Forum* 28(3), 205–236.

Beattie, V. (2014). Accounting narratives and the narrative turn in accounting research: Issues, theory, methodology, methods and a research framework. *The British Accounting Review*, 46(2), 111–134.

Bowman, E. H., & Haire, M. (1976). Social impact disclosure and corporate annual reports. *Accounting, Organizations and Society*, 1(1), 11–21.

Brown, N., & Deegan, C. (1998). The public disclosure of environmental performance information – a dual test of media agenda setting theory and legitimacy theory. *Accounting and Business Research*, 29(1), 21–41.

Busco, C., Frigo, M. L., Riccaboni, A., & Quattrone, P. (Eds.). (2013). *Integrated Reporting: Concepts and Cases that Redefine Corporate Accountability.* Berlin: Springer Science & Business Media.

Campbell, D. (2003). Intra-and intersectoral effects in environmental disclosures: evidence for legitimacy theory? *Business Strategy and the Environment*, 12(6), 357–371.

Carroll, A. B. (1999). Corporate social responsibility: Evolution of a definitional construct. *Business & Society*, 38(3), 268–295.

Catturi G., (1993). Sul contenuto specifico dell'ecologia aziendale. In *Scritti in onore di Carlo Masini, Tomo I.* Milano: Istituzioni di economia d'azienda.

Caulfield, P.A. (2013). The evolution of strategic corporate social responsibility. *EuroMed Journal of Business*, 8(3), 220–242, https://doi.org/10.1108/EMJB-05-2013-0030.

Coda, V. (1992). *L'orientamento strategico dell'impresa.* Torino: UTET.

Dechow, P., Ge, W., & Schrand, C. (2010). Understanding earnings quality: A review of the proxies, their determinants and their consequences. *Journal of Accounting and Economics*, 50(2), 344–401.

Endrikat, J., Guenther, E., & Hoppe, H. (2014). Making sense of conflicting empirical findings: A meta-analytic review of the relationship between corporate environmental and financial performance. *European Management Journal*, 32(5), 735–751.

Hooks, J., & Van Staden, C. J. (2011). Evaluating environmental disclosures: The relationship between quality and extent measures. *The British Accounting Review*, 43(3), 200–213.

IASB (2010). *Management commentary.* London: IFRS practice statement, International Accounting Standards Board.

IEA (2013). *Global EV Outlook Understanding the Electric Vehicle Landscape to 2020.* Retrieved from www.iea.org/topics/transport/subtopics/electricvehiclesinitiative/publications/ (accessed 29 July 2017).

IIRC (2013). *Consultation draft of the international integrated reporting framework.* International Integrated Reporting Council. Retrieved from www.theiirc.org/consultationdraft2013 (accessed 29 July 2017).

ISA No. 315 (2009). *Identifying and assessing the risks of material misstatement through understanding the entity and its environment.* International Federation of Accountants.

Jones, M. J., & Shoemaker, P. A. (1994). Accounting narratives: A review of empirical studies of content and readability. *Journal of Accounting Literature*, 13, 142.

Jones, M., & Smith, M. (2014). Traditional and alternative methods of measuring the understandability of accounting narratives. *Accounting, Auditing & Accountability Journal*, 27(1), 183–208.

Lindblom, C.K. (1994). The Implications of Organizational Legitimacy for Corporate Social Performance and Disclosure. In Proceedings of the Critical Perspectives on Accounting Conference, New York, NY, USA, 13–15 June 1994.

Krippendorff, K. (2013). *Content analysis: An introduction to its methodology.* New York: Sage.

Matacena, A. (1984). *Impresa e Ambiente.* Bologna: Clueb.

Oberhofer, P., & Fürst, E. (2012). Environmental management in the transport sector: findings of a quantitative survey, *EuroMed Journal of Business*, 7(3), 268–279, https://doi.org/10.1108/14502191211265325

Patten, D.M. (1995). Variability in social disclosure: a legitimacy-based analysis. *Advances in Public Interest Accounting*, 6, 273–286.

Porter, M.E., (1985). *Competitive advantage: Creating and sustaining superior performance*. New York: Free Press.

PWC (2006). *La gestione del rischio aziendale – ERM Enterprise Risk Management*. Milano: Il Sole 24Ore.

PWC (2014). *Europe: The Great Electric Hype?* Pricewaterhouse Coopers, Autofacts, November. Retrieved from www.pwc.com/en_GX/GX/automotive/autofacts/analyst-notes/pdf/pwc-analyst-note-eu-market-survey-nov14.pdf (accessed 29 July 2017).

Rusconi, G. and Dorigatti M. (2004). *La responsabilità sociale*. Milano: Franco Angeli.

Scaltrito, D. (2016). Voluntary disclosure in Italy: Firm-specific determinants and empirical analysis of Italian listed companies. *EuroMed Journal of Business*, 11(2), 272–303, https://doi.org/10.1108/EMJB-07-2015-0032

Stokes, D. P., Moore, D. N., Brooks, D. S., & Wells, P. C. A. J. (2013). Sustainable and responsible business: focal cases, sectors and contexts. *EuroMed Journal of Business*, 8(3) https://doi.org/10.1108/EMJB-05-2013-0029

Teodori, C., and Veneziani, M. (editors) (2013). *L'evoluzione della disclosure nella sezione narrativa. L'impatto dei principi contabili internazionali e del processo di armonizzazione*. Torino: Giappichelli.

Terzani, S. (1984). Responsabilità sociale d'impresa. *Rivista Italiana di Ragioneria ed Economia Aziendale*, n. 7–8, July–August.

Trotman, K. T., & Bradley, G. W. (1981). Associations between social responsibility disclosure and characteristics of companies. *Accounting, Organizations and Society*, 6(4), 355–362.

Weber, R.P. (1988). *Basic Content Analysis*, Sage University Paper Series on Quantitative Applications in the Social Sciences, Series No. 07-049. Beverly Hills, CA and London: Sage.

11 Human and task integration during post-merger integration

Yaakov Weber

Introduction

Despite their popularity, and dismal performance track record, mergers and acquisitions (M&A) remain poorly understood and poorly executed (Weber, Tarba and Oberg, 2014; Weber and Tarba, 2010). For example, in 2011, global M&A activity shattered previous years deal volume records and recent surveys reveal that despite the financial market crisis, executives remain upbeat about their M&A plans around the world. However, recent meta-analyses examining the most widely studied variables in the M&A literature (King, Dalton, Daily, and Covin, 2004; Stahl and Voight, 2008) have not clearly established the reasons for the high failure rate of M&As.

One reason why the research on acquisition performance in several disciplines, such as industrial economics, strategic management, and finance, has not produced consistent results is that it has failed to account for the role of human resource (HR) practices and mechanisms implemented during M&As stages, especially during the post-merger integration process (Weber, 2013; Weber, Oberg and Tarba, 2014). Furthermore, the post-merger integration process requires contradicting efforts and trade-off between the use of resources for both human and task integration (Birkinshaw, Bresman and Hakanson, 2000; Bjorkman, Stahl and Vaara, 2007; Weber, Oberg and Tarba, 2014). Moreover, simultaneous human and task integration is likely to increase conflicts due to cultural differences and thus may impede both human and task integration (Bjorkman, Stahl and Vaara, 2007; Weber and Tarba, 2010). This trade-off becomes even more complex when considering that M&A have various levels of cultural differences and synergy potential that require a high degree of balance and alignment of systems and resources: namely, Organizational Ambidexterity (OA). Ambidexterity is an organization's capacity to address two organizationally-incompatible objectives equally well.

Yet, the concept of OA needs development and application in various organizational situations. Although O'Reilly and Tushman (2013) indicate that scholars have recently refined the concept of OA, they conclude that:

> To be successful at ambidexterity, leaders must be able to orchestrate the allocation of resources between the old and new business domains. How

Post-merger human and task integration 169

they actually do this is seldom addressed in the research on ambidexterity but is at the core of the leadership challenge.

The OA concept seems appropriate to deal with the complexity and contradiction of the post-merger integration process faced by HR managers and other leaders. The goal of this chapter is twofold: a) to develop the concept of ambidexterity about major HR issues such as the balance between human and task integration, and b) to articulate different balance options for human and task integration in different post-merger integration situations. Thus, this chapter clarifies how HR managers and leaders can manage the inevitable conflicts that arise during post-merger integration as well as pointing to future research directions.

Contextual ambidexterity

A central part of what firms do is manage the tensions that exist between competing objectives; that is, they seek to achieve some form of ambidexterity (Birkinshaw, 2012). For example, to what extent do the systems work coherently to support the objectives of the organization? (Very limited extent/very great extent).

Organizational ambidexterity offers at least two ways to deal with the conflicting demands on organizations. Each way focuses on the competing or complementary facet of managers' decisions and actions. The former try to solve the conflicting demands on organizational resources by structural ambidexterity in a cyclical or sequential manner emphasizing temporal cycling between long periods of one demand and short periods of the other demand. However, this involves changes in formal routines and systems and may create conflicts due to the switch between the two and requires maintaining effective interpersonal relations that may be a challenge in the first place in M&A due to cultural differences and removal of autonomy required for the integration (Weber and Tarba, 2010; Weber, Shenkar and Raveh, 1996; Weber, Tarba and Reichal, 2011b). This form of OA requires high coordination costs (Simsek et al., 2009).

The second way is contextual ambidexterity that considers the two demands as complementary organizational activities (Simsek et al., 2009). This approach sees OA as a multidimensional construct where activities can take place simultaneously with different levels of effort. The advantage of this approach is that the combined firm is geared towards the integration of the two demanding tasks through a process of learning, thus avoiding the switching and coordination costs associated with the first approach. In the case of M&A it does not require a greater burden on interpersonal relations. Instead, it offers better relationships among people from both sides due to the emphasis on human integration, as will be explained below.

Despite its benefits, contextual ambidexterity is exceptionally challenging to implement because it requires not only organizational slack resources for

170   *Yaakov Weber*

the various activities but also effective mechanisms to integrate these activities (Gibson and Birkinshaw, 2004). Essentially, contextual ambidexterity can be viewed as a distinctive organizational capability that is complex, widely dispersed and time consuming to develop. However, while contextual ambidexterity emphasizes the integration of contradicting activities and their required resources within a single business unit, it allows for differentiated effort among both activities in M&As.

Contextual ambidexterity for integration approaches in M&A

Conceptually, the pursuit of contextual ambidexterity must be intertwined in the ongoing operating and strategic activities of a business unit (Simsek et al., 2009). In M&As, contextual ambidexterity epitomizes the integration of both firms during post-merger integration (PMI) geared towards the balance and alignment of human and task efforts through the division of efforts and resources in various integration approaches (Weber, Tarba and Reichal, 2009; Weber and Tarba, 2010), thus avoiding the coordination costs incurred due to structural separation and the transition costs due to temporal separation (Simsek et al., 2009).

PMI efforts are of utmost importance for extracting potential synergies between the acquired and acquiring firms (Haspeslaph and Jemison, 1991; Weber, Tarba and Reichal 2011; Weber, Tarba, and Rozen-Bachar, 2011a; Weber, 2013). Following a review of the literature that shows mixed, contradicting and confusing empirical evidence of the effects of cultural compatibility and strategic fit on M&A performance, Weber, Tarba and Reichal (2011) proposed a new concept that revised previous integration approaches matrices (see Figure 11.1) and tested it (Weber, Tarba and Rozen-Bachar (2011a). This framework is useful as a platform for the various options of balance between human and task integration efforts and resource allocation. Human integration refers to the creation of shared identity, trusting relationships and minimizing conflicts between members of the combined organization. The results of good human integration in M&A are lower post-merger behavior effects such as stress, negative attitudes, higher commitment and cooperation as well as lower turnover among key talents and top executives. Task integration refers to procedural and physical integration as gauged by the extent to which the M&A standardizes work procedures and systems, transfers capabilities and removes overlapping operations. These tasks are used to realize potential synergies that result from the M&A. At the same time, task integration involves autonomy removal from acquired managers that, like cultural differences, causes conflicts and behavioral problems.

This framework emphasizes cultural differences and synergy potential as pre-merger determinants of M&A performance. (Note: The uncertainty avoidance is just one example for one cultural dimension, among others. It will be used below in hypotheses development.) One implication of this framework is that implemented integration approaches are mediators of the

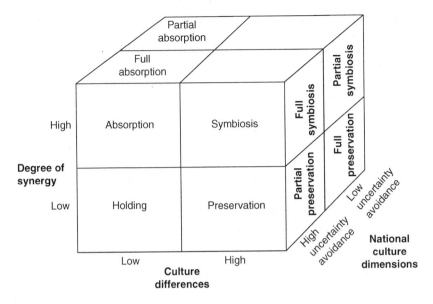

Figure 11.1 Corporate cultural differences, national cultural distance and optional integration approaches

relationships between these sources and M&A performance. This framework and recent empirical findings published in another special issue on M&A provide promising support for the mediation role of integration approaches to M&A performance (Weber, Tarba and Rozen-Bachar, 2011a).

The *absorption* approach requires a high level of integration for achieving a high level of synergy. *Preservation* reflects the lowest level of integration in low synergy potential M&As. *Symbiosis* is for moderate levels of synergy and reflects a moderate level of integration.

The human and task integration and the role of HR manager are related to the cube dimensions shown in Figure 11.1. Human integration has to deal with human effects of cultural differences, while task integration refers to the resources and efforts used to seize synergy potential. However, the loss of autonomy that usually results from the integration process can be detrimental to the performance of the specific M&A deal (Weber, Shenkar and Raveh, 1996). This issue, among others, causes conflicting demands on management of human and task integration, and thus, requires ambidexterity. These conflicting demands ask for balance between efforts and resources dedicated to human and task integration and alignment of each to the specific synergy potential and cultural difference issues.

In practice, post-merger integration is an interactive and gradual process in which individuals from both organizations at M&A must learn to work together and cooperate. "Creating an atmosphere that can support it [the

172   *Yaakov Weber*

integration] is the real challenge" (Haspeslagh and Jemison, 1991, p. 107). Thus, while the integration process is aimed at improving performance based on synergy potential, it may also lead to human resource problems, such as stress, negative attitudes, low cooperation with and commitment to the success of the merger, and high turnover among top executives (Bjorkman, Stahl and Vaara, 2007; Weber, Shenkar and Raveh, 1996; Lubatkin, Schweiger and Weber, 1999). Furthermore, transferring knowledge and integrating other resources during the post-merger integration is also difficult because of cultural differences that create conflicts, communication problems and employee resistance (Weber, Tarba, and Rozen-Bachar, 2011a; Weber and Tarba, 2010).

Moreover, the contact between the two top management teams not only reduces the autonomy of the acquired top executives but also exposes the diverse national and corporate cultures of the management teams to each other and makes the differences salient (Weber, 1996). To the extent that cultural distance produces a 'culture clash', such a clash may be strongest at high synergy expected where the contact between the adherents of the opposing culture is the greatest (in high level of integration).

Thus, there is an explicit trade-off between high and low levels of integration. High levels of integration may be needed to exploit high levels of synergy, but a high level of integration may also cause human resource problems that have the potential to destroy the value of the acquired firm and increase costs to an extent that offsets the benefits expected from the merger.

In sum, human integration to deal with the consequences of cultural differences and autonomy removal due to integration process and tasks integration (to seize synergy potential) are not sufficient to explain M&A performance. Post-merger integration is a complex process that appears to need a better conceptualization than the simple linear relationship suggested by earlier studies. The following section, Proposition development, suggests using a combination of these two factors together with the concept of contextual ambidexterity to explain integration effectiveness.

Proposition development

Gibson and Birkinshaw (2004) propose *contextual* ambidexterity (as opposed to *structural* ambidexterity) as a mechanism to reconcile conflicting demands. By this they meant that the organization ought to design the appropriate context that would encourage and support each manager to achieve an appropriate level of balance between the conflicting demands. Thus, resource allocation is all about trade-offs between two or more sets of priorities, such as that for human versus task integration. Most of the important things that happen within organizations involve making choices that emphasize one objective ahead of another. They can therefore be positioned as potentially ambidextrous situations.

Each integration approach aims to achieve a different level of synergy. Yet, each faces a different level of cultural differences (see Figure 11.1).

Thus, each integration approach aims to a different level of integration that is associated with a different level of removed autonomy from acquired managers. The preservation approach is characterized by low levels of integration due to low synergy potential. In fact, an unnecessarily high level of integration in the full preservation approach has the potential to cause conflicts due to culture clash and removal of autonomy from acquired managers with no clear explanation for the need for such autonomy removal. Therefore, the recommended balance of efforts between human and tasks integration will be to invest less in efforts to achieve synergy, and thus, less effort will be necessary to invest for human integration. However, the cube that presents the integration approaches also refers to a partial level of integration. For example, when the acquirer nationality is characterized by a high level of uncertainty avoidance, the acquirer needs some level of control to lower the levels of uncertainty (Weber, Tarba, and Reichal, 2011b). In the case of partial preservation, such an acquirer will remove some autonomy from acquired managers to reduce its uncertainty and will follow partial preservation. This integration approach will bring greater necessity for taking care of the human side than is needed in full preservation. This leads to the following propositions:

> **Proposition 1:** Full preservation will require low efforts for human and task integration during the post-merger integration process
>
> **Proposition 2:** Partial preservation will require low efforts for task integration and higher efforts for human integration

The symbiosis approach is characterized by a moderate level of synergy but with a high level of cultural differences. Here, moderate levels of integration due to a moderate level of synergy potential will be required, thus, there is a moderate level of task integration efforts. Yet, the high level of cultural differences requires high efforts for human integration. In partial symbiosis managers would like to avoid the expected culture clash, and use a lower level of autonomy removal, willing to be satisfied with less, but more viable, synergy. Hence,

> **Proposition 3:** Full symbiosis will require moderate efforts on task and human integration
>
> **Proposition 4:** Partial symbiosis will require less task integration efforts and higher human integration efforts relative to full symbiosis.

The absorption approach is characterized by both a high level of synergy and a high level of cultural differences. Here, highest levels of integration due to the high level of synergy potential will be required, thus, there is a high level of task integration efforts. Similarly, the high level of cultural differences will require a high level of effort for the human integration. In partial absorption managers would like to avoid the expected culture clash, and may use a lower

174 Yaakov Weber

level of integration focusing on the most promising synergy rather than trying to have it all. Therefore,

> **Proposition 5:** Full absorption will require high efforts on task and human integration
> **Proposition 6:** Partial absorption will require lesser task integration efforts and human integration efforts relative to full absorption, but both will be higher than in the symbiosis integration approach

Discussion and conclusion

The management literature has been trying for the last three decades to explain the enduring paradox of the high rate of M&A failure vs. the growing activity and volume of M&As. Two streams of research, organizational behavior with a focus on cultural distance, and strategic management with a focus on synergy potential, have been overly simplistic in assuming that either cultural differences or synergy potential may affect acquisition outcomes in isolation from the other factor in post-merger integration processes. This chapter offers a more sophisticated conceptualization of the effect of human integration and task integration.

The chapter builds on organizational ambidexterity theory to address a major M&A challenge during post-merger integration of managing the trade-off between organizationally incompatible objectives. Most M&As aim to seize synergy. This requires task integration that usually creates conflict between members of both organizations. This conflict may be detrimental not only to synergy potential but to M&A performance.

It is suggested, first, to treat each M&A according to the best integration approach that fits its own characteristics, such as cultural differences and level of potential synergy. Following this, the chapter develops propositions on the best balance of effort for human integration and task integration.

This offers ample opportunities for future research. First, testing hypotheses based on the suggested propositions may reveal the best balance for various M&A performance. For example, balance may vary in domestic versus international M&A, different industries, various size differences between the buying and target companies, etc. Second, top management turnover after the merger was found to reduce M&A performance. It will be interesting to find how different balances between human and task integration affect top management turnover. Similarly, because domestic and international M&A have different impact on human behavior during PMI (Weber, Rahman-Mor, and Tarba, 2012; Weber, Shenkar, and Raveh, 1996), these balances may have different effects. Thus, the exploration of how different balances between human and task integration affect human behavior such as stress, attitudes, commitment and cooperation of the acquired managers and employees can help to accomplish successful PMI.

In all these research avenues, it will be interesting to see the impact of HR practices on human behavior and eventually M&A performance. Such practices as communication, training, incentive systems and more, will be critical to human behavior and may have different impact on various ways to balance human and task integration in various integration approaches.

Acknowledgments

This study was supported by the research unit at the school of Business Administration, The College of Management Academic Studies, Rishon Lezion, Israel.

References

Björkman, I., Stahl, G. K. and Vaara, E. (2007). Cultural Differences and Capability Transfer in Cross-border Acquisitions: The Mediating Roles of Capability Complementarity, Absorptive Capacity, and Social Integration. *Journal of International Business Studies*, 38, 658–672.

Birkinshaw, J., Bresman, H. and Håkanson, L. (2000). Managing the Post-acquisition Integration Process: How the Human Integration and Task Integration Processes Interact to Foster Value Creation. *Journal of Management Studies*, 37, 395–425.

Haspeslagh, P.C. and Jemison, D.B. (1991) *Managing Acquisitions: Creating Value Through Corporate Renewal*. New York: Free Press.

King, D. R., Dalton, D. R., Daily, C. M. and Covin, J. G. (2004) Meta-analyses of Post-Acquisition Performance: Indications of Unidentified Moderators. *Strategic Management Journal*, 25, 187–200.

Lubatkin, M. and Schweiger, D., Weber, Y. (1999). Top Management Turnover, Following Mergers: A Longitudinal Study of Perceptual and Attitudinal Determinants. *Journal of Management*, 49 (9), 1181–1202.

Weber, Y. (2013). *Handbook for Research on M&A*. Edward Elgar Publishing Limited, Cheltenham, UK.

Weber, Y., Oberg, C and Tarba, S. (2014). *A comprehensive Guide to Mergers and Acquisitions Management: Integration and Implementation*. Financial Times Press, New York, NY.

Weber, Y., Rahman-Mor, D. and Tarba, S. (2012). Managing Cross Cultural Conflicts in Organizations. *International Journal of Cross Cultural Management*, 12(1), 73–99.

Weber, Y., Shenkar, O. and Raveh, A., (1996). National and Corporate Culture Fit in Mergers/Acquisitions: An Exploratory Study. *Management Science*, 42 (8), 1215–1227.

Weber, Y. and Tarba, S. (2010). Human Resource Practices and Performance of Mergers and Acquisitions in Israel. *Human Resource Management Review*, 20, 203–211.

Weber, Y., Tarba, S and Rozen-Bachar, Z. (2011a). Mergers and Acquisitions Paradox – the Mediating Role of Integration Approach. *European Journal of International Management*, 5 (4), 373–393.

Weber, Y., Tarba, S. and Reichal, A. (2011b). A Model of the Influence of Culture on Integration Approaches and International Mergers and Acquisitions Performance. *International Studies of Management and Organizations*, 41 (3), 9–24.

12 An integrated cross-functional model of strategic innovation management in business

The implications of ten cross-functional business areas

S. M. Riad Shams, Demetris Vrontis, Yaakov Weber and Evangelos Tsoukatos

Introduction

In terms of strategic innovation management in business, in general, cross-disciplinary knowledge plays an instrumental role in long-term success (Bresciani et al., 2012; Rossi et al., 2014, Christofi et al., 2015, 2017; Chebbi et al., 2016; Festa et al., 2017). This is why this book attempts to develop insights from cross-disciplinary business knowledge streams to originate a cross-functional business innovation management model, in order to underpin research and practice in management innovation. In general, novel cross-disciplinary business and management knowledge plays an important role in business and management innovation. Also, we know that innovative management processes have significant implications for effective cross-functional management, and overall business and management success. From this context, the aim of this book is to extend our understandings of how different cross-functional business and management functional areas individually and collectively can underpin innovation in business management, in order to proactively explore/exploit business opportunities and/or offset business risks. Following this context, each chapter of this book presents different novel theoretical insights on diverse business knowledge streams and their innovative applied implications for cross-functional business management practices. Following these cross-disciplinary business theories and their cutting-edge, discipline-specific practical implications, this chapter proposes and justifies a cross-functional strategic business innovation management model (Figure 12.1).

In terms of academic research, these cross-disciplinary contexts of theoretical developments offer a number of innovative theoretical propositions, which are comprehensively supported by rigorous conceptual developments and state-of-the-art empirical analyses, focusing on the diverse management functional areas. Alongside presenting the new research, this book also offers generous scope for further research in innovative business models and cross-functional management. In terms of practical implications, first, the different chapters offer the varied business discipline-specific fresh insights and their relevant management functional area-specific implications. For example, the new insights from neuroscience or marketing as academic disciplines and the implications of those new insights for strategic management or international business practices as management functional areas. Second, the cross-functional business innovation management model (Figure 12.1) of this book appears as instrumental to enable the cross-functional management teams to proactively underpin organisation-wide business innovation processes.

In order to pursue the aim of this book, an inductive constructivist approach of critical reasoning is followed as an analysis method (Shams, 2015, 2016a) in this current chapter to summarise the overall findings of the rest of the chapters of the book and propose an innovative business model that will have implications for cross-functional management practice. In order to summarise the key insights of this book and to develop and justify the cross-functional strategic business innovation management model of Figure 12.1, the remainder of this chapter first discusses the ten cross-functional perspectives in business that are extracted from Chapter 2 to Chapter 11. Second, an integrated cross-functional model of strategic innovation management in business is proposed and justified. Finally, this chapter presents the conclusions, limitations and future research areas on the core cross-functional concept of this book for strategic innovation management in business.

The ten cross-functional perspectives in business

The ten chapter-specific (Chapter 2 to Chapter 11) cross-functional perspectives of strategic innovation management discussed in this book are outlined below:

- Chapter 2 – neuroscience and its impact of marketing;
- Chapter 3 – information and communication science and its impact on stakeholder relationships and engagement;
- Chapter 4 – international trade and export management before and after the economic transitions;
- Chapter 5 – entrepreneurship for knowledge management;
- Chapter 6 – financial management and profitability;
- Chapter 7 – persuasion science for business communication;
- Chapter 8 – strategic innovation management for stakeholder/customer satisfaction in the higher education industry;
- Chapter 9 – stakeholder relationship management and marketing for entrepreneurial innovation;
- Chapter 10 – business risks, strategies and environment; and
- Chapter 11 – cross-cultural issues for HRM and mergers and acquisitions.

178   S. M. Riad Shams et al.

Based on the following definition of strategic innovation in business, this section attempts to summarise and discuss the key driving factors and mediating factors of strategic innovation, centred on the discussion and insights of the ten cross-functional perspectives in innovation management of Chapter 2 to Chapter 11:

> [...] a firm's tendency to engage in and support new ideas, novelty, experimentation and creative processes that may result in new products, services or technological processes. Innovativeness represents a basic willingness to depart from existing practices and venture beyond the current state of the art (in order to sustain the competitive advantage underlying the innovation).
>
> (Lumpkin and Dess, 1996, p. 142, as cited in Vrontis et al., 2012, pp. 422–423; Shams and Kaufmann, 2016, p. 1257)

Here, the focus of discussion is to illustrate insights on the ideas, novelty, experimentation or creative processes that are planned and implemented, based on the ten cross-functional business perspectives in innovation management, in order to develop a new product, service, idea or technological process. Table 12.1 demonstrates these insights.

Table 12.1, first, summarises the chapter-specific cross-functional perspectives for strategic innovation management process in business. Second, it illustrates the key driving and mediating factors of strategic innovation management to develop and nurture ideas, novelty, experimentation or creative processes for business innovation. These driving and mediating factors are extracted from Chapter 2 to Chapter 11, in relation to the chapter-specific arguments on product, service, idea or technological process innovation. Third, Table 12.1 shows the newly innovated/proposed products, services, ideas or technological processes that are presented in this book. Finally, the table exhibits the innovation outcome, based on the implications of the chapter-specific arguments.

Building on the concept of Table 12.1, the next section of this chapter presents and justifies an integrated cross-functional model of strategic innovation management in business.

An integrated cross-functional model of strategic innovation management in business

Figure 12.1 is structured based on the cross-functional driving and mediating factors of strategic innovation management process in business. The first constituent of Figure 12.1 is "entrepreneurial orientation and market data collection". Entrepreneurial orientation can be defined as "understanding target market-specific conditions" (Shams, 2016b, p. 140), related to the needs, wants and expectations of the target market, and the relevant economic and political environment, in order to organise a process of both tangible and

Table 12.1 Cross-functional business perspectives for strategic cross-functional innovation management in business

Chapter number	The cross-functional business perspectives for strategic innovation management	The key factors of strategic innovation management (ideas, novelty, experimentation or creative processes)		Innovated product/service/idea/technological process	Innovation management outcome (corresponding to the arguments of Figure 1.1)
		Driving factors	Mediating factors		
2	Neuroscience and its impact on marketing management	Data collection about the target market. Influencing the behaviour of the target market	- Cognitive/Perceptual image of the target market	Applications of neuroprosthetic devices for gathering data and influencing behaviour of the target market	Internal and/or external (intra and/or inter firm and other stakeholders') use of the innovated product/service/idea/technological process for optimising value for all associated stakeholders, in order to ensure a superior competitive advantage
3	Information and communication science and its impact on stakeholder relationships and engagement	Information sharing among the key stakeholders	Availability/Accessibility of right information at the right time for right target audience	An original process of classifying the role of information sharing and communication strategies in supporting the emergence of the preconditions for stakeholder engagement	
4	International trade and export management before and after the economic transitions	Establishing and Sustaining Competitive advantage	Capability to enter into the new market(s)	New insights on proactive and prolific international trade management in economic transitions	
5	Entrepreneurship for knowledge management	Entrepreneurial orientation	Absorptive capacity of knowledge exploitation	A new idea on the influence of entrepreneurial orientation on the exploitation of knowledge	
6	Financial management and profitability	Value creation	Growth strategy	Perceptive influence of value creation on the growth strategy in the banking sector	

(continued)

Table 12.1 (Cont.)

Chapter number	The cross-functional business perspectives for strategic innovation management	The key factors of strategic innovation management (ideas, novelty, experimentation or creative processes)		Innovated product/service/idea/technological process	Innovation management outcome (corresponding to the arguments of Figure 1.1)
		Driving factors	Mediating factors		
7	Persuasion science for business communication	Means of persuasion: Public relations Advertising Digital media Stakeholder consultation	Efficacy of the action-based persuasion techniques	A unique method of the commercialisation of innovation	
8	Strategic innovation management for stakeholder/customer satisfaction	Stakeholder expectation	Stakeholder feedback	An innovative model of stakeholder/customer satisfaction	
9	Stakeholder relationship management and marketing for entrepreneurial innovation	Analysing and Understanding stakeholder causal scopes (the cause and consequence of stakeholder relationships and interactions	Integration of the stakeholders' needs, wants and expectations in the business innovation management process	A planned and organised process of alignment/re-alignment of new idea/novelty/experimentation and creative input towards product/service innovation	
10	Business risks, strategies and environment	Business risk and environmental issues	Long-term strategic plan	Insights on legitimacy framework in interpreting risk and environmental reporting strategies	
11	Cross-cultural issues for HRM and mergers and acquisitions	Cross-cultural issues (corporate culture difference and national culture distance)	Balance in between the cross-cultural issues	Human and task integration during post-merger integration	

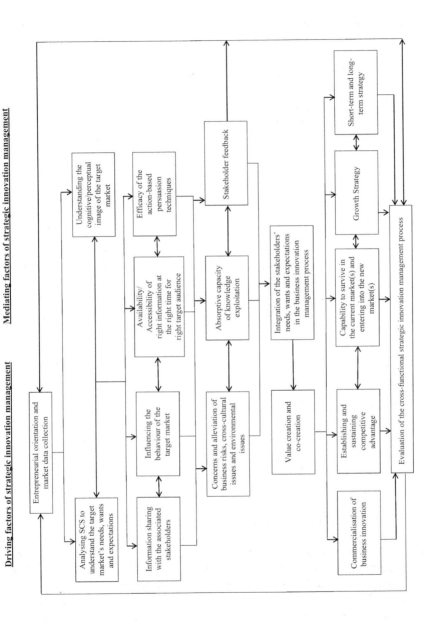

Figure 12.1 Cross-functional driving and mediating factors of strategic innovation management in business

182 S. M. Riad Shams et al.

intangible resource allocation/reallocation, with an aim to deliver those market needs, wants and expectations cost-effectively, competitively and sustainably, in a way that would be expected and accepted by the target market. Entrepreneurial orientation therefore is an "organization-wide generation of market intelligence that pertains to current and future customer needs, dissemination of intelligence across departments, and organization-wide responsiveness" (Hurley and Hult, 1998, p. 43). Generating market intelligence to develop a proper entrepreneurial orientation generally requires ongoing monitoring of the target market conditions (Kohli and Jaworski, 1990; Narver and Slater, 1990; Shams, 2013).

The target market, generally, includes not only the customers or consumers of an organisation, but also all associated key internal and external stakeholders of the organisation, which includes, but is not limited to, employees, shareholders, suppliers, intermediaries, other government and non-government agencies and even the general public, if the activities of the organisation impact on these groups. From this context, the efforts related to market data collection for successful market orientation should involve collecting data about all associated stakeholders, including customers, since the relevant data and information about the associated stakeholders is one of the key elements for successful market orientation (Shams, 2017a, 2017b).

The key focus of entrepreneurial market orientation and market data collection in the process of cross-functional strategic innovation in business that is portrayed in Figure 12.1 is to analyse stakeholder causal scope to develop a detailed understanding of the needs, wants and expectations of the target market(s), in order to develop a cognitive or perpetual image of the target market.

> The cause and consequence of stakeholder relationships and interactions in a network, as a stakeholder causal scope (SCS) helps to collaborate with the stakeholders, with an on-going understanding on the contemporary and latent needs, and subsequent value-anticipation of the associated stakeholders.
>
> (Shams, 2016c, p. 676)

"The image of a (target market) is the blend of beliefs, ideas and impressions that (the entrepreneurs or marketers) have about the (target market)" (Kotler et al., 1993, as cited in Shams, 2016d, p. 143). From this context, analysing SCS would be instrumental for entrepreneurs or marketers to develop beliefs, ideas, impressions and an overall image of their target market, in relation to understanding the cognitive behaviour or perceptions of the target market, related to the target market's needs, wants and expectations. Developing such insights, in general, is useful to comprehensively understand the target market's value anticipation, based on their needs, wants and expectations, in order to deliver that value in a way that the target market expects and accepts.

On the one hand, analysing SCS is valuable to understand the target market's cognitive or perceptual image. On the other hand, developing insights on the target market's cognitive or perceptual image would also be valuable for further analysing SCS as a continuous part of entrepreneurial orientation and market data collection. The double-headed arrow sign in Figure 12.1 shows the dynamics of the interrelationship between SCS analysis and understanding the target market's cognitive image. This is useful for sharing the relevant information with the key stakeholders at the right time, with the right information, targeting the right target audience, in order to persuade/influence the behaviour of the target audience/stakeholder, in favour of the organisation's or entrepreneur's or the marketer's value proposition.

In these communication dynamics, a proper exploitation of the acquired knowledge (i.e. market data and information) is instrumental to receive and respond to stakeholder feedback, as well as to analyse the potential business risks, cross-cultural issues and environmental concerns, with an aim to mitigate them. Following the analysis of the business risks, cross-cultural issues and environmental concerns, the acquired knowledge can be exploited to integrate the target market's needs, wants and expectations in the planning and implementing process of innovative products/services/ideas or technological processes, in order to create or co-create value with the involved stakeholders (Shams and Belyaeva, 2017). In this planning and testing stage, upon or during the value creation or co-creation for the anticipated innovative products/services/ideas/technological processes related to the target market's needs, wants and expectations, the other key issues that need to be planned are:

- the short-term and long-term strategy for the newly innovated products, services, ideas or technological processes, in order to optimise the internal and external use and the competitive advantage of the innovation; and
- the commercialisation or launching strategy, in association with the strategies to survive in the organisation's existing market(s), as well as the strategies to enter into the new market(s) with the innovated products, services, ideas or the technological process, with an aim to attain and sustain the competitive advantage of the innovation.

The final stage of Figure 12.1 is the evaluation of the cross-functional strategic innovation management process. Figure 12.1 exhibits that the cross-disciplinary driving and mediating factors of strategic business innovation that are extracted from the arguments of this book are the core elements to plan, implement and monitor the impact of this cross-disciplinary innovation management process, in order to underpin research and practice in management innovation, which is further discussed in the next section.

Conclusions, limitations and future research

This final chapter summarises the overall findings of the rest of the cross-disciplinary chapters of the book to propose an innovative cross-functional innovation management model (Figure 12.1). This business model will have implications for cross-functional management practice across diverse industries and markets. However, in order to appropriately exploit the insights and implications of Figure 12.1 across different industries and markets, they need to be adapted to the industry-specific and market-specific issues, ideas and phenomena, since different industries and markets have different variables that would not be equally effective or important in all different markets and industries.

A key limitation of the cross-disciplinary strategic business innovation model of Figure 12.1 is it is developed based on only ten cross-disciplinary perspectives, which are (1) neuroscience and its impact of marketing, (2) information and communication science and its impact on stakeholder relationships and engagement, (3) international trade and export management before and after the economic transitions, (4) entrepreneurship for knowledge management, (5) financial management and profitability, (6) persuasion science for business communication, (7) strategic innovation management for stakeholder/customer satisfaction in the higher education industry, (8) stakeholder relationship management and marketing for entrepreneurial innovation, (9) business risks, strategies and environment, and (10) cross-cultural issues for HRM and mergers and acquisitions. Other cross-functional perspectives in business, such as corporate social responsibility, quality control and quality assurance, supply chain management and so forth are either not completely covered in this book or entirely overlooked, because of the limited scope of a single book. From this context, the other cross-functional perspectives in business bring an ideal opportunity for future research, focusing on the core cross-functional concept of this book.

Another limitation of the cross-disciplinary strategic business innovation model of Figure 12.1 is it is structured based on the arguments of studies that focus on specific socio-economic contexts, industries and markets. As a result, future research can also be extended to investigate the arguments and insights of Figure 12.1 in other markets, socio-economic contexts and industries across the world, in order to strengthen the contribution of this study, as well as to progress the debate on this cross-disciplinary concept of strategic innovation management in business. Similarly, the competitive advantage that would be derived from the entrepreneurial orientation and cross-functional innovation management process can be perceived differently by different stakeholders.

> Based on different age, income, gender and other relevant market characteristics, the extent of perceived competitive advantage would be different to different stakeholders. For example, the competitive advantage that is originated from the same outcome of a co-ordinated entrepreneurial process would appear as extremely advantageous, moderately advantageous and even entirely disadvantageous to different customers and other stakeholders, based on their different perspectives.
>
> (Shams and Kaufmann, 2016, p. 1262)

From this context, analysing the associated stakeholders' diverse extents of perceived experience on competitive advantage would provide new insights to the entrepreneurial orientation and cross-functional innovation management concept of Figure 12.1. In future research "a longitudinal data collection process would be valuable to ascertain how the mutual application of…(the discussed driving and mediating factors of cross-functional innovation management in business) has progressed" (Shams, 2016c, p. 687). "Beside the academic interest, further research will also satisfy the need for explicit guidance for practice" (Shams and Lombardi, 2016, p. 234).

References

Bresciani, S., Thrassou, A. and Vrontis, D. (2012). Human Resource Management – Practices, Performance and Strategy in the Italian Hotel Industry. *World Review of Entrepreneurship, Management and Sustainable Development,* 8 (4), 405–423.

Chebbi, H., Yahiaoui, D., Vrontis, D. and Thrassou, A. (2016). The Impact of Ambidextrous Leadership on the Internationalization of Emerging Market Firms (EMF): The Case of India. *Thunderbird International Business Review,* 59 (3), 421–436.

Christofi, M., Vrontis, D., Kitchen, P. and Papasolomou, I. (2015). Innovation and Cause-related Marketing Success: a Conceptual Framework and Propositions. *Journal of Services Marketing,* 29 (5), 354–366.

Christofi, M., Leonidou, E. and Vrontis, D. (2017). Marketing Research on Mergers and Acquisitions: a Systematic Review and Future Directions. *International Marketing Review* (published online ahead of print, DOI: 10.1108/IMR-03-2015-0100).

Festa, G., Ciasullo, V.C., Vrontis, D. and Thrassou, A. (2017). Cooperating for Competing – a Small Italian Wineries' Internationalisation Strategy Case Study. *Global Business and Economics Review,* 19 (5), 648–670.

Hurley, R. F. and Hult, G. T. M. (1998). Innovation, market orientation, and organizational learning: An integration and empirical examination. *Journal of Marketing,* 62, 42–54.

Kohli, A. and Jaworski, B. (1990). Market orientation: The construct, research propositions and managerial implications. *Journal of Marketing,* 54 (2), 1–18.

Kotler, P., Haiderr, D. H., and Rein, I. (1993). Marketing places. New York, NY: The Free Press.

Lumpkin, G.T. and Dess, G.G. (1996). Clarifying the entrepreneurial orientation construct and linking it to performance. *Academy of Management Review, 21* (1), 135–72.

Narver, J. and Slater, S. (1990). The effect of a market orientation on business profitability. *Journal of Marketing,* 54, 20–36.

Rossi, M., Vrontis, D. and Thrassou, A., (2014). Agro Business in a Changing Competitive Environment – Campania firms' strategic, marketing and financial choices. *World Review of Entrepreneurship, Management and Sustainable Development,* 10 (2), 321–333.

Shams, S. M. R. (2013). Implications of relationship marketing indicators to enable organisational growth: A stakeholder causal scope analysis. In Kaufmann, H., and Panni, M. F. A. K. (Eds.), *Customer Centric Marketing Strategies: Tools for Building Organizational Performance* (214–244). Hershey, PA: Business Science Reference.

Shams, S. M. R. (2015). Stakeholders' perceptions and reputational antecedents: A review of stakeholder relationship, reputation and brand positioning. *Journal of Advances in Management Research, 12*(3), 314–329.

Shams, S. M. R. (2016a). Stakeholder relationship management in online business and competitive value propositions: Evidence from the sports industry. *International Journal of Online Marketing, 6* (2), 1–17.

Shams, S. M. R. (2016b). Sustainability issues in transnational education service: A conceptual framework and empirical insights. *Journal of Global Marketing, 29* (3), 139–155.

Shams, S. M. R. (2016c). Capacity building for sustained competitive advantage: A conceptual framework. *Marketing Intelligence & Planning, 34* (5), 671–691.

Shams, S. M. R. (2016d). Branding destination image: A stakeholder causal scope analysis for internationalisation of destinations. *Tourism Planning and Development, 13* (2), 140-153.

Shams, S. M. R. and Kaufmann, H. R. (2016). Entrepreneurial co-creation: a research vision to be materialised. *Management Decision, 54* (6), 1250–1268.

Shams, S. M. R. (2017a). Transnational education and total quality management: A Stakeholder-centred model. *Journal of Management Development, 36* (3), 376–389.

Shams, S. M. R., and Lombardi, R. (2016). Socio-economic value co-creation and sports tourism: Evidence from Tasmania. *World Review of Entrepreneurship. Management and Sustainable Development, 12*(2/3), 218–238.

Shams, S. M. R. (2017b). International education management: Implications of relational perspectives and ethnographic insights to nurture international students' academic experience. *Journal for Multicultural Education, 11* (3), 206–223.

Shams, S. M. R. and Belyaeva, Z. (2017). Quality assurance driving factors as antecedents of knowledge management: A stakeholder-focussed perspective in higher education. *Journal of the Knowledge Economy*, 1–14 (published online ahead of print, DOI: https://doi.org/10.1007/s13132-017-0472-2).

Vrontis, D., Tharassou, A., Chebbi, H. and Yahiaoui, D. (2012). Transcending innovativeness towards strategic reflexivity. *Qualitative Market Research: An International Journal, 15* (4), 420–437.

Index

absorptive capabilities 60
advertising 11, 13, 42, 88, 89, 90, 91, 94, 95, 96, 100, 101, 102, 103, 104, 105, 122, 134, 180
agriculture 44, 45, 47, 48, 54, 56, 57
agri-food 44, 45, 46, 48, 50, 51, 52, 53, 54, 55, 56
annual report 41, 140, 147, 152, 153, 154, 155, 156, 157, 158, 159, 160, 163, 164, 165, 166
augmentation 12, 14

brain 12, 13, 14, 16, 18, 19, 20, 21, 22, 23, 24, 88, 89, 92, 101, 104, 105
brain-computer interfaces 22, 24
brain spyware 20
brand 16, 42, 45, 66, 89, 91, 98, 99, 100, 101, 102, 103, 104, 119, 123, 134, 135, 136, 144, 148, 150, 186
branding 57, 123, 134, 150, 186
business risk 7, 154, 155, 176, 177, 180, 181, 183, 184
B2B (Business-to-business) 36, 125, 127, 128, 129, 130, 131, 132, 136, 141, 142, 143, 145
business strategy 10, 41, 154, 166

case study 8, 51, 52, 57, 72, 121, 122, 131, 148, 151, 185
change management 4, 9
CO2 emission 157
co-creation 8, 10, 36, 39, 42, 43, 124, 129, 150, 181, 183, 186
cognitive 6, 11, 12, 14, 15, 16, 18, 19, 20, 21, 22, 24, 37, 38, 75, 89, 103, 179, 181, 182, 183
competition 55, 56, 90, 94, 108, 134, 135, 137, 138
competitive advantage 2, 3, 10, 38, 54, 58, 59, 61, 67, 68, 69, 108, 123, 126,

127, 128, 130, 144, 146, 150, 165, 167, 178, 179, 181, 183, 184, 185, 186
communication strategy 29, 34
competitiveness 25, 27, 34, 35, 36, 45, 46, 54, 55, 56, 59, 74, 120
competitive environment 106, 120, 123, 149, 185
conceptual framework 8, 10, 11, 15, 21, 38, 43, 55, 83, 101, 107, 111, 112, 113, 115, 118, 122, 123, 147, 150, 185, 186
consumer behaviour 12, 23, 43, 89, 98, 101, 104, 155
consulting 93, 98
content analysis 90, 152, 153, 155, 156, 163, 164, 165, 166, 167
correlation 31, 32, 59, 64, 76, 77, 80, 81, 93, 100, 113, 114, 115, 116, 117, 158, 163, 164
corporate communication 30, 36, 38, 42, 43, 154
corporate entrepreneurship 68, 70
corporate governance 36, 39, 76, 81, 82, 83
corporate management 155
creative 2, 7, 88, 89, 90, 100, 102, 103, 127, 128, 129, 133, 142, 144, 149, 150, 178, 179, 180
credit cooperative 71, 73, 74, 80, 81, 84
cross-cultural 6, 7, 9, 38, 42, 57, 84, 149, 177, 180, 181, 183, 184
cross-functional 1, 2, 4, 5, 6, 7, 8, 9, 10, 130, 176, 177, 178, 179, 180, 181, 182, 183, 184, 185
cross-functional business 1, 2, 5, 6, 7, 130, 176, 178, 179, 180
cross-functional management 177, 184
cross-functional model 5, 7, 176, 177, 178
cross-functional team 2, 4, 5, 6, 9
customer satisfaction 7, 36, 102, 107, 108, 121, 177, 180, 184

188 *Index*

culture 38, 41, 97, 103, 129, 133, 140, 149, 163, 171, 172, 173, 175, 180
cultural management 9, 42, 57, 84, 149, 175
cybernetics 11, 12, 14, 15, 16, 18, 21, 24

decision making 37, 48, 55, 59, 61, 66, 88, 89, 103, 104, 119, 131
demographic factor 111, 112, 114, 118, 119
digital 23, 37, 87, 93, 97, 104, 105, 147, 180
digital marketing 87, 93, 97
disclosure 29, 30, 33, 34, 36, 37, 39, 40, 41, 42, 43, 152, 154, 155, 156, 159, 163, 165, 166, 167
dynamic capabilities 58, 59, 61, 62, 66, 67, 68, 69, 70

economic efficiency 45, 46, 50, 56
economic growth 74, 84, 125, 139, 146
economic performance 29, 35, 43, 82, 129, 149, 152, 158, 163, 164, 165
electric mobility 152, 153, 154, 155, 156, 157, 158, 159, 160, 161, 162, 163, 164, 165
entrepreneur 4, 129, 146, 182, 183
entrepreneurship 7, 8, 10, 36, 37, 59, 68, 69, 70, 121, 122, 123, 124, 149, 150, 177, 179, 184, 185
entrepreneurial 7, 8, 9, 10, 58, 59, 60, 62, 63, 64, 65, 66, 67, 68, 69, 70, 103, 123, 124, 125, 127, 129, 130, 131, 132, 139, 145, 146, 149, 150, 151, 177, 178, 179, 180, 181, 182, 183, 184, 185, 186
entrepreneurial challenge 8, 123, 149
entrepreneurial capabilities 139
entrepreneurial co-creation 10, 124, 150, 186
entrepreneurial culture 129
entrepreneurial development 10, 69, 150
entrepreneurial initiative 125, 131, 132, 145, 146
entrepreneurial innovation 7, 125, 127, 129, 177, 180, 184
entrepreneurial mindset 129, 151
entrepreneurial organisation 129, 130, 131
entrepreneurial orientation 9, 58, 59, 60, 62, 63, 64, 65, 66, 67, 68, 69, 70, 178, 179, 181, 182, 183, 184, 185
ethical 11, 15, 18, 21, 22, 23, 24, 85, 89, 96, 100, 102
ethically 13, 15

environment 1, 3, 5, 7, 15, 19, 37, 39, 41, 57, 58, 59, 61, 66, 68, 70, 88, 95, 96, 97, 99, 104, 106, 110, 120, 123, 136, 149, 152, 154, 155, 157, 159, 162, 166, 177, 178, 180, 184, 185
environmental 5, 19, 37, 39, 41, 57, 58, 70, 152, 154, 155, 156, 157, 158, 159, 163, 165, 166, 167, 180, 181, 183
environmental aspect 155, 156
environmental change 5, 58
environmental concern 183
environmental disclosure 41, 156, 165, 166
environmental impact 152, 154, 155, 157, 158, 159, 163, 165
environmental initiative 163
environmental management 167
environmental performance 165, 166
environmental issues 154, 155, 158, 180, 181
environmental strategies 37
electric car 157, 160, 161, 162
export 7, 44, 45, 46, 47, 48, 49, 50, 51, 52, 53, 54, 55, 56, 59, 62, 65, 66, 69, 177, 179, 184
export management 7, 177, 179, 184

finance 5, 40, 43, 74, 82, 83, 146, 168
financial management 7, 177, 179, 184

global 9, 10, 36, 38, 54, 55, 56, 72, 83, 105, 122, 123, 128, 136, 147, 148, 150, 155, 166, 168, 185, 186
globalisation 8, 56, 102, 148

higher education 7, 10, 36, 43, 104, 106, 107, 108, 109, 111, 120, 121, 122, 123, 124, 150, 177, 184, 186
HRM (Human Resource Management) 5, 6, 7, 177, 180, 184

image 12, 16, 33, 92, 104, 119, 121, 123, 134, 150, 179, 181, 182, 183, 186
import 45, 56
information management 37
information sharing 25, 26, 28, 34, 35, 36, 37, 179, 181
information security 11, 23
information technology 153
innovation 1, 2, 3, 4, 5, 6, 7, 8, 9, 10, 36, 37, 38, 40, 42, 54, 55, 57, 58, 60, 63, 64, 65, 66, 68, 81, 83, 84, 101, 122, 124, 125, 127, 128, 129, 130, 131, 133, 140, 141, 142, 143, 145, 146, 147, 149,

150, 151, 176, 177, 178, 179, 180, 181, 182, 183, 184, 185
innovation capacity 54
innovation incubator 129
innovation management 1, 2, 3, 4, 5, 6, 7, 8, 9, 10, 40, 149, 150, 176, 177, 178, 179, 180, 181, 183, 184, 185
innovation model 184
innovation process 1, 2, 7, 125, 129, 133, 140, 141, 142, 143, 145, 146, 147, 177
innovative 3, 4, 8, 9, 10, 11, 58, 102, 106, 122, 127, 130, 133, 135, 141, 142, 146, 148, 151, 176, 177, 178, 180, 183, 186
innovative management 176
innovative model 180
institutional factor 111, 112, 113, 114, 115, 116, 118, 119, 120
international 7, 8, 9, 10, 23, 24, 36, 37, 39, 42, 43, 47, 54, 56, 57, 65, 67, 68, 69, 70, 72, 83, 84, 97, 101, 102, 103, 104, 107, 113, 121, 123, 124, 134, 135, 136, 137, 147, 148, 149, 151, 155, 163, 166, 174, 175, 177, 179, 184, 185
international business 54, 69, 121, 175, 177, 185
international education 149, 186
internationalisation 84, 121, 122, 123, 148, 150, 185, 186
international marketing 38, 147, 148, 185
international trade 7, 177, 179, 184
internet 9, 42, 57, 84, 124, 149, 151
internet of things 9, 42, 57, 84, 124, 149, 151

knowledge 5, 6, 7, 8, 9, 10, 13, 16, 18, 20, 25, 26, 27, 28, 29, 37, 38, 39, 40, 42, 43, 54, 57, 58, 59, 60, 61, 62, 63, 64, 65, 66, 67, 68, 75, 83, 84, 86, 88, 92, 98, 101, 103, 109, 128, 142, 143, 149, 150, 172, 176, 177, 179, 181, 183, 184, 186
knowledgeable 142
knowledge acquisition 60
knowledge economy 10, 38, 150
knowledge exploitation 58, 60, 61, 62, 64, 65, 66, 67, 179, 181
knowledge integration 5, 8, 42
knowledge management 5, 7, 9, 10, 37, 38, 57, 84, 149, 150, 179, 184, 186
knowledge production 10, 39
knowledge society 38
knowledge transfer 40, 61

management 1, 2, 3, 4, 5, 6, 7, 8, 9, 10, 13, 27, 29, 36, 37, 38, 39, 40, 41, 42, 43, 56, 57, 58, 59, 61, 62, 66, 67, 68, 69, 70, 72, 74, 77, 80, 82, 83, 84, 102, 103, 104, 110, 121, 122, 123, 124, 125, 126, 129, 130, 131, 132, 133, 136, 146, 148, 149, 150, 151, 154, 155, 163, 165, 166, 167, 168, 171, 172, 174, 175, 176, 177, 178, 179, 180, 181, 183, 184, 185, 186
management insight 5, 7
management model 176, 177
management research 43, 150
management vision 8
market capital 26, 28, 30, 33, 34, 35, 36
marketing 4, 5, 6, 7, 8, 9, 10, 12, 15, 18, 36, 38, 39, 41, 42, 43, 45, 46, 54, 55, 69, 83, 85, 87, 88, 89, 90, 92, 93, 94, 95, 96, 97, 98, 99, 101, 102, 103, 104, 105, 106, 107, 121, 122, 123, 125, 126, 127, 128, 130, 131, 133, 135, 137, 138, 139, 140, 141, 142, 143, 145, 146, 147, 148, 149, 150, 151, 177, 179, 180, 184, 185, 186
marketing communication 42, 85, 87, 88, 97, 99, 100, 102, 104, 122
marketing management 6, 102, 149
marketing research 5, 9, 42, 89, 96, 147, 185
market value 26, 30, 33, 34, 35, 57
multinational 36, 156

neural 11, 12, 13, 14, 15, 16, 18, 19, 20, 22, 23
neuromarketing 11, 12, 13, 15, 16, 17, 18, 19, 20, 21, 22, 23, 86, 88, 89, 90, 92, 96, 97, 99, 100, 101, 102, 103, 104, 105
neuroprostheses 13, 14, 15, 16, 17, 18, 19, 20, 21, 24
neuroprosthetics 11, 23, 24
novelty 2, 3, 7, 104, 127, 128, 129, 144, 145, 178, 179, 180

online 8, 9, 10, 62, 88, 95, 96, 97, 99, 100, 121, 132, 147, 149, 185, 186

packaging 13
perception 30, 34, 35, 41, 88, 100, 101, 102, 106, 107, 109, 110, 111, 120, 121, 123, 150, 156, 165, 182, 186
persuasion 7, 85, 86, 87, 88, 89, 90, 91, 92, 93, 94, 95, 96, 97, 98, 99, 100, 101, 102, 103, 104, 105, 177, 180, 181, 184

190 *Index*

persuasion method 86, 87, 90, 91, 92, 93, 95, 96, 97, 98, 99, 100
persuasion principle 86, 88, 95, 98, 99, 100
persuasion science 7, 85, 177, 180, 184
persuasion theory 87
positioning 10, 12, 16, 29, 123, 150, 186
positive relationship 26, 28, 30, 33, 34, 35, 111, 112, 114, 120
privacy 23
proactively 1, 35, 59, 176, 177
profit 2, 71, 72, 74, 75, 76, 77, 78, 79, 80, 81, 84, 91, 142
profitability 7, 56, 71, 75, 76, 81, 82, 84, 121, 177, 179, 184, 185
profit efficiency 72, 84
profitability factor 84
profit margin 76, 77, 78, 79, 81
project management 8, 36, 38, 39, 41

quality 5, 10, 36, 38, 45, 54, 106, 107, 108, 109, 110, 111, 112, 119, 120, 121, 122, 123, 124, 140, 141, 142, 145, 149, 150, 154, 165, 166, 184, 186
quality assurance 10, 122, 123, 150, 184, 186
quality control 5, 36, 184
quality management 5, 10, 38, 122, 186
quality perception 121

RBV (Resource-based view) 58
relationship management 7, 37, 41, 42, 125, 126, 149, 177, 180, 184, 186
relationship marketing 9, 10, 123, 125, 130, 148, 149, 150, 151, 185
relationship value 144, 145, 146
reputation 39, 43, 119, 123, 148, 150, 186
return on equity 73, 76, 82, 158
risk 4, 7, 12, 25, 37, 58, 59, 60, 63, 64, 65, 66, 72, 73, 74, 83, 84, 99, 124, 129, 130, 137, 142, 145, 151, 152, 154, 155, 156, 157, 158, 159, 162, 163, 165, 166, 167, 176, 177, 180, 181, 183, 184

satisfaction 5, 7, 36, 38, 87, 102, 106, 107, 108, 109, 110, 111, 112, 113, 114, 115, 116, 117, 118, 119, 120, 121, 122, 124, 177, 180, 184
SCS (Stakeholder causal scope) 181, 182, 183
security 11, 21, 23
service 1, 2, 3, 7, 8, 10, 13, 35, 36, 37, 38, 39, 40, 41, 42, 43, 47, 48, 55, 73, 74, 83, 84, 101, 102, 106, 107, 108, 109, 110, 111, 112, 113, 116, 119, 120, 121,

122, 123, 124, 125, 126, 127, 128, 129, 130, 131, 132, 133, 134, 135, 136, 137, 138, 139, 140, 141, 142, 143, 144, 145, 146, 147, 149, 150, 178, 179, 180, 183, 185, 186
service dominant logic 37, 40, 42
service encounter 108, 143
service innovation 125, 128, 129, 130, 131, 133, 141, 145, 180
service marketing 107
service quality 106, 107, 108, 109, 110, 111, 112, 121, 122, 123, 124, 140
service quality model 108, 122
service research 41, 42, 121
social 5, 6, 9, 11, 15, 25, 26, 27, 29, 30, 31, 32, 33, 34, 35, 36, 37, 38, 39, 40, 41, 42, 43, 47, 61, 63, 64, 71, 74, 77, 82, 83, 84, 86, 87, 94, 95, 96, 99, 100, 101, 102, 103, 104, 108, 110, 143, 144, 149, 154, 155, 156, 157, 163, 166, 167, 175, 184
social media 11, 38, 39, 40, 94, 95, 96, 97, 99, 100, 103
stakeholder 1, 2, 3, 4, 5, 7, 8, 9, 10, 12, 22, 25, 26, 27, 28, 29, 30, 33, 34, 35, 36, 37, 39, 40, 41, 42, 43, 58, 86, 93, 106, 123, 125, 126, 127, 128, 129, 130, 131, 132, 133, 134, 136, 137, 138, 139, 140, 141, 142, 143, 144, 145, 146, 149, 150, 152, 154, 177, 179, 180, 181, 182, 183, 184, 185, 186
stakeholder commitment 41, 132, 141, 145
stakeholder engagement 10, 25, 26, 27, 28, 29, 30, 33, 34, 35, 36, 37, 39, 40, 130, 150, 179
stakeholder management 37, 39, 40, 41, 42, 133
stakeholder relationship 5, 7, 37, 39, 123, 125, 126, 129, 130, 132, 133, 138, 140, 145, 150, 177, 179, 180, 182, 184, 186
stakeholder theory 26, 37, 38, 39, 40, 41, 42
stimuli 11, 12, 13, 15, 16, 18, 19, 21
stimulation 16, 19, 20, 21, 22, 23, 24, 88
strategic management 5, 36, 37, 39, 40, 58, 61, 67, 68, 69, 168, 174, 175, 177
strategic innovation 1, 2, 3, 4, 5, 7, 8, 176, 177, 178, 179, 180, 181, 182, 183, 184
strategy 4, 8, 10, 27, 28, 29, 33, 34, 35, 40, 41, 43, 44, 45, 58, 60, 66, 68, 69, 102, 121, 122, 130, 139, 148, 151, 154, 155, 157, 158, 159, 162, 163, 166, 179, 181, 183, 185

structural equation model 31, 37, 40, 41
supply chain 5, 6, 9, 184
sustainability 5, 9, 10, 38, 41, 42, 55, 70,
74, 81, 83, 123, 147, 150, 154, 163, 186
sustained competitive advantage 10, 123,
130, 150, 186

technology 1, 3, 4, 9, 12, 13, 15, 20, 22,
23, 24, 40, 41, 66, 69, 88, 98, 153
transnational 10, 123, 149, 150, 186

value 1, 2, 3, 4, 8, 10, 23, 26, 27, 30, 32,
33, 34, 35, 37, 39, 40, 41, 42, 43, 46,
47, 50, 51, 53, 57, 58, 62, 64, 65, 67,
74, 75, 80, 81, 84, 86, 89, 90, 91, 102,
115, 116, 117, 121, 122, 123, 124,
125, 126, 127, 128, 129, 130, 131,
132, 133, 134, 139, 140, 141, 142,
143, 144, 145, 146, 147, 148, 149,
150, 154, 181, 183, 157, 172, 175,
179, 181, 182, 183, 186
value-creation 74, 75, 81, 84, 154, 175,
179, 181
value co-creation 8, 10, 39, 43, 123, 124,
149, 150, 186
value proposition 183, 186
values 26, 29, 36, 43, 47, 51, 64, 71, 132,
133, 155
value innovation 142, 143, 146
value network 127, 129, 143

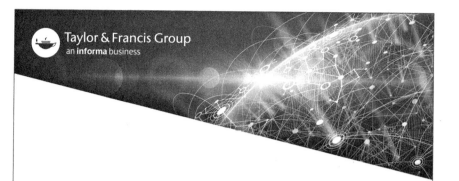